Recreation Programs that Work for At-Risk Youth:

The Challenge of Shaping the Future

Edited by
Peter A. Witt and John L. Crompton

Acknowledgements

Many individuals are responsible for the production of the case studies contained in this book. First and foremost, appreciation is expressed to the professionals from each of the 38 communities who supplied materials that make up each case study. The bases for the case studies were the presentations they made at the Colloquium held in Fort Worth, Texas in February, 1995, *"The Challenge of Shaping the Future: Recreation Programs that Work for At-Risk Youth."* In addition, they generously supplied follow-up materials which we requested after the Colloquium, and invested their time to review and amend final drafts of the cases.

Another group of people who were directly responsible for bringing this project to fruition was the team that organized the Fort Worth Colloquium. Thus, we wish to thank Richard Zavala, Diane Darnell, and the dedicated staff of the Fort Worth Department of Parks and Community Services who hosted the conference; and Laura Kurk from the Department of Recreation, Park and Tourism Sciences at Texas A&M who coordinated the Colloquium's registration and program development activities.

Dean Tice, Executive Director of the National Recreation and Park Association, one of the sponsors of the Colloquium, provided vigorous support, as he has for other ongoing efforts at Texas A&M University associated with evaluating and improving recreation services for at-risk youth.

This project also would have not been possible without the support of the officers and members of the American Academy of Park and Recreation Administration who endorsed the initial idea of the Colloquium and are furthering the process of information exchange begun at the national Colloquium through their support of a series of follow-up regional conferences.

We are indebted to staff in the Department of Recreation, Park and Tourism Sciences, especially Jennifer Jahedkar, Susan Buzzingham, Liz Harrison, Glenda Simmons, and Teresa Mireles for transcribing tapes from the Colloquium and typing the case study drafts. Dwayne Baker and Kent Wall assisted by diligently recording all the Colloquium presentations. Cindy Hansel from the National Recreation and Park Association provided invaluable initial editorial assistance in the preparation of the final drafts for some of the case studies. Joyce Nies provided similar assistance at the end of our editing process by giving the document a final careful reading before it was sent to Venture for publication.

Finally, we are indebted to Geof Godbey and the staff at Venture Publishing (particularly the efforts of Richard Yocum, Diane K. Bierly, Michele L. Barbin, and Katherine Young) for undertaking production of this volume.

Peter A. Witt and John L. Crompton
February, 1996

Table of Contents

Section I
Introduction and Overview

Chapter 1
Background and Organization
of the Book

Background

The problems created by youth dropping out of school, using drugs or alcohol, joining gangs, becoming teenage parents, and being involved in antisocial and delinquent acts are widely recognized. Many agencies—educational, social service, law enforcement, recreational, and health—are responding to these issues through targeted prevention and intervention strategies. With the problems created by at-risk youth emerging as a central concern in many communities, there are increasing pressures on the political system to "do something about them."

The pressure of dealing with these problems offers an opportunity for recreation and park departments to position themselves (Crompton, 1993) so they are perceived to be alleviating a problem which is a prevailing political concern of the public and those policymakers who are responsible for allocating tax funds. The field has a distinguished heritage in this area. Indeed, a primary cornerstone upon which public recreation services were founded was the belief that recreation can make a substantive contribution to alleviating the impact of nonproductive, personally destructive, and/or antisocial actions by youth. Positioning themselves to address the at-risk youth issue requires agencies to move beyond a "fun and games" mandate, under which they offer programs that enhance participation in leisure for its own sake, to a problem-solving mandate requiring that programs contribute to ameliorating societal problems. This shift in orientation facilitates public recreation and park services being seen positively as part of the solution to a community's problems, rather than negatively as a drain on the tax resources of its general fund.

Recognition of the magnitude of the challenge presented by at-risk youth has sparked a renaissance of interest in this issue among some park and recreation agencies. The prospect in the immediate future is that many more agencies will be involved in developing services in this area. Unfortunately, relatively little information is currently available about programs and services for at-risk youth being offered by park and recreation agencies. The dearth of information makes it difficult for those agencies already offering services to refine and improve them, and for agencies seeking to initiate programs to know how to develop them most effectively.

With this need in mind, the American Academy for Park and Recreation Administration initiated efforts to increase information available about recreation services for at-risk youth. These efforts were consistent with the Academy's mission which is to advance knowledge related to the administration of recreation and parks, to encourage scholarly efforts by both practitioners and educators that enhance the practice of park and recreation administration, and to promote broader public understanding of the importance of parks and recreation to the public good. Its membership is comprised of approximately 125 elected members who have served for at least fifteen years in a high level of park and recreation administration or as a senior educator in the field.

The efforts of the Academy led to a cooperative project with the National Recreation and Park Association; the Department of Recreation, Park and Tourism Sciences at Texas A&M University; and the Fort Worth Parks and Community Services Department to convene a Colloquium in Fort Worth, Texas, on the theme *Recreation for At-Risk Youth: Programs that Work.* One hundred and forty invited participants from approximately 80 agencies in the United States and Canada attended the Colloquium, with 37 participants providing lead case examples.

The intent of this book is to build on the presentations made at the Colloquium and to provide state-of-the-art information other communities can use to improve or initiate their own services in this area. The case studies which constitute this book are based on written papers which were prepared by Colloquium presenters. The editors have supplemented these papers with information gleaned from tapes of the presentations and discussions and from extensive additional background resources derived from files, newspapers, reports or other materials which were supplied by the presenters. Efforts were made to check with presenters that the edited material accurately portrayed their programs, but any errors contained in the volume remain the responsibility of the editors.

Organization of the Book

The book is organized into sections which group together cases that address similar issues. In the second chapter, the editors have attempted to provide an overview of the commonalities and major themes which emerged from the case studies.

In Section II, case studies are presented for five cities which have had relatively long experience and an extensive array of programs targeted at at-risk youth. The city of Commerce, California, with a population of 12,000, offers an extraordinary range of programs and a thorough holistic approach aimed at preventing the gang warfare in adjacent Los Angeles from spilling over into its community. Commerce demonstrates that full-spectrum programs need not be confined to large cities. Of the remaining cities in Section II, Anaheim is a medium-sized community, while Minneapolis, Phoenix, and Seattle all are larger cities. All four provide case studies of model at-risk youth programs which other municipal recreation and park departments may want to emulate.

When the political forces enable and/or direct a recreation and park agency to concentrate more resources on at-risk youth, the temptation often is to plunge unilaterally ahead and implement programs that agency staff anticipate might work. This approach fails to recognize that a comprehensive thrust in this area cannot be successful without the involvement of other stakeholders seeking to impact at-risk youth, such as residents in affected neighborhoods, community leaders, business interests, nonprofit organizations, and other public agencies. The five case studies which constitute Section III focus on mobilizing and organizing multiple resources in the community to address the issue. They offer a wide variety of approaches to achieving this and illustrate that local circumstances dictate which is likely to be most successful in a particular context.

The times at which youth are most at-risk are those when they are not in school. In Section IV, three time blocks are recognized: after school (and teacher training days); summer; and evening/late night. The case studies in this section discuss six programs that focus on the after-school period, four summer programs, and two which cover both of these time periods. In addition, three evening/ late night programs are presented.

Case studies in Section V describe efforts in Boulder, Colorado, and in Columbus, Mississippi, targeted at public housing areas, and a program organized by Calgary Parks and Recreation which aims to keep youth who are identified as likely high school dropout candidates in school.

In Section VI, particularly innovative programs are featured. Most of them are nontraditional. The programs represent responses to needs which have emerged by "thinking outside the envelope." They are testimony to the creativity and imagination which some recreation agencies exhibit in addressing the needs of at-risk youth.

Problems associated with at-risk youth are not unique to North America. Section VII includes two cases from other countries. In the "new" South Africa, a very large proportion of African youth are both uneducated and unemployed. In some areas they have been exposed to violence for much of their lives. The situation was explained to the Colloquium by a senior South African official, an invited guest of the Colloquium organizers. Finally, one of the editors reports on a widely adopted program in the United Kingdom, where youth who are placed on probation for the first time by the juvenile court system have the opportunity to participate in recreation programs. These are staffed by recreation professionals, funded by the probation service, and used as a vehicle to rehabilitate and direct youth away from further deviant or illegal behavior.

References

Crompton, J. L. (1993). Repositioning recreation and park services: An overview. *Trends, 30*(4), 2-5.

Chapter 2
Major Themes Emerging
from the Case Studies

The programs described in the 38 case studies in this volume evolved in response to local community circumstances, and each was molded by constraints and opportunities afforded by local administrative practices. However, several key themes such as the stimuli underlying program initiation, program objectives, the need for collaborative efforts, and the degree of involvement of participants in program planning, among other issues, emerged across the various local situations. These commonalities are reviewed in this chapter.

The themes emerging from the case studies complement, and were frequently consistent with, the results of a recent national survey of 661 park and recreation agencies concerning the services they offer for at-risk youth (Espericuerta-Schultz, Crompton & Witt, 1995). Data from this survey are periodically inserted in this chapter since they provide a generalizable context for some of the insights and specifics provided through the case studies. On the other hand, the presentations provide a richness and depth of information that could not be captured in a survey.

Stimuli for Launching At-Risk Programs

The national survey revealed that targeting separate programs to at-risk youth is a relatively recent occurrence. Only 28% of agencies that offered these programs launched them before 1989. Another 31% of agencies initiated these programs between 1989 and 1991, while the remaining 41% started targeted programs after 1991. The recent expansion of programs that target at-risk youth has been stimulated by several factors, one of which is an increase in gang membership. For example, the number of gangs in Fort Worth increased from 77 to 211 between 1987 and 1992, while gang membership rose from 1,316 to 3,448. In the national survey, 57% of agencies which targeted programs for at-risk youth indicated that gangs were perceived to be a problem by residents in their jurisdictions.

This national pattern was reflected in the case studies. With only a few exceptions, the case studies reveal that most communities launched targeted services in the late 1980s and early 1990s. Many factors contributed to the emergence of these programs, but four major stimuli were identified as being particularly prominent. They were:

(1) changed demographics;
(2) emergence of negative youth behaviors in smaller communities;
(3) growth in the number of latchkey children; and
(4) increased high-visibility violent incidents.

Changed Demographics

The demographics of many major cities, particularly the inner-city areas, significantly changed during the 1980s. The proportion of African Americans, Hispanics, and, in some cities, immigrants, increased. For example, since 1980 the Black population of North Miami has grown 377%, primarily as a result of the immigration of Caribbean peoples. In many instances, the age distribution of recent migrants to the inner cities was younger than that of the general population. Typically, inner cities have had high rates of unemployment and a larger percentage of families living below the poverty level. During the late 1980s and early 1990s, many cities reported substantial increases in drug use among youth and violent crime committed by and to youth; school dropout rates accelerated, not only among high school students, but also among middle school students; and rates of teen pregnancy increased. These factors galvanized local residents and political forces to demand solutions to these spiraling societal problems.

Emergence of Negative Youth Behaviors in Smaller Communities

Many of these same factors, which were thought previously to be confined to "big cities," began to appear in suburban and smaller communities in the late 1980s and early 1990s.

• In both Boulder, Colorado, and Columbus, Mississippi, growing concerns about high poverty levels and unemployment, high drug use and gang activity, and lack of meaningful activities for Housing Authority residents led to the development of recreation and drug education programs at these sites in 1991. A Federal

program sponsored by the U.S. Department of Housing and Urban Development (HUD) was initiated that year which made the development of these types of programs possible.
- In Scottsdale, Arizona, there was a 44% increase in juvenile crime between 1989 and 1994.

Growth in the Number of Latchkey Children

Problems associated with a lack of adult supervision at home were prevalent in communities of all sizes due to the growing number of two-wage earner families and the number of single-parent households. Many localities have developed after-school and summer camp programs in response to the need for affordable, supervised out-of-school programs for children, with some communities also beginning to develop programs for middle and high school students as well.

- Longview and Kelso, Washington, initiated after-school programs in 1992 in response to concerns about the high number of distress calls received by the police from children who were "home alone" after school.
- A 1993 NBC *Dateline* segment about latchkey children featured a Tucson, Arizona, single mother who was forced to leave her children home alone while she worked a minimum wage job. Along with concerns about gang activity and youth violence, the story spurred the expansion of after-school and summer program efforts which had been initiated in 1989.
- In 1992, North Miami, Florida, developed after-school programs for children and youth ages 8 to 15 in response to concerns from business owners about problems in the downtown area. When school recessed in the afternoon, teenage students swarmed into thoroughfares, businesses and shops to hang out, wait for rides, and visit. The business community was disrupted, and many citizens were afraid to go into the district because of the large teenage presence.
- In 1993, Houston, Texas, implemented an extensive after-school program because of concerns expressed by children about gangs, drugs and lack of things to do after school.
- Summer day camp programs were launched in 1989 in Oklahoma City for children 8 to 13 years of age as a substitute for the

typical drop-in summer playground program. The Parks and
Recreation Department recognized that more structured prevention and intervention activities were needed for youth living in
high crime, poverty, and gang member areas of the city.

Increased High Visibility Violent Incidents

The late 1980s witnessed unprecedented levels of violence involving
young people, due in part to increased gang activity and the highly
competitive illegal narcotics market. In many communities dramatic
events such as drive-by shootings moved the communities to implement targeted intervention and prevention strategies.

* Although Cincinnati, Ohio, had already established a comprehensive citywide program to address at-risk youth problems, in
  1993 the city expanded program efforts in the Winton Hills community as a result of an FBI drug raid and a shooting in the
  neighborhood.
* In Fort Worth, Texas, a 1991 drive-by shooting after a Sunday
  church service led to the mobilization of at-risk youth and gang
  intervention efforts.
* Commerce, California, had been dealing with gangs in the community since 1982, but a drive-by shooting in 1989 intensified
  and expanded prevention and intervention efforts.

Task Forces

These stimuli served as a catalyst which galvanized political leaders
"to do something." Actions had to be more than putting additional
police officers on the street because, as the Fort Worth Police Chief
stated, "We can't arrest our way out of social problems." The Mayor
of Fort Worth offered a trenchant analogy: "I compare it to smoking
and the progress we've made with lung cancer. We didn't get there
because we perfected surgery. We got there because we educated
people into prevention."

The case studies indicate, in most instances, that "something"
was establishment of a task force whose typical charge was to solicit
broad community input to identify all dimensions of the problem and
its magnitude, recommend actions to alleviate the problem, and
coordinate and mobilize community resources so these actions could

be undertaken efficiently and effectively. The national survey indicated that 71% of agencies that targeted at-risk youth had established a communitywide task force.

Task force action plans usually embrace *prevention*, designed to lower the number of children and youth engaging in undesirable behaviors in the future, and *intervention*, intended to change the attitudes, behavior, and "life course" of individuals causing problems.

- In 1991, the Mayor of Cincinnati, Ohio, formed a Youth Steering Committee, comprised of the Directors of a number of municipal departments including the Recreation Commission, to deal with youth problems stemming from "historical disenfranchisement, poverty, discrimination, inadequate education and skill levels, damaged self-esteem, and thwarted aspirations." The development of a comprehensive approach to youth services, "Back on the Block," was the result.
- In Anaheim, California, gangs began to be recognized as a problem in the early 1980s. However, a 1984 report indicated that the city's efforts were only marginally effective in dealing with the problems of gang violence and drug use. Project S.A.Y (Save-A-Youth) was created in 1986 and expanded in 1991 to address those problems.

In many of the case study communities, task forces remained in place after formulating their recommendations and were charged with coordinating and overseeing subsequent service delivery. Task forces are perceived to be an effective mechanism for coordinating the actions of overlapping jurisdictions, mandates, programs, and resources.

Prevention Versus Intervention

Most of the case studies stress prevention rather than intervention. This is consistent with findings of the national survey which indicated that 67% and 21% of the total resources invested by recreation and park departments were targeted at "potential at-risk youth" and "at-risk youth," respectively. Only 10% and 2% of these resources were committed to programs impacting "juvenile delinquents" and "chronic delinquents," respectively.

With limited resources recreation and park agencies have to make choices. Prevention programs seek to pro-actively change the behavior of at-risk individuals, rather than undertake reactionary efforts after children have dropped out of school, started using drugs, become pregnant or become involved with the legal system. These programs may be more feasible to implement than intervention programs, which frequently require resources and expertise beyond those available to many recreation and park systems.

Program Mission and Objectives

In general, the case studies demonstrate congruence between program objectives and the problems and issues that stimulated development of programs. However, some of the objectives were too vague to be operationally useful for guiding specific program design and delivery decisions, even though they expressed laudable sentiments and platitudes.

The lack of clear objectives is consistent with findings from the national survey and highlights a key limitation of at-risk youth programs. The lack of specific objectives written in an operational format leads to the inference that many agencies have not identified specific standards by which to evaluate the success of their programs. Properly formulated objectives help form the basis for program design. Structured, attainable objectives offer an incentive for improvement, if they are properly communicated and understood by staff, and specific and written objectives enable personnel and taxpayers to conclude that programs are successful. A good example of specific objectives are those used by the Sunnyvale, California, Recreation and Parks Department. They include:

(1) increase middle school performance by coordinating educational, health and social services to students and community members. The results will (a) increase student performance by 5% on standardized achievement tests; (b) reduce absences by 20%; (c) reduce disciplinary referrals by 10%, and (d) increase parent contacts by 10%.

(2) provide rehabilitation, predelinquency, neighborhood education, leisure services, youth employment and neighborhood volunteer services. This will reduce the FBI Crime Rate by 5% and help maintain an annual juvenile offender recidivism rate of 4% or less.

Objectives of the case study programs are specified at a macro or societal level and at a micro or individual level. The investment of public funds is usually justified by a desire to ameliorate societal problems such as violent crime, drug and alcohol abuse, the percentage of school dropouts, youth involvement in unsafe sexual activity, and the number of children born to unmarried teenage mothers. For example, Anaheim's Project S.A.Y. has an overall objective "to assist youth with gang and drug involvement to reach adulthood as productive law-abiding citizens."

Attainment of these societal objectives, however, is achieved through inducing social-psychological and behavioral changes in individuals. The Anaheim program, therefore, has a series of specific behavioral change objectives such as reducing school absenteeism/truancy and decreasing the incidence of failing grades plus a series of social-psychological objectives related to increasing self-esteem, self-confidence, and cultural pride.

Another example of the relationship between the societal and individual youth objectives is provided by the Oakland Summer Performing Arts Day Camp which targets children and youth ages 6 to 16. The societal objective is:

> to provide an affordable, accessible, high-quality creative arts experience in a safe and nurturing environment to occupy Oakland-area children's available time with positive, constructive alternatives to prevent crime and delinquency.

At the individual level the objective is:

> to foster and nurture appreciation for all forms of creative expression, and by doing so, emphasize the importance of each child's vision and voice and improve his or her self-esteem.

Moving Beyond the Front Gate

The case studies repeatedly demonstrate that to reach at-risk youth effectively, it is necessary to move beyond the boundaries of an agency's facilities. For example:

- The Phoenix At-Risk Youth Division views itself as a mobile
  outreach service providing recreational, educational, social, and
  cultural programs for teens at outreach sites such as malls,
  schools, and park sites at which there was no regular programming. One manifestation of this philosophy is the Mobile Unit
  Partnership developed in collaboration with the Girl Scouts.
  Each week a renovated "bookmobile" serves approximately
  1,000 youth.
- Rather than expecting those engaged in an unhealthy or alternative lifestyle to participate in traditional recreation programs and
  services, Olympia, Washington, utilized two counselors to meet
  with these high-risk youth one-on-one in the downtown area.
  Their charge was to identify and develop relationships with these
  youth and ultimately to connect them to appropriate public
  healthcare, job opportunities, education, recreation, and other
  social services. These counselors also develop training programs
  for recreation and police department staff which address the
  changing issues and needs of troubled youth.

The important role of outreach leaders is reinforced by several of
the case studies. For example, in Anaheim, program leaders are
trained in conflict resolution, are bilingual, college educated, and
come from backgrounds similar to those of the clients they serve. In
addition to their education and training, they are described as being
sensitive and understanding as well as savvy and street-smart.

Returning to Our Roots:
Moving Beyond Fun and Games

These case study presentations demonstrate that at least some park
and recreation agencies have moved beyond a "fun and games"
philosophy to one in which recreation programs serve as vehicles for
an agency's objectives for serving at-risk youth (Tice & Tindall,
1994). Thus, Seattle Park and Recreation Department's (PARD) at-
risk youth staff do not talk about recreation. Rather they talk of the
"re-creation" of human lives. Many examples are presented where
the definition of what constitutes a recreation program has been
broadened considerably, such as:

- YO! Hott Shotts is a job training program organized by Seattle PARD. It is intended to inspire at-risk youth to take an interest in business and entrepreneurial self-direction. Seattle includes specifications in their concession contracts which require concessionaires to hire and train at-risk youth.
- Teen Teamworks is a summer employment program for 200 at-risk youth which has been operated by the Minneapolis Parks and Recreation Board since 1986. Its mission is to offer a positive park maintenance work experience, recreational opportunities, and educational sessions to unemployed youth ages 14–18.
- Midnight Basketball in Kansas City, Missouri, includes a required educational component in which participants are exposed to opportunities for personal development, motivational training, entrepreneurial skills, job interviewing skills, antidrug and other health programs. Basketball is an attractive hook used to achieve broader educational and entrepreneurial goals for youth.
- Phoenix, Arizona, and Commerce, California, park and recreation departments offer a tattoo removal program. Youth who have been persuaded to leave gangs find tattoo insignia make it difficult to find employment, avoid fights in school, and convince peers they have left a gang.

The types of services now being offered are in some ways reminiscent of those which were prominent in the 1950s and 1960s. Jim Colley, Director of the Phoenix Parks, Recreation, and Libraries Department reminds us that during that period, "We did mobile recreation centers, school campus lunchtime programs, after-school programs, teen councils, gang out-reach programs and so on, but we then we got away from this type of approach to services."

The case studies also indicate that many agencies are returning to the mission and objectives that spurred the launching of the public recreation movement in the late 1800s and early 1900s. Public recreation services emerged in response to negative social conditions in major cities. There was a humanistic concern for the welfare of those who found themselves with few resources, places to recreate, and/or skills to undertake recreational activities. Comments made by Jane Addams in 1893 are reminiscent of those made by commentators today:

> The social organism has broken down through large
> districts of our great cities. Many of the people living
> there are very poor, the majority of them without leisure
> or energy for anything but the gain of subsistence. They
> move often from one wretched lodging to another. They
> live for the moment side-by-side, many of them without
> knowledge of each other, without fellowship, without
> local tradition or public spirit, without social organiza-
> tion of any kind. Practically nothing is done to remedy
> this. The people who might do it, who have the social
> tact and training, the large houses, and the traditions and
> custom of hospitality, live in other parts of the city. The
> clubhouses, libraries, galleries, and semipublic conve-
> niences for social life are also blocks away. (Addams,
> [1893]1960, p. 4)

In response to this situation, Addams established Hull House, a settlement house in Chicago, which was in many respects the precursor of the modern recreation center. Facilities such as the Columbia Neighborhood Center being developed in Sunnyvale, California, are reminiscent of Addams' philosophy and a reaffirmation of the importance of a holistic approach to serving at-risk youth.

Program Leadership

Leadership is perhaps the most important element in determining the positive impact of a program, since it shapes what participants derive from their experience. The types of programs described in the case studies move recreation professionals into a different mode of operation and require different leadership skills than those possessed by many park and recreation professionals in the past. The Director of Phoenix Parks and Recreation Department, Jim Colley, observed:

> My staff say we are becoming counselors and social
> workers. That's fine, I believe we should be. We have
> always done this, but there is much more emphasis on it
> now than there has been in a couple of decades. My
> philosophy is that if a young man comes in on drugs or a
> young woman comes in who is pregnant, we have to
> help. Young women come to my female staff and say

'I'm pregnant, will you come home with me and help me talk to my mom.' They are scared, so of course we help. We respond as best we can to whatever they need. I would not have a problem with my Department being called a Department of Community Services. Our job is to make young people whole in any way we can, and offering wholesome recreation activities is only one aspect of that. It's a way of reaching them and gives us an opportunity to help them straighten out other parts of their lives.

Many cities are thus making major investments in creating full-time, adult leadership positions based on the principle that the single most important factor in reaching healthy adulthood is a positive relationship with a caring adult. The motivation for utilizing nontraditional sources of leadership in some of the cities was the realization that departments were losing touch with their clients and that in some cases employees hired during a different era cannot relate to the type of direct service responsibilities that need to be undertaken today.

To address this problem, some departments (e.g., Seattle and Fort Worth) have hired former gang members to provide primary leadership. They are role models with whom the youth identify. They have lived in an environment where there are gangs and have experienced what it feels like to be in a gang, and what it feels like to get out of a gang. This policy has aroused controversy since some residents challenge the appropriateness of placing former gang members in positions where they can influence others, and of rewarding them with employment opportunities.

Former athletes are also a good source of potential role models, likely to have the respect of at-risk youth. Thus, when North Miami launched its after-school program in the city's middle school, a former Miami Dolphin football player was hired to direct the daily activities. This added a considerable amount of credibility to the program in the minds of the students.

In Columbus, Mississippi, residents of the housing projects were trained to provide leadership for on-site recreation programs. Similarly, Cincinnati hires at-risk youth from the neighborhood in which a swimming pool is located to work at the facility, and the Kansas City Night Hoops program trains participants to become basketball referees.

Many of the after-school programs utilize teachers to provide activity leadership since many of the activities involve a learning component and have learning goals built into the program. This creates a reimbursement conundrum because teachers typically are compensated at their professional salary rate for these additional duties, while recreation leaders doing similar work typically receive $5 to $7 per hour. This disparity, combined with the emotional intensity of the work and the difficult nature of the clientele, often results in high staff turnover. The Seattle Parks and Recreation Department has responded to this dilemma by paying their at-risk youth program leaders $10.50 to $15.00 per hour. Ultimately, however, it is the depth of commitment of program leaders which secures a program's longevity and success:

> Dealing with these kids is more than a job. These leaders have to be extraordinarily dedicated. You can't pay for that or buy it. It has to be in their hearts. They don't count hours, they'll spend weekends, nights, whatever— they are always there when the kids need them.
> (Jim Colley, Director, Phoenix Parks, Recreation and Library Department)

Local Champions

Over a decade ago, Peters and Waterman (1982) reported that a primary characteristic of excellent companies was their ability to innovate and be responsive to the changing external environment. Frequently this innovation occurred because there was a "champion"—a dedicated individual or small group who believed in an idea, regarded it as a personal crusade, advocated it to others, and bullheadedly persisted until it came to fruition. Similarly, the case studies reveal the profound influence of individuals or small groups who have championed the launching of at-risk programs:

* Internationally renowned tennis players Arthur Ashe and Butch Buchholz were instrumental in the genesis of Metro Dade County's Good Life Mentoring Project. Ashe and Buchholz were concerned that many school-age children in their home community were not being exposed to the opportunities they had experienced in their youth. They involved others to refine and develop their ideas and to launch the program.

- A Youth-In-Action program was launched and has been operating under the leadership of a parent volunteer for ten years in Hanover, New Hampshire. This visionary parent saw the need for high-school-age young people to use free time in a constructive manner to benefit themselves and their community. The vehicle for achieving this goal was the creation of volunteer opportunities. This program was subsequently adopted by the Lebanon, New Hampshire, Recreation Department.

Collaborations with Other Agencies and Organizations

In a number of communities the guiding principle and philosophy of program approaches is rooted in the old African proverb, "It takes a whole village to raise a child." Charles Jordon, Director of Portland, Oregon, Parks and Recreation, has observed that:

> While retaining our uniqueness and autonomy, we in the field of recreation, who share the same values and goals, can accomplish more by working together than we can on our own. This is the chance for us to demonstrate the full value of who we are and what we can do....[S]ociety needs help with its youth, and we have a piece of the solution.

To encourage this cooperation, the Portland Parks and Recreation Department organized a series of Youth Summits which bring together all organizations in the community involved in serving at-risk youth. This facilitates pooling resources and coordinating program efforts.

A contributing factor to the success that the programs described in this volume have achieved is the strong collaborative arrangements they have developed to launch, operate, and finance programs with participants and their parents, other municipal agencies, voluntary sector agencies, foundations, and businesses. Examples of collaborations include:

- The Summer Performing Arts Program is planned in partnership with the Oakland, California, Public School District, the Office of the Mayor, prominent members of the local arts community (e.g., Michael Morgan, Director of the Oakland Symphony), Laney Community College, and the Office of Parks and Recreation/Cultural Arts Division. Additional implementation partners include the Federal Lunch Program, Summer Youth Employment Training Program (SYETP), Studio One Teen Club teaching assistants, community members, and parent volunteers.

• The Community Services, Police, and Parks, Recreation and Cultural Services Departments cooperate in Olympia, Washington, to provide a street outreach program targeted at troubled, runaway, and homeless youth.

• The recreation program at the Public Housing sites in Boulder, Colorado, is a cooperative effort between the Housing Authority of Boulder, Boulder Parks and Recreation Department, the YMCA, Salvation Army, various church groups, Boy/Girl Scouts, Sierra Club, Rural Transportation District, and a variety of volunteers from the community.

• The after-school programs in Corpus Christi, Texas; Sunnyvale, California; North Miami, Florida; and Tucson, Arizona, are coordinated or operated in partnership with their local school districts.

• The Good Life Mentor Program in Metropolitan Dade County, Florida, involves the Greater Miami Chamber of Commerce, the public schools, the parks and recreation department, the Miami Police, a local university, the YMCA, and a variety of professional sport organizations.

The case studies are also reflective of a national trend regarding collaborative efforts. The national survey data indicated that 97% of agencies offering programs targeted at at-risk youth worked directly with nonprofit organizations or other government agencies. The most frequent collaborations were with education agencies (85%), law enforcement agencies or officials (79%), youth serving organizations such as YMCAs or Boys and Girls Clubs (66%), and adult service organizations such as Lions or Elks (54%). Few park and recreation agencies serving at-risk youth have the capacity, or perceive the necessity, to operate alone without substantial involvement with other social service organizations.

Program Security

A primary requirement of all at-risk youth programs is the guaranteed safety of participants. Safety issues often present an additional obstacle in areas of high crime and gang activity, where members of rival gangs may be interacting in recreational and social activities, and nongang members may need to be protected from the actions of gang members.

Some communities have resorted to metal detectors and hand wands to screen youth as they enter a facility. Others are considering the use of ID cards with card readers to check participants in and out of program sites. These procedures would also enable attendance patterns to be monitored and would provide useful data for program evaluations.

Most of the reported programs note the involvement and input of police departments through the utilization of on-duty or off-duty police officers at program sites as security guards. This relationship breaks down existing barriers of suspicion and distrust and gives the police the opportunity to better know individual young people. In addition, the juxtaposition of police and recreation staff working together may lead to enhanced appreciation by police for the contributions made by recreation staff in alleviating at-risk youth problems.

Youth Involvement

In addition to addressing larger societal needs, programs must be relevant and interesting in order to attract young people, many of whom have been exposed to the "action" and "excitement" of illicit activities. "It's not fun to be a good kid," observed one gang leader after joining a recreation program. After being on both sides of drive-by shootings and engaging in all kinds of illegal activities, such young people require challenging, high-skills programs to keep their interest. According to one parks and recreation director,

> We didn't respond to the needs of these youth very well
> for many years. We did traditional programs—for ex-
> ample, we always had to have a Maypole dance on May
> 1, irrespective of whether anyone came. The youth

wanted more exciting programs, but we weren't responsive to their needs. We told them what they needed. We
never asked them what they wanted.

Similarly, the director of another park and recreation department
said:

Often, the programs aren't exciting enough because the
staff aren't excited enough. They don't know what
teenagers want, so the teenagers don't come to our programs. When we establish steering committees, task
forces, and programs we have to involve teenage leadership or the youth we want to attract won't show up.

In short, young people are tired of adults making decisions that
effect them regardless of their interest and input. Empowerment is
an important theme that runs through these case studies. Empowerment enables youth to take ownership and responsibility for their
recreational and social activities.

Teen councils are one widely used empowerment method:

• In Montreal, Canada, teenagers are fully involved in conceiving,
  developing, and implementing programs which respond to their
  needs and expectations. Rather than proposing a schedule of
  activities based on a conventional program, teenagers are assisted in their efforts to develop and carry out activities which
  they have proposed. A key principle in the Montreal Youth 2000
  program is that efforts should be *by* and *for* teens. Thus emphasis is placed on young people's capacities to take initiative, on
  their organizational and managerial abilities, and on their creativity.
• The Youth Recreation Council in Rockford, Illinois, has promoted projects that enabled teens to take major responsibility for
  planning and carrying out projects designed to meet their needs.
  Teens planned, helped design, build, and program "The Gate-
  way" teen playground, a high-quality, custom-designed, supervised play structure which offers a unique community experience
  for teens.
• Phoenix has 25 teen councils throughout the city. They meet
  weekly or bimonthly to plan activities, trips, special events,

educational and community service programs with professional recreation staff. Teen council members advise recreation staff on these issues. The local councils are complemented by a citywide Youth Advisory Board which plans an annual teen conference. The day long program of youth planned workshops brings together teen councils from across the city.

Communication and Marketing

Faced with the inefficiencies of using traditional promotional materials such as brochures, many agencies have developed innovative media strategies to communicate with at-risk youth and their families. The most successful rely on young people themselves to develop and disseminate messages. Direct mail newsletters or cable television shows created for and by teens give youth a medium to discuss current issues affecting their lives while promoting relevant recreation-based programs and services:

- Wuzz-Up Teens is the name chosen by Phoenix youth for a quarterly newsletter and cable television program targeted at teens.
- 9teen Talk is a 30-minute television talk show on which Seattle teens express their opinions on issues that generally affect their lives, but about which they often feel powerless. Youth are involved in the "behind the scenes" production of the show.

For most recreation programs, word-of-mouth information transmitted by existing participants appears to be the most effective form of communication. Special circumstances necessitate unique, client-responsive approaches, as observed by a program manager in Olympia, Washington, whose program targets homeless and "street" youth:

> Street youth typically do not have access to the traditional forms of program marketing such as the print, television, or radio media. Postings in public places usually go unnoticed. Yet, many of these displaced youth have a finely refined network of communicating with each other on the street. As a result, most know how, when, and where to connect with one of our street workers.

In Indianapolis, Indiana, recreation personnel have gone door-to-door in target neighborhoods to promote the summer camp program. Similarly, Madison, Wisconsin, employs two regular part-time outreach workers who identify needy families through school social workers and other sources, then call or go door-to-door with fee waiver, transportation, and other information.

Resource Support

Because many at-risk youth programs target clientele in economically distressed areas, services often need to be offered either free of charge or at a nominal fee. These programs need substantial resource support which may come from either local government sources or external sources, such as state and federal grant programs, or private entities.

The golden years of tax-supported funding for local park and recreation agencies were from 1984 to 1991 (Crompton & McGregor, 1993). In contrast, the most recent era of downsizing and "reinventing government" has been characterized by a shortage of resources, a political climate which has emphasized law enforcement and incarceration, and a reluctance to invest in preventive actions. Many of the case studies reveal that at-risk youth programs, many of which started since 1989, receive minimal government investment and must rely heavily on external funds.

The limitations and danger of this strategy were pointed out by David Fisher, Executive Director of the Minneapolis Park and Recreation Board. He suggested that agencies might actually be contributing to the problems of youth by building expectations through short-term, one-shot recreation programs, then failing to follow-through with long-term, ongoing services:

> We will undertake a disservice to our clients, who already are beset by part-time parents and part-time education, by offering part-time programs. To be effective, programs must be consistent, constant, and sustainable. Otherwise I believe we simply feed the loop of failing to fulfill our promises.

Fisher called on each agency to develop a strategy for program continuance. He noted that the current federal strategy of avoiding hard decisions by providing block grants to states, which in turn are avoiding difficult decisions by making block grants to counties, eventually leaves the hard decisions about priorities and responsibilities at the local level:

> Unfortunately, while the 'control' for making decisions will be local, this system of allocating money will leave less funds to allocate at the local level. To avoid creating false expectations, we will need to make the hard decisions now about what we can realistically support in the future; we will need to build political alliances that will provide the advocacy and support base for programs; we will need to build ownership of programs among political and consumer constituencies; and we will need to find *long-term* corporate support. More importantly, we will need city government to invest local tax dollars on a continuing basis to support programs. We can be creative in our financing, but it will take long-term commitments and continuing support if we are to build sustainable programs.

In some communities, obtaining general fund support has not been possible, due to the reluctance to increase taxes. However, elected officials have been persuaded to create dedicated funds for these programs by imposing a surcharge on other recreation users, especially golfers:

- Portland, Oregon, has initiated an added fee of 50¢ for each round of golf played at one of the city-owned golf courses. An additional fee is also charged to nonresidents ($2 per round). Together these fees bring in close to $1 million per year which goes into a Parks and Youth Trust Fund.
- Phoenix generates $150,000 per year for at-risk youth programs through a 25¢ surcharge on each round of golf.

External Sources of Resources

Federal and state grants were the initial funding source for several of the programs described in the case studies:

- *The Drug Elimination/Youth Sports Program* of the U.S. Department of Housing and Urban Development has been used by

Boulder, Colorado, and Columbia, Mississippi, to establish rec-
reation-drug prevention programs in public housing.
- *Urban Park and Recreation Recovery Act (UPARR)* funds administered by the Department of the Interior gave the funding
  impetus for Tacoma, Washington's, Youth Outdoor Adventures
  program. It continues with support from a variety of public and
  private entities.
- Crime reduction funds from the Arizona Supreme Court funded
  staff and programming as part of Phoenix's City Streets initiative.

In order to be competitive for these grant funds, some agencies
have invested in staff specialists. For example, the Phoenix At-Risk
Youth Division hired a full-time grants researcher and coordinator in
1994. In the first full year, the Division submitted 25 applications
for funds, of which 15 were successful. This process yielded almost
$1 million in additional resources. To support this grant application
work, a resource library of data and statistical findings related to
youth was developed.

These grant resources, however, are short term, and the prevailing political climate in Washington, DC, and in state capitals sug-
gests that such opportunities will decline in the future. Hence, other
local public or private sector support for continuation of these programs will be essential.

The case studies demonstrate that support from local sources,
particularly the business community, voluntary organizations and
foundations is possible. For example:

- Advanced Micro Devices contributed $1 million towards the cost
  of constructing the Columbia Service Center in Sunnyvale, California.
- Along with funding received from local service clubs and at least
  one other foundation, the Longview and Kelso, Washington,
  after-school programs sought and received a substantial three-
  year funding commitment from the Weyerhaeuser Company
  Foundation. The three-year commitment was crucial to the
  program's success because it provided funding for a time period
  sufficient for the program to demonstrate its viability.
- In Seattle, Washington, the Ackerley Youth Foundation was
  formed by the owners of the SuperSonics basketball team in

1993 to support Seattle's at-risk youth programs. The foundation donated five vans to community centers; funded ten new teen leader positions, refurbished basketball courts, and facilitated the involvement of professional basketball players in educational programs.

External funding sources may be necessary to initiate programs, or to provide matching resources for them, but local government has to accept long-term responsibility for the continuance of these programs when they have been shown to be effective, if they are to be successful. This pattern has been used extensively in Oakland, California:

> The Oakland Summer Performing Arts Day Camp received its initial funding from the Mayor's Office with some private monies used to supplement these city funds. After demonstrating success, the City Council was approached for funding for future years.

In the national survey, 86% of the park and recreation agency respondents reported that the business community contributed resources to their at-risk youth programs. Voluntary organizations (85%) and foundations (46%) were also major resource contributors. The type of assistance received from these entities consisted of monetary donations (91%), volunteering of personnel (75%), equipment donations (56%), and provision of organizational leadership or expertise (53%).

Observations on Future Funding Sources

Future resources for at-risk youth programs may come from three sources: redirecting resources from other recreational programs, additional appropriations from legislative bodies, or additional reliance on external partners. The first option is, of course, likely to be resisted by the users of existing programs, and perhaps also by staff who may perceive a loss of personal power. Lowering service standards for existing client groups frequently leads to political protest. Opposition from staff to changes in emphases may occur since the changes may threaten an individual's status, area of expertise, or self-confidence. For example:

> In Montreal, some employees were very negative about
> hiring 'youth specialists,' and the assumption of respon-
> sibilities by partners which had traditionally been the
> employees' domain. They saw it as representing a loss
> of their personal power since they were no longer the
> sole front-line experts. They resented their loss of hier-
> archial control, as partners became involved.

Reallocation of resources is likely to occur only when a program's
life cycle nears its end and when turnover of staff occurs. This is
likely to be a gradual process.

Reluctance to raise tax rates means that if any additional appropriations are made, they are likely to be small, especially in major
cities where the tax base is declining. In order to justify tax increases for at-risk youth services to their constituents, legislators
have to be provided with evidence that these programs are effective.
Hence the current interest in developing evaluation measures which
provide this evidence.

Evaluation of Program Outcomes

Evaluating the extent to which programs have reached their goals is
crucial to their continued funding. Local elected officials often require indicators of a program's success before investing public tax
dollars in its continuation. Systematic evaluation procedures, unfortunately, have not been instituted by most agencies.

In a follow-up to the national survey of 120 agencies offering at-
risk youth programs, approximately 30% of the sample indicated that
they undertook *no* evaluation of their programs (Witt, Garteiser, &
Crompton, 1995). The remaining respondents were categorized
along a continuum of data sophistication. Thirteen percent of the
agencies used mainly participation data, the least sophisticated form
of evaluation; approximately 14% undertook some effort to collect
testimonials or case studies; 19% used surveys to obtain participant,
parent or other stakeholders' input about program quality or outcome; 20% used or planned to use crime statistics as an indicator of
program impact; and only 4% had undertaken any form of evaluation
utilizing a pre/post study of changes in such indicators as school
grades, test scores, leisure-related attitudes or behavior. These data

suggest increased efforts are needed by recreation and park agencies to build evaluation procedures into their program development efforts.

For the programs presented in this volume, evaluation methods cover the full spectrum of approaches described above. Unfortunately, few of the programs are utilizing methods beyond testimonials from participants, parents, program leaders, or other stakeholders. For example, the programs in Boulder, Colorado; Calgary, Alberta; and Tucson, Arizona, offered compelling testimonial evidence from participants, program leaders, parents and/or other stakeholders about the positive impact of their programs on participants.

In a few cases, postprogram surveys have been undertaken. For example, Longview and Kelso, Washington, and Tucson, Arizona, provided data from postprogram surveys, designed to elicit information about program quality and outcomes.

Finally, in a few cases, systematic procedures had been used to determine—through school, police or other data sources—the impact of at-risk programs. For example:

- Cincinnati, Ohio, reported a 31% decrease in crime incidents in the first six months after the Winton Hills prevention programs began.
- Commerce, California, compared gang-related assaults in their city with neighboring East Los Angeles to demonstrate program effectiveness. In East Los Angeles there were 140 gang-related assaults and 11 homicides in 1993, compared to seven gang-related assaults and zero homicides in Commerce.
- Kansas City, Missouri, reported a 25% decrease in the rate of juvenile apprehensions compared to the previous year in the areas abutting centers in which midnight basketball programs were offered.
- In Fort Worth, Texas, crime statistics supplied by the Police Department indicated in a one-mile radius of the community centers where midnight basketball was provided, crime dropped 28%. At five other community centers where these programs did not exist, crime rose an average of 39%.

Four agencies reported undertaking some form of formal evaluation using pre/post evaluation methodologies. For example:

- Raleigh, North Carolina, used the Self-Concept Attitudinal (SCAT) Inventory to compare children ages 6–12 who participated in their structured summer leisure education program, with children who used other playground sites but did not participate in the leisure education program. Results indicated significant improvement in scores for children participating in the more structured leisure education program, while participants in the traditional playground programs did not show as much improvement in their SCAT scores.
- University of Wisconsin researchers have undertaken several studies of the after-school programs sponsored by the Madison School-Community Recreation Department. Results showed a greater positive impact on school grades and conduct ratings associated with children in structured after-school programs, compared to others who were in self-care or less-structured programs. The differences may be attributable to children in the Madison programs spending more time in enrichment activities and sharing more activities with adults and peers.
- Impact evaluation of the Northern Fly-In Sports Camps program in Manitoba, Canada, has indicated a decrease in crime rate in communities where the sports camps are offered. Results also showed the program has had a positive effect on participants' levels of happiness, enjoyment, interest, perceptions of leisure and feelings about the Royal Canadian Mounted Police.
- Anaheim, California, tracks the progress of youth involved in their gang and drug intervention program. The tracking system allows leaders to determine the long-term impact of intervention efforts. In addition, Anaheim conducts nine different types of surveys to evaluate different components of the program.

Achieving meaningful evaluations of at-risk youth programs may be a difficult. As Reco Bembry, Seattle's teen program coordinator, noted:

> Part of the problem of doing a cost-benefit evaluation analysis of the program is that you cannot measure what didn't happen. We save lives, but how can you measure a shooting that didn't occur because the kid was in this program?

One way of doing this may be to place a cost on each of the crimes (and the costs of prosecuting and incarcerating guilty individuals associated with them) and document the dollars saved by any drop in crime rates which appear to be related to the program.

Concluding Comments

> The human services view of recreation and parks as practiced in many urban communities places the recreation and park movement at a crossroads. One path travels down the narrow road of traditionally defined, segmented activities based on economic values; the other path leads to a multidisciplinary community services approach that places recreation, parks and amenities in the center of the urban policy debate. (Foley & Pick, 1995, p. 70)

The case studies provide evidence that many recreation and park agencies are returning to the roots of the profession by investing more resources in providing programs for at-risk children and youth. The service priorities of responsive recreation and park agencies are shaped by external forces which they cannot control, but to which they must adapt. In the late 1970s and throughout the 1980s, the external political forces directed that an agency's primary concern should be to increase efficiency or to "do more with less." This was accomplished by reducing an agency's tax subsidy, while maintaining or expanding its range of offerings. This resulted in focusing on target markets with the ability and willingness to pay prices high enough to cover most service costs, and reducing resources invested in high-subsidy programs.

Since 1988, political forces have continued to stress reducing tax subsidies, but this has been accompanied by a priority emphasis "to do something about" juvenile crime and delinquency. Explosive, high-profile incidents involving young people have grown exponentially in recent years, and each horrific event directs more political attention to this issue. Recreation programs have been viewed by some as a means through which these problems may be addressed.

Despite being labeled by some critics as "wasteful social spending" and "pork," recreation programs have been embraced as one means to address problems associated with high-risk youth. Smith (1991) noted the cost benefits in her report to the Carnegie Council on Adolescent Development:

> The provision of community recreation services is a good investment. Participation in organized recreation provides for the constructive use of free time and develops skills for the management of discretionary time and thereby reduces the need for, and the costs of, providing other governmental and social services that deal with the management of antisocial behaviors after they occur. (p. ii-iii)

Repositioning, however, takes time. Agencies that have focused for a decade or more on middle-class target markets cannot immediately reorient staff and resources to serving at-risk youth. Unfortunately today's youth, indeed society, cannot wait. We therefore present the following profiles of successful park and recreation programs and strategies with the ultimate hope that they can be replicated to benefit communities of all sizes, demographic composition, and needs across the country.

References

Addams, J. [1893] (1960). The subjective necessity for social settlements. In *Philanthropy and Social Progress*, pp. 1-26. Freeport, NY: Books for Libraries Press.

Crompton, J. L. & McGregor, B. (1994). Trends in the financing and staffing of local government park and recreation services. *Journal of Park and Recreation Administration, 12*(3), 19-37.

Espericuerta-Schultz, L., Crompton J. L., & Witt P. A. (1995). A National Profile of the Status of Public Recreation Services for At-Risk Children and Youth. *Journal of Park and Recreation Administration, 13*(3), 1-26.

Foley, J. & Pick, H. (1995). Healthy cities: Survival strategies for recreation and parks. *Parks and Recreation, 30*(4), 68-72.

Peters, T. J. & Waterman R. H. (1982). *In Search of Excellence.* New York, NY: Harper & Row.

Smith, C. (1991). *Overview of youth recreation programs in the United States.* Washington, DC: Carnegie Council on Adolescent Development.

Tice, R. D. & Tindall, B. (1994). *Beyond fun and games: Emerging roles of public recreation.* Arlington, VA: National Recreation and Park Association.

Witt, P. A., Garteiser, M., & Crompton, J. L. (1995). *Status of evaluation of recreation programs for at-risk youth.* Unpublished paper. College Station, TX: Department of Recreation, Park and Tourism Sciences.

Section II
Mature Full-Spectrum Programs

Chapter 3
Youth Diversion Program
in Commerce, California

Presenter:
Robert Chavez
    Social Services Division Manager, City of Commerce Youth
    Division

Background

Commerce, a heavily industrialized city with 12,500 residents, is located six miles southeast of Los Angeles, bordered by East Los Angeles on the north and Bell Gardens on the south. Incorporated in 1960, the city has a strong tradition of commitment to youth through education, libraries, and sports. The city has been working on issues related to gangs since 1982.

In late 1989, the city of Commerce suffered its first drive-by shooting. In early 1990, staff of the Social Services Division of the City of Commerce Department of Parks and Recreation and other members of the community noted attempts by a local gang to expand its membership into previously unaffected areas of Commerce. Residents complained to City Council regarding drug activity, graffiti, and vandalism produced by gang members.

As a result the Social Services Division established a Community Youth Gang Task Force, drawing individuals from City Council, law enforcement agencies, the Probation Department, schools, community-based organizations, and the community at large to address the issue of youth delinquency in Commerce. The Task Force currently meets on the second Wednesday of every month, or when an emergency arises requiring collaboration amongst agencies.

Program Description

Purpose and Goals

The purposes of the Community Youth Gang Task Force are to:

(1) coordinate community resources, discuss and develop policies, and recommend programming geared to controlling delinquent activity in Commerce;

(2) unite as a community to insure the public safety of Commerce residents; and

(3) maintain and protect the city's image as a safe environment to live and raise a family.

Special goals of the Task Force are as follows:

a. *Gangs:* To reduce gang membership amongst city of Commerce youth. Ultimately to control the existence of gangs within the boundaries of Commerce.

b. *Graffiti Eradication*: To reduce incidents of graffiti and recover restitution for damages incurred. To encourage and support legislation addressing gang-related issues.

c. *Parent Education/Awareness*: To assist city of Commerce families by helping them to analyze their needs and providing parents with the knowledge to regain control of their own children. To help parents understand their legal rights, responsibilities, and liabilities.

d. *Prevention*: To continually educate Commerce children that gang activity is unacceptable behavior. To establish an early identification system of tracking and diverting high-risk youth to positive activity at an earlier phase of child development.

e. *Employment*: To develop employment opportunities and training for youth 14–21 years of age.

f. *Community Mobilization*:

   i. To develop a spirit of community pride and involvement amongst residents, employees, churches, and local businesses.

   ii. To unite efforts between City Council, the community, law enforcement, courts, the probation department, schools, all city departments, neighborhood watch groups, community-based organizations, etc.

   iii. To plan, implement, and enforce a comprehensive community plan of action that ensures the utilization of available resources.

   iv. To communicate actively and effectively toward the goal of controlling gangs in the city of Commerce.

Programs

Through the efforts of the Task Force and a number of agencies in the community, a variety of services have been developed to help meet these goals. The City of Commerce Youth Diversion Program (YDP) helps to coordinate many of these strategies to prevent and divert youth from becoming involved in illegal and/or gang-related activities.

The Youth Diversion Program is sponsored by the Social Services Division of the Parks and Recreation Department. The Division operates on an annual budget of $1,774,783 targeting approximately 4,227 youth (see Exhibit 3A). The Division's budget is 6% of the total city budget.

Exhibit 3A

Youth Diversion Program Budget—1994

G.A.P.P. Los Angeles County Probation	42,000
Social Services Advisors	333,024
Community Safety Specialist	376,614
Special Problems Team East Los Angeles Sheriff's Office	316,614
Dedicated Sergeant East Los Angeles Sheriff's Office	244,376
Community Psychologist	10,000
Graffiti Removal	200,000
Parenting Classes	4,155
Employment Referral Office	240,000
50/50 Program	8,000
Total	$1,774,783

Commerce's YDP features a community psychological services partnership with the Los Angeles County Probation Department's Gang Alternative Prevention Program (with an in-house probation officer), the Community Gang Task Force, in-house parenting classes, local job placement programs, close work with the Sheriff's Department through the Special Problems Team and Community-Based Policing Program, and education programs focusing on prevention (grades K–6) and intervention (grades 7–12).

Parent Education: Through a cooperative effort between Montebello Unified School District (MUSD) and Commerce Social Services, bilingual parenting classes are conducted year-round. Other specialized classes focus on issues such as self-esteem, communicating with one's child, and developing listening skills. In addition, guest speakers who deal with topics such as alcoholism or the juvenile justice system, are part of the program. All classes are run by MUSD faculty and a Social Services advisor. Staff time, materials, and the facility are provided by the city, and MUSD Adult Education assumes the cost of the instructor.

In-House Counseling: A licensed psychological therapist is also available to work directly with troubled youth and parents enrolled in the Gang Alternative and Prevention Program (G.A.P.P.). The psychologist's services are not limited to G.A.P.P. cases, but are also available to residents requesting counseling.

Counseling Services: Commerce also contracts with Consolidated Youth Services Network (CYSN) which provides professional licensed counseling dealing with behavior modification, drugs, alcohol, potential suicide, parenting, and other issues. The Sheriff's department diverts arrested Commerce youth to CYSN, which later refers them to Commerce Social Services for follow-up.

Educational Seminars: These sessions provide a forum to discuss current topics affecting the city and its residents (e.g., drugs, graffiti). Residents have the opportunity to express their opinions and provide the city with viable solutions for dealing with problems.

Information and Referral: Some families have serious problems, e.g., a family member's addiction, a battered spouse, an elderly relative in need of special services, or an unemployed family member. Often people seek support from friends and relatives, but prefer to avoid the embarrassment of sharing problems with relatives and turn elsewhere for assistance. The Commerce Social Services Division staff is trained to listen to the needs of residents and refer them to the local, state, and federal agencies best qualified to assist them. Social Services staff may also communicate with these agencies on their behalf to explain special circumstances or schedule appointments.

Employment: The Employment Referral Office places local residents and youth in local industry free of charge. The service averages approximately 500 placements per year.

Job Training Partnership Act and **Summer Youth Employment Program**: The city, along with the West San Gabriel Valley

Consortium, participates in providing summer employment opportunities for low-income youth between the ages of 14 and 21. Youth must meet eligibility criteria set by the Job Training Partnership Act (JTPA)/Summer Youth Employment Program (SYEP). Job sites are found throughout city departments. Typical types of work experiences include: gardening, clerical work, and park and recreation assistants. Social Services Division staff are responsible for collecting eligibility paper work of local Commerce youth, and monitoring work sites to ensure credible work experiences.

50/50 Program: The city utilizes Job Training Partnership Act (JTPA) funding to provide low-income youth temporary employment. However, in cases when youths do not meet state eligibility criteria, 50/50 program funds are allocated to partially pay for a youth's salary. This program is utilized for youth 18–21 years of age who respond positively to G.A.P.P. The program is not solely for G.A.P.P. minors; there are cases where Social Services have utilized the program for other youth of Commerce who display the desire to redirect their lives. This program entices local businesses to give troubled youth an opportunity to become employed. The agency says to a business, "Are you looking for an employee? We have somebody here who is at-risk, but has been through our program. He is trying to turn his life around. We believe he can. Give him a shot at this job and we will pay his wages for the first two weeks. If you like him, you keep him. If you don't, then you can terminate him and it has not cost you anything."

Youth Leadership Development: The Youth Advisory Committee (YAC) is made up of five members (ages 13–19) appointed by the City Council. YAC's primary purpose is to help City Council and staff understand the needs and concerns of Commerce youth. The appointed youth hold two meetings monthly to discuss current events and plan educational projects. All youth are invited to attend meetings. A Social Services Advisor serves as a liaison between the Council and YAC. He or she oversees meetings, trips, and other special events occurring in the city.

The primary objective of the Youth Leadership program is to use YAC and other park development teen groups to teach fundamental management and positive organizational skills, and to promote and increase college enrollment amongst Commerce youth. Youth are taught to take pride and become actively involved in the community. The program provides an alternative for youth who are not active in sports programs sponsored by the city.

Drug Education: The Substance Abuse Narcotics Education (SANE) and Drug Awareness Resistance Education (DARE) programs are taught by the Los Angeles County Sheriff's Department in conjunction with the Social Services Division. SANE is a drug awareness program taught to all third and fourth graders at local schools. DARE is implemented in all fifth and sixth grade classes at Suva and Bell Gardens intermediate schools.

G.A.P.P.: Gang Alternative Prevention Program

The Gang Alternative Prevention Program (G.A.P.P.) is a comprehensive approach to prevention. Minors who have demonstrated gang-related behavior such as graffiti, gang-style dress and/or associating with other known gang members (see Exhibit 3B) are referred to the programs by a parent, school, police, probation, and/or local park personnel. Contrary to popular stereotypes, a majority of the cases—52%—came from two-parent homes. Thirty-three percent of the G.A.P.P. cases are known gang members who are considered to be a stage beyond "at-risk" status. Of the 57 cases that have come to G.A.P.P. only one case has been remanded and sent to a youth probation camp.

Youth are directed to G.A.P.P. only after all youth diversion alternatives offered by the Social Services staff are exhausted. To participate, parents and the minor must agree to join G.A.P.P. as a voluntary probationer under the 654 Welfare and Institutions code.

Under the terms of agreement, the minor is required to attend ten weeks of individual or group therapy sessions. If further counseling is needed, the G.A.P.P. Officer will require the youth to attend other sessions. While this is occurring, the youth's parents are required by the Deputy Probation Officer (DPO) to attend ten parenting classes offered by the city in conjunction with the Montebello Unified School District.

Networking Resources: G.A.P.P. success is attributable to the vast network of resources it utilizes, including schools, juvenile camps and courts, local police departments and other youth referral agencies. The Commerce G.A.P.P. Office has established this kind of network to ensure that it has all the information on a case, information on possible disciplinary alternatives for each case, and a full range of assistance as necessary.

Local Schools: Local elementary, junior high, and high school teachers and counselors assist the DPO in evaluating the behavior of G.A.P.P. cases.

Exhibit 3B

Dress/Style Found Among Youth in Commerce—1994

Rave: Nonviolent, baggy clothing, usually colorful and/or containing a lot of denim material. Unusual haircuts or shaved heads (often dyed). Piercing of both ears in males (as well as nipples or navels) is common. This group often enjoys dancing for long periods of time.

Party Goers: Underground and warehouse parties and nightclubs.

Music: Techno/house similar to disco sound, imported music.

Drug Use: Focuses on hallucinogens. Amphetamines and methamphetamines are popular. Marijuana and alcohol are also common.

Hip Hop: This group wears baggy clothing, baseball/hockey jerseys, baseball hats, expensive tennis shoes, and baggy Levis.

Party Goers: Underground, house (backyard) and warehouse parties and nightclubs.

Music: Rap music (not necessarily gangsta rap).

Drug Use: Alcohol and marijuana are prevalent. Cocaine is also common.

Cholo: Gang members with violent tendencies who favor baggy clothing, Pendleton or flannel shirts, solid colors, Ben Davis clothing (thick material) which is usually found in swap meets. Neat creases on shirts and pants, Nike "Cortez" style shoes (dark blue/black with white stripe), heads shaved to the skin or short hair slicked back (using hair net, palm comb, or hair oil [typically "Three Flowers"]). Some with shaved heads have a braid at the base of the neck. Goatee or moustache is common.

Party Goers: Frequent most events of which they are aware.

Music: Oldies, old funk, gangsta rap.

Drug Use: Marijuana, alcohol, heroin and PCP are traditional among this group. A new trend in this group's drug use is amphetamines (speed) and crack cocaine.

Taggers: Cross section of Rave, Hip Hop, and Cholo that focuses on "tagging" or marking graffiti on walls either individually or in groups called *crews*. This classification draws on facets of the other three in locations frequented, music listened to, and also in drug use. Existent drug use in this group can vary as in the other groups but is commonly like that of Cholos.

Special Probation Team (SPT): The DPO receives much of its information on the G.A.P.P. caseload or potential G.A.P.P. minors by maintaining a relationship with the Special Problems Team and other local police officers from the Sheriff's Department. In some instances where positive redirection cannot be achieved, an alternative must be sought. In cases such as these, the DPO will recommend to the court that the youth be sent to a youth probation camp or an alternative educational institution.

Tattoo Removal Services: G.A.P.P. believes that an important factor in helping the client start a new life is by changing the youth's image. However, there is a problem when aspects of that image are permanent, as is the case with tattoos. To deal with this, the Beckman Laser Institute and Medical Clinic has joined forces with Interagency Gang Task Forces in Los Angeles and Orange Counties to provide reduced-cost laser therapy for the removal of gang tattoos.

Antigraffiti Campaign: Developing a more positive community image is the goal of antigraffiti efforts. Commerce Public Works, Community Development, Community Services, Park and Recreation, East Los Angeles Probation Department, and the East Los Angeles Sheriff's Department coordinate information and resources in this effort.

The graffiti removal team and painters from Public Works and Community Development take Polaroid pictures of graffiti prior to removal. Expedient removal of graffiti is essential to cut down on communication between gangs using this medium and "tagging" (i.e., placing one's name on anything with an artistic flare). Taggers and gang activity are not always related. The Social Services Manager monitors graffiti on a daily basis working with Social Services staff, parks staff, local school officials, informants, and Public Safety staff to identify nicknames, insignias, etc. Law enforcement and city staff make direct contact with alleged graffiti producers, known gang members, and parents to advise them that they are being watched. Occasionally, arrests are made.

Evidence of Effectiveness

Proactive action is taken to redirect youth activities away from gang or other detrimental activities before juvenile court proceedings are necessary. The concept of G.A.P.P. has become so popular that it has been replicated by other incorporated cities. In December 1990 there were ten contracted DPOs; today there are 18. G.A.P.P. has been instrumental in undermining local gang recruitment efforts in Commerce. The G.A.P.P. Officer provides early intervention to at-risk youth, juveniles on court-ordered probation, and youth returning to the community after court-ordered placements.

The impact of Commerce's YDP is clearly illustrated by the statistics contrasting neighboring East Los Angeles and Commerce. In 1993, East Los Angeles experienced 140 gang-related assaults and 11 homicides. Commerce reported seven gang-related assaults and zero homicides. More recently Commerce's G.A.P.P. Deputy Probation Officer reported five straight months (March—July, 1994) with an arrest-free caseload of 40 probationers, half of whom are youth on voluntary probation.

During the first year of G.A.P.P., there was only one homicide in Commerce. However, it is important to emphasize that the G.A.P.P. officer came into a virtually homicide-free situation. Since 1984 there have only been three gang-related homicides. Hence, the G.A.P.P. officer is not dealing with a particularly violent population which means the program has a high probability of success.

Another potential indicator of the success of the G.A.P.P. program is to look at the high-school graduation rate of youth who have been in the G.A.P.P. program. While the number of high school graduates does not appear impressive (six) in relation to the number of G.A.P.P. cases, if placed in proper perspective it is quite respectable. The number of minors who were of age to graduate between September 1993 and February 1995 was between ten and 15, so a graduation rate of at least 40% was achieved. The case study in Exhibit 3C (see page 46) provides evidence of the program's effectiveness for one individual.

Exhibit 3C

How It Works: A Case Study

- In early 1993, Juan Costello was a junior at Bell Gardens High School. School officials noted that problems, including truancy, were interfering with his education. "I was involved in too many gang-related activities," Costello said, "I didn't feel I had to be there regularly."
- In August, Costello was recruited for Soledad Enrichment Action, an independent study program aimed at helping participants earn a high-school diploma or the GED equivalent. "The city of Commerce called me," Costello said. "They actually called me. People here make you want to come to their program."
- Through G.A.P.P. Costello received additional counseling and employment placement.
- Costello then worked with the city Employment Referral Office to find a job. "The same day I was interviewed, they found me a job at a fast-food restaurant," Costello said.
- By December, Costello became the first student to obtain his high-school diploma through the Soledad Enrichment Action program. His job has allowed him to move into his own apartment. "I stuck to it all the way through," said Costello. "My main interest is computers. I want to learn and get into that profession. Maybe go to trade school."

Chapter 4
Project S.A.Y. (Save-A-Youth)
in Anaheim, California

Presenter:
Mark Deven
    Recreation/Community Services Superintendent, Recreation and
    Community Services Department

Background

Anaheim is a city of 266,406 residents, 31% of whom are Hispanic
and 59% are Caucasian. Spanish is spoken at home in 16% of the
households. While the median family income in Anaheim is
$45,407, in certain segments of the city (particularly where there are
high concentrations of minorities) the median income is approximately $27,000.

As early as 1984, the Anaheim Parks, Recreation and Community Services Department recognized that the community was facing
a problem relative to its youth.

- Groups of unorganized youth between the ages of 13 and 21
  were increasingly responsible for such crimes as vandalism,
  substance abuse, graffiti, assaults, burglaries, and thefts.
- Existing youth-related service programs were only somewhat
  effective because of: (a) limited bilingual/bicultural staff; (b) the
  absence of networking among city, community-based schools,
  parents, and private sector interests; (c) the lack of programs
  targeted at gang prevention/intervention; and, (d) the city's cri-
  sis-oriented rather than preventive service delivery.

These findings prompted the 1986 creation of Project S.A.Y.
(Save-A-Youth), a youth-oriented gang/drug intervention program.
The initial program dealt with youth between the ages of 13 and 21;
however, city staff realized that a large number of younger, more
impressionable youth were still not being reached. These youth were
falling under the influence of gangs, though in most cases they had
not made up their minds about participating in them.

As a result, the city sought and received a grant from the U.S. Department of Health and Human Services, Family and Youth Services Bureau, to create Kids-in-Action, a prevention component for Project S.A.Y. with activities focusing on self-esteem and confidence building for children 5–12 years of age. Thus, the city was able to mount a three-pronged approach to youth gang/drug problems to include prevention, intervention, and suppression components. The suppression component was already being provided by the Anaheim Police Department.

Despite these initial efforts to address the problem, gangs and drug usage continued to be a growing concern. Therefore, in 1991, the Parks, Recreation and Community Services Department helped facilitate an interdepartmental task force to address the problem comprehensively. Task force recommendations led to the formation of a Citizens' Task Force comprised of a broad coalition of citizen representatives from businesses, schools, human service organizations, civic groups, and religious organizations. Grass-roots neighborhood residents were also represented. City staff, including the Police Chief, Parks, Recreation and Community Services Director, Planning Director, Fire Chief, and other city staff served as ex-officio members of the Task Force.

The Task Force convened public forums throughout the city and gathered the input from more than 600 residents. This information was used to help create a strategy for addressing Anaheim's gang and drug issues. The strategy identified ten gang and drug issues and recommended over 90 actions to address these issues. School, religious, and nonprofit organizations, the business community, and numerous city departments were delegated specific tasks to implement the strategy.

In June 1992 the Anaheim City Council adopted the "Citizen Task Force Report" and appointed a full-time city staff position to work with the community to help coordinate and facilitate implementation of the recommendations. In 1995 the Task Force was replaced by an interdepartmental neighborhood services committee composed of executive managers representing various departments including Parks, Recreation and Community Services. The full-time city staff position formerly assigned to gang/drug prevention is now responsible for implementing a broad range of services designed to revitalize depressed and deteriorating neighborhoods. Project S.A.Y. is a critical component of the overall neighborhood revitalization strategy.

Program Description

Goals and Objectives

The long-term goal of Project S.A.Y. is to assist youth in avoiding gang and drug involvement, and become productive, law-abiding citizens. Specific short-term objectives which give context to the long-term goal are as follows:

(1) to keep youth in school (reduce absenteeism/truancy);
(2) to return youth to school (prevent students from dropping out);
(3) to assist youth in achieving passing grades (reduce incidence of failing);
(4) to assist youth in completing informal/formal probation (reduce repeat offenses);
(5) to assist youth in reducing drug activity; and
(6) to assist youth in reducing gang activity.

Key Players

Project S.A.Y. works closely with public and private nonprofit agencies to facilitate the delivery of services to target neighborhoods. Private businesses provide support through contribution of funds and/or in-kind services. The most significant key players are the Anaheim Religious Community Council (ARCC), the Anaheim Boys and Girls Club, Anaheim Family YMCA, Salvation Army, Anaheim Union High School District, Anaheim City School District, Centralia School District, Anaheim Police Department Gang and Community Policing Details, Orange County Probation Department, Anaheim Private Industry Council (PIC), and YWCA Youth Employment Service. Several Anaheim businesses including Rockwell Corporation, Carl Karcher Enterprises, Disneyland, the California Angels, and the Mighty Ducks of Anaheim have consistently supported Project S.A.Y. activities.

Program Content

Project S.A.Y. consists of a combination of outreach, paraprofessional counseling, recreation, and sports activities to encourage youth involvement in positive activities.

Prevention: Kids-in-Action targets children ages 5–12 and provides comprehensive, nontraditional recreation, sports, and outreach programs in eight targeted neighborhoods of the city. Programs are offered in community centers, elementary schools, or on park sites. Recreational and educational activities are designed to promote positive self-esteem, build confidence, develop cultural pride, and reinforce and support various classroom prevention programs in place in the Anaheim elementary schools such as Drug and Alcohol Resistance and Education (D.A.R.E.) and Wipe-Out Graffiti, a graffiti abatement and educational curriculum.

An early assessment, referral, and evaluation tracking method is used on youths participating in the program. A procedure and referral system documents behavioral problems in participants for assessment and follow-up by the outreach worker. With this linkage the outreach worker and recreation staff can address the behavior of the child and work with the parents and community resources to affect positive change.

On the surface, a Kids-in-Action site looks similar to other after-school programs currently being offered across the United States. College-age staff in uniform interact with groups of children and conduct activities ranging from arts and crafts to sports.

Upon closer observation, subtle differences between Kids-in-Action and other after-school programs address the root causes of youth gang involvement and substance abuse. The sites have a distinct identity through the prominent display of the multicolored Kids-in-Action logo in activity areas and on participants' shirts. A minimum of two bilingual/bicultural staff work at each site, each trained to recognize social problems and provide referrals to community service outreach workers. Staff members' cultural sensitivity enables them to establish trust with parents which in turn leads to more consistent participation by the children.

Kids-in-Action sites are open fifty weeks per year with early afternoon and evening program hours to accommodate Anaheim's growing year-round school population. Many activities emphasize cultural pride, including Ballet Folklorico dances and holiday celebrations such as Cinco de Mayo, 16 de September, and Dia del Muerte. Off-site excursions to local businesses involve the participation of the Hispanic owner and/or manager as a positive role model in order to send a "can-do" message to the children. Youngsters are encouraged to join each site's Community Club and participate in neighborhood clean-ups, graffiti "paint outs," and tree planting/beautification efforts to promote environmental stewardship and community responsibility. Recreation programs emphasize skill development, sportsmanship, and team play over winning and losing. A specialized curriculum which discourages gang affiliation, antisocial behavior, and substance abuse is introduced into small group activities such as arts and crafts, and role-playing.

Intervention: Project S.A.Y.'s intervention component targets youth ages 13–19 and works extensively on junior and senior high school campuses. Together, the city and the Anaheim Union High School District have developed a paraprofessional antigang and drug counseling and behavior guidance program. Gang-awareness training for school administrators and teachers enables school personnel to make appropriate referrals to one of the city's five Community Service Outreach Workers. The outreach workers are assigned to areas of the city which correspond to specific high-school attendance boundaries and their supporting junior high and elementary feeder schools.

Outreach workers are trained in conflict resolution and provide mediation assistance between individuals and groups to prevent potentially violent situations. All of the current staff are bilingual, college educated, and come from backgrounds similar to the clients they serve. Workers are usually sensitive and understanding as well as savvy and street-smart. They have proven equally adept at communicating with educators, corporate officers, city administrators, police officers, high-school students, and gang members.

Each outreach worker carries an average load of 50 active clients, although they involve many more in recreation activities including summer camp, sports, tournaments, workshops, educational programs, special events, excursions, and rap sessions. Outreach workers also conduct parenting workshops which focus on recognizing youth gang involvement and the resources available for referrals.

Outreach workers have offices at high schools and junior high schools to maintain close relationships with clients and school truant officers. The Anaheim Police Department's school-based gang investigator works with outreach workers in intervention programs including assemblies and rallies.

Outreach workers spend the majority of their time in one-on-one paraprofessional counseling and assessment sessions with clients and members of their families, usually in the client's home. The outreach workers are able to make referrals to a variety of public and nonprofit sources. A tracking procedure is followed for all participants, to assure appropriate evaluation, referral, and follow-up.

Supporting elements tied to prevention and intervention activities include efforts by the Anaheim Religious Community Council in parental education, and the work of the Boys and Girls Clubs and YMCA in recreation programming. Breakfast and lunch are available through a U.S. Department of Agriculture funded program at selected sites including neighborhood centers where the Kids-in-Action programs operate.

Suppression: The third component of Anaheim's antigang/drug strategy focuses on law enforcement. In 1991, the Anaheim Police Department formed a Gang Unit to investigate and prosecute gang-related crimes proactively. However, at the same time the Police Department strengthened prevention and intervention programs by assigning a gang investigator to work directly with Project S.A.Y. and the schools to identify potential problems on campus and in the neighborhood, and to strategize jointly in resolving conflicts and issues. The gang investigator operates in an enforcement capacity to deal with situations of a criminal nature, but also counsels youth and parents to try to avoid problematic situations that will involve "suppression" responses in the future. In a related effort, the Police Department's Community Policing Detail is forming a Police Athletic League which will target at-risk youth and further enhance the recreation activities associated with Project S.A.Y.

Evaluation and Program Impact

Tracking System

Project S.A.Y. participants are closely tracked, beginning with their initial assessment and continuing through high school and beyond as feasible. While statistics exist to measure program participation and criminal incidents, a true evaluation of the program's effectiveness needs to be measured on an individual basis. The long-term impact of Project S.A.Y. is evaluated according to the following criteria:

A. *Basic Education*
   Achieves high school equivalency (GED), *or*
   Achieves high school graduation
B. *Higher Education/Employment*
   Enrolls/attends trade school, *or*
   Enrolls/attends community college, *or*
   Enrolls/attends university/four-year college, *or*
   Gains full-time employment (self-supporting)

C. *Criminal Activity*
Remains off probation, *and*
Is not incarcerated in the criminal justice system, *and*
Does not exhibit criminal behavior

"Long-Term Tracking Cards" are kept on each client (see Exhibit 4A, page 54) within the first month of initial contact. The outreach workers make three status report entries per year. The tracking cards become a permanent part of the client's files and are maintained in perpetuity.

Other Evaluation Components

In addition to the tracking system, a variety of other surveys are utilized to help evaluate the success of the intervention and prevention components of the program. These include:

(a) *Test group—Kids-in-Action:* Pretest and posttest surveys are conducted at a park site during the summer program.
(b) *Periodic surveys of specific activities:* Surveys are conducted at all Kids-in-Action sites throughout the year to determine the effectiveness of specific activities.
(c) *Special event surveys:* Surveys are conducted at the conclusion of all special events.
(d) *Participant surveys:* Surveys of participants in both Project S.A.Y. and Kids-in-Action are conducted three times per year to determine the effectiveness of the program.
(e) *Parent surveys:* Annual parent surveys of Kids-in-Action children are conducted to determine the effectiveness of the program from the parents' point of view.
(f) *School personnel surveys:* Surveys of elementary and junior high/high school personnel are conducted to determine the effectiveness of the program.
(g) *Evaluations at Kids-in-Action sites:* Site evaluations are conducted three times per year to evaluate attractiveness of the site as it relates to encouraging participation in the programs.
(h) *Evaluation by program staff:* Staff complete a program evaluation three times per year to determine effectiveness of the program.
(i) *Police personnel survey:* Annual surveys of police personnel are conducted to determine effectiveness of the program.

Exhibit 4A   Project S.A.Y.—Outreach Long-Term Tracking Card

Client Name: _____   Date: _____

Address: _____   Phone: _____

Enrolled In School
- Yes
- No
- Jr. High
- Sr. High
- Trade
- Jr. College
- University

Attendance
- Reg. Att.
- Freq. Abs.
- Freq. Tardy
- Truant
- Formal Withdrawal

Grades
- Good (A/B)
- Passing
- Failing

Probation
- Informal
- Formal
- 1st Offense
- 2nd Offense
- Completion Date

Employment
- P.T. Job
- F.T. Job
- Skilled
- Unskilled
- Self-Supporting

Illegal Activity
- Gang Related
- Drugs
- Weapons
- Assault
- Theft
- Murder/Attempt
- Other: _____

Today's Date: _____   Age of Client: _____

Comments: _____

Enrolled In School
- Yes
- No
- Jr. High
- Sr. High
- Trade
- Jr. College
- University

Attendance
- Reg. Att.
- Freq. Abs.
- Freq. Tardy
- Truant
- Formal Withdrawal

Grades
- Good (A/B)
- Passing
- Failing

Probation
- Informal
- Formal
- 1st Offense
- 2nd Offense
- Completion Date

Employment
- P.T. Job
- F.T. Job
- Skilled
- Unskilled
- Self-Supporting

Illegal Activity
- Gang Related
- Drugs
- Weapons
- Assault
- Theft
- Murder/Attempt
- Other: _____

Today's Date: _____   Age of Client: _____

Comments: _____

Enrolled In School
- Yes
- No
- Jr. High
- Sr. High
- Trade
- Jr. College
- University

Attendance
- Reg. Att.
- Freq. Abs.
- Freq. Tardy
- Truant
- Formal Withdrawal

Grades
- Good (A/B)
- Passing
- Failing

Probation
- Informal
- Formal
- 1st Offense
- 2nd Offense
- Completion Date

Employment
- P.T. Job
- F.T. Job
- Skilled
- Unskilled
- Self-Supporting

Illegal Activity
- Gang Related
- Drugs
- Weapons
- Assault
- Theft
- Murder/Attempt
- Other: _____

Today's Date: _____   Age of Client: _____

Comments: _____

Further testimony to Project S.A.Y.'s effectiveness occurred in June 1994. A grass-roots group of churches, the Orange County Community Congregation Organization (OCCCO), successfully persuaded the City Council to allocate an additional $250,000 to services targeting youth and families in central Anaheim. OCCCO's justification included numerous references to how Project S.A.Y. has met the community's gang and drug prevention and intervention needs. Approximately $170,000 of the allocation was directed to Project S.A.Y. activities, with the balance directed to other human services which indirectly support gang prevention and intervention.

Chapter 5
An Integrated Approach to Services for Children and Youth
in Minneapolis, Minnesota

Presenter:
David Fisher
  Superintendent, Minneapolis Park and Recreation Board

Background

The city of Minneapolis (population 367,924) has experienced dramatic changes in population in the last decade. Nearly 28% of the
city's 1990 population migrated to Minneapolis since 1985. About
one-half of these persons moved from out of state, while nearly 30%
moved into Minneapolis from a suburb. The racial and ethnic distribution of the population moving to Minneapolis resemble closely the
racial composition of the city's 1990 population as a whole. However, the age distribution of the recent migrant population is significantly younger than that of the general population.

In the past decade there has been an increase in poverty, single-
parent households, alcohol and other drug abuse, teenage sexual
experimentation and pregnancy, gang activity, crime, and school
dropout rates. These trends created a significant need to provide
prevention programs. Currently, 32% of children in the city live with
a single, female parent; about 13% of the population is African
American; 3% each are either Native American or of Asian backgrounds. In 1992 slightly more than one-half of all Minneapolis
children received some form of economic assistance. Beginning in
the late 1980s working, two-parent families and single-parent families were finding it increasingly difficult to identify safe and affordable childcare.

Dave Fisher, Superintendent of the Minneapolis Park and Recreation Board, noted:

> All of us have a vital stake in the healthy development of
> today's children and adolescents, who will become

tomorrow's parents, workers, and citizens. Young
people do not become mature adults without assistance.
They are profoundly influenced by experiences they
have at home and in school, and are also affected by
experiences in their neighborhoods and the larger community during nonschool hours. The importance of
communities in contributing to the development of
young people is well-supported by both research and
practice. The opportunity to make that contribution
exists primarily during the after-school hours.

Program Description

The Minneapolis Park and Recreation Board has assumed a leadership role in supporting youth and their families through the development of four key programs. These programs provide a "continuum
of services" which serve the needs of elementary school children
through high-school-aged youth. This follows the recommendation
of a recent report of the Carnegie Corporation, which the Minneapolis Park and Recreation Board has embraced as a guiding statement
of philosophy:

> In a youth-centered America, every community would
> have a network of affordable, accessible, safe and chal-
> lenging opportunities that appeal to the diverse interests
> of youth. Youth development services would provide
> meaningful opportunities for young people to pursue
> individual interests as well as contribute to their commu-
> nities. They would grant youth appropriate degrees of
> autonomy. They would be organized through responsive
> program, organizational and community structures.
> They would be rooted in a solid foundation of research-
> and practice-based knowledge of the needs of children
> and adolescents and supported by a dependable and
> diverse financial base. Finally, they would be grounded
> on suggestions from youth themselves (Carnegie Corpo-
> ration, 1992, p. 77).

A brief description of the four programs that form the continuum of
services follows:

- *Recreation Plus+*: Kindergarten- and elementary-school-age childcare.
- *Youth in Minneapolis After-school Program (Y-MAP)*: After-school program for middle-school-age youth.
- *Youthline Outreach Mentorship Program*: Program for 12- to 16-year-old youth providing positive leisure activities.
- *Teen Teamworks*: Summer youth employment for at-risk youth.

Recreation Plus+

In the fall of 1988 Recreation Plus+ opened at 13 parks throughout Minneapolis. The program offers traditional childcare with an emphasis on recreation skill-building in after-school, before-school, school-release and summer break time periods. It is funded through the Park Board operating budget and user fees. The program places special emphasis on serving the needs of Minneapolis children from low-income, single-parent, and minority families. Children in kindergarten through sixth grade participate in a recreation program which includes social, cultural arts, physical, and environmental activities at their neighborhood park, with Civil Service certified care coordinators. On school-release days and during vacation periods and summer, full-day childcare is provided and the program is expanded to include field trips and day-long experiences. All activities and program materials project heterogeneous racial, gender and cultural attributes. In 1995 Recreation Plus+ served approximately 500 children during the school year, and 700 during the summer at 22 parks.

A Parent Advisory Council contributes to the development of the program and provides a strong base of support. The program has received three grants for supplies and equipment and a Network Mentoring Grant for staff development. Through the mentoring grant, 80 park board staff have received training in cultural diversity awareness; 50 staff have received at least 24 hours of childcare training; and a program to teach staff how to develop the prosocial skills of children is being planned.

The State Department of Education provides guidelines from which a set of Recreation Plus+ standards were developed. The Minneapolis Public Schools provide transportation to and from the schools to the parks during the school year.

Youth in Minneapolis After-school Program (Y-MAP)

Former Minneapolis Mayor Don Fraser initiated the program in 1992 in response to the lack of after-school recreational programs for middle-school-age youth and the complications created for working parents by a new school schedule that released middle-school-age youth at 1:45 p.m. Y-MAP is a citywide collaboration of more than 100 parks, schools, libraries, churches and other youth-serving agencies.

Intramural sports, life skills, community involvement, academic skills and creative expression programs are offered Monday through Friday, from 2 p.m. to 6 p.m. during the school year. Neighborhood advisory councils composed of parents, youth, and agency staff identify needs and select activities. A citywide advisory council (composed of parents, youth, and youth workers) is also involved in overall program development through a review of neighborhood recommendations. Finally, a steering committee of youth program professionals from all areas of the city meets regularly to determine program needs and to advise on program development.

Y-MAP divides the city into 12 "hubs" (areas) for which an agency director or key staff member is the appointed "hub facilitator" (an unpaid position). Hub facilitators are responsible for coordinating all Y-MAP activities including receiving proposals, scheduling meetings of the hub's program providers and community member advisory council to determine which programs should be recommended for funding, and ensuring that the hub is meeting Y-MAP requirements. The hub facilitator is assisted by a "hub coordinator," which is a paid, 20-hour-per-week position.

The outreach workers have a significant role in overall program growth and development. Outreach workers (one per hub) visit the participating agencies weekly to stay abreast of program offerings, observe participation and assist with activity planning and implementation.

In the fall of 1992 Y-MAP served 500 youth with no tax dollar funding. Resources were acquired by the participating agencies changing their program schedules to accommodate the youths' needs. Since 1993 the program grew dramatically (with $1.2 million from the city of Minneapolis in 1993; and $870,000 in 1994) and currently serves 4,000 of the city's 10,000 middle-school-aged youth. A full-time coordinator and 12 outreach workers, along with part-time leaders and many volunteers, work with a Parent/Youth Advisory Council to provide input and guidance for program development.

Youthline Outreach Mentorship Program

This program was implemented in 1991 after discussions with community leaders, parents and youth revealed that youth had a significant amount of discretionary time (40%), much of which was unstructured, unsupervised, and unproductive for the youth.

Youthline's primary objective is to involve 12- to 16-year-old youth in positive leisure-time activities, introduce them to community resources and encourage a strong sense of belonging. Youth are involved in program development through participation in Teen Councils. Youthline focuses on four major activity components: (1) community involvement and service; (2) creative expression; (3) life skills learning; and (4) wish list (e.g., field trips, special events). Another important objective of Youthline is to provide a girls' program that promotes their interests and health through innovation in recreation programs, investment in community support systems, and the identification of women mentors.

The structure of Youthline includes two major mentorship components—in-park and outreach:

(a) *In-Park Activities* consist of developing a teen council and working with the youth to plan and implement activities, organize community service projects and identify part-time job opportunities.

(b) *Outreach Activities* include developing working relationships with youth workers at other agencies and assisting with the service delivery plan for each youth.

Youthline is based in Minneapolis parks with youth (ages 12–16) targeted in the six blocks surrounding the area of each park. Approximately 30 of the 45 recreation centers were identified as being in need of a youth program. The parks were prioritized, based on the demographic and economic need of the neighborhood to determine the final eleven parks that would receive the program. An additional 25 parks have a Youthline summer program.

Youthline also provides part-time employment combined with leadership development through the WE WHO CARE program. Youth work as assistants to the Youthline mentor at the park and participate in monthly experiences focusing on leadership development.

In 1993, the Search Institute completed an evaluation of the Youthline program. Stakeholders, including parents, youth, community groups, the Mayor, City Council Members and Minneapolis Park and Recreation Board Commissioners and staff were interviewed. Focus groups met in the community, and the evaluators visited parks to see the program in action. A sampling of comments made in the focus interviews by youth participants are listed in Exhibit 5A. The report indicated that Youthline met the needs of some of the most severely underserved and challenged youth in Minneapolis. The Search Institute noted that this program is:

> a shining example of youth development programming
> which is designed to promote the healthy psychosocial
> and physical development of all young people without
> labeling them 'at-risk.'

According to the report, the typical young person in Youthline boards a school bus immediately after school and is dropped off at the park. Participants have a snack if available; run off energy in the gym if one is available; and do their homework, particularly if someone is available to work with them. Many parks close from 5:30 to 6:30 p.m. to encourage young people to go home for dinner. Most youth, however, simply wait outside the door until the park building opens again. Participants said that supper is either not waiting for them at home, or no one cares whether they return home for dinner. When the doors reopen, the youth remain at the park until it closes at around 9 p.m.

An average of 50 youth per park spend an average of five hours a day, five days a week at the park. Two thousand to three thousand more youth participate in Youthline sports, special events, and citywide activities. The Search Institute report summarized the attitudes of youth toward the program as follows:

> Youthline was a safe place, with people who cared about
> you and taught you things you needed to know in order
> to succeed in life, where you could get off the streets and
> do positive things and still have fun.

Exhibit 5A

Comments from Youthline Participants

I'm the new me. I used to get kicked out all the time because I was disrespectful. Now the little kids look up to me.

I used to be very shy and a loner. Then I started comin' down here and got to know a lot of people. Now I help out every day.

We learned about leadership skills, like taking the lead to do whatever needs to get done.

You get to go somewhere different. Like a lot of people don't get to go with their parents to these places.

I'm a better person. I help out more. I helped to coach a team. This helped me get a job.

I've matured. I don't act like a child anymore. I'm not such a nuisance.

Here, you can talk to the staff and your friends about anything. Especially things you wouldn't talk to your parents about, like sex and relationships and stuff.

It's kept me from learning how to kill somebody.

We learned to think about consequences, like if you steal someone's bike or something.

We've cleaned up our acts. We're more polite and more responsible.

I've learned that there's better things than doing drugs.

I got to see how other people live. Playing cribbage with senior citizens was fun!

You learn about cooperation. When we go on field trips, you have to cooperate or you can't go.

We even set goals here, like selling T-shirts in order to earn money for more trips.

How to deal with other people. They taught us that we should be proud of Youthline and that when we're out in public, we represent Youthline. It's like you represent a company, like a job.

Teen Teamworks

The Teen Teamworks summer youth employment project has been a model for turning the energy and ambition of at-risk youth into positive results for themselves, their neighborhood, and the city of Minneapolis. This project was developed in 1986 as a response to employment vulnerability as well as many other special needs of at-risk Minneapolis youth. The overall goal of Teen Teamworks is to offer a nine-week positive park maintenance work experience, recreational opportunities and educational sessions to unemployed at-risk youth ages 14–18. Additional goals for youth working with Teen Teamworks include the opportunity for all youth to:

(a) earn money as well as have the experience of being able to get a job and then have the opportunity to master job-keeping skills;
(b) develop positive relationships both with an adult role model and other youth;
(c) learn the value of teamwork;
(d) acquire gardening and landscaping skills;
(e) develop increased initiative and independence;
(f) increase responsibility and maturity levels; and
(g) identify learning skills necessary for successful work experience and be motivated to acquire those skills.

Specific objectives include:

(1) hire 200 youth (who meet "at-risk" requirements) referred by Minneapolis agencies for summer employment in the parks;
(2) provide basic job-skill development through daily experiences under the supervision of an adult supervisor with "youth work" skills;
(3) organize biweekly educational sessions focusing on social skill development and independent living skills development;
(4) plan biweekly recreational activities that allow for individual exploration of interests and abilities and the learning of positive use of leisure time; and
(5) provide an opportunity for youth to spend time with caring, supportive adults who can serve as adult role models.

From the beginning, partnerships were built with community-based youth-serving organizations, the juvenile justice system, and other public/private organizations with a youth focus. A referral process ensures that youth receive the support they need throughout the summer for assistance with issues, problem behavior, and most important, for recognition of positive efforts.

The prime reason for youth unemployment is not a shortage of available jobs, but the lack of basic skills and the existence of unrealistic attitudes and expectations of what is required to succeed in the work world. In earlier decades, youth could drop out of school and begin working on an assembly line, mastering the necessary skills for advancement through on-the-job training experience. Today, however, the relationship between dropping out of school in adolescence and chronic unemployment or underemployment as adults, is due to a significant deficiency in the work skills and attitudes needed in the workplace.

Over the last nine years, Teen Teamworks has received funding support from the Minneapolis Park and Recreation Board, city of Minneapolis, Hennepin County, state of Minnesota, and the Federal government, as well as numerous charitable foundations.

Partnerships for providing jobs were built with the spectrum of community-based youth-serving organizations, the juvenile justice system, and other public/private organizations with a youth focus. Youth are referred to agencies for summer employment, with the requirement that the agency staff assist with issues, problem behavior, and most important, support the youth's positive efforts.

Special relationships were developed with Junior Achievement members, who shared insights into their career pathways, and with the staff of Lutheran Social Services who conducted group sessions to dramatize how choices youth make in regards to music, friends and the way they dress may carry both positive as well as negative consequences, now and in the future.

Through this project, youth are introduced to the concept of maintaining parks as a viable career option. "Parkkeeping" is critical to the maintenance of safe, environmentally-sound, and aesthetically pleasing parks within the city and throughout the country, and it offers a living-wage job through which individuals can support themselves and their families.

Adults are hired to be in charge of a work crew consisting of eight youth employees. Each supervisor is also a working member of the crew and serves as a mentor and positive role model. A 1990 Search Institute study reported that "youth being connected with adults" is one of four key factors associated with developing youth who show behaviors of caring for self and others. In fact, the support system provided by peers and nonparental adults is often of extreme importance for lower-income youth.

Tasks completed by the work crews include: serving as support staff at community events, spreading wood chips, cleaning up lake shorelines and swimming pool areas, cutting grass, edging park lawns and paths, as well as general park maintenance.

New collaborations each year create opportunities for nontraditional work crews. For example, in 1993 a collaboration with the Walker Art Center resulted in a work crew for which tasks included learning about various artists and art pieces in the Sculpture Garden, how to properly maintain art sculptures, and serving as tour guides for other youth, park commissioners, city council members and Walker Art Center education staff.

All youth employees receive a biweekly performance rating that measures progress and identifies concerns in twelve job areas: attendance and punctuality, initiative, attitude, judgment, public image presented, productivity, adherence to directions, adherence to safety rules, communication ability, use of equipment, quality of work, and disciplinary actions.

The recreational component of Teen Teamworks is an integral part of its structure and success. Youth participated in recreational opportunities on a voluntary, no-pay basis after work and on payday Fridays when the youth did not work. These opportunities not only served as a reward for hard work, but, just as important, they aided in the development of teamwork and a sense of community involvement for each work crew.

The recreational activities were also times when youth from different backgrounds and cultures would come together and experience positive, cultural, social and ethnic interrelationships. When asked which recreational events were special to them, work crews considered their picnics, pick-up court games and informal get-togethers at their neighborhood parks as being very memorable. The groups also went out to shop and to eat, learned to open a savings account, and went to the movies.

One of the original program objectives was to give all youth employees a "symbolic chit or token" in exchange for a day's labor.

After the concept was instituted, it became apparent that the youth employees were enthusiastic about acquiring the tokens; therefore, a plan was developed whereby they could earn additional tokens in recognition of:

- *Initiative*—asking for another assignment when completing an assigned task and/or suggesting a task that needed to be done;
- *Follow Through*—getting out the proper tool, completing the assigned task, putting the tool back;
- *Positive Peer Relationships*—befriending another worker, stopping arguments, suggesting group social activities for the work crew; and
- *Punctuality*—mornings, breaks, lunch.

At the end of the project celebration party, the youth workers were able to exchange these tokens for various prizes. The tokens soon became known as the "good guy tokens" as youth perceived that they had to behave like a "good guy or gal" to earn them. From a supervisory perspective, the tokens became a motivating and behavior modification tool that could be used to deal with negative and/or antisocial behavior.

References

Carnegie Council on Adolescent Development. (1992). *It's a matter of time: Risk and Opportunity in the nonschool hours.* New York, NY: Author.

Chapter 6
City Streets/At-Risk Youth Division
in Phoenix, Arizona

Presenter:
Cynthia D. Peters
> Recreation Supervisor, City of Phoenix Parks, Recreation and
> Library Department

Background

Phoenix is the eighth largest city in the United States with a population of 1.07 million (3 million in the metropolitan area). The city
covers an area of 450 square miles which is geographically larger
than Chicago or San Francisco. Sixty-eight percent of the residents
are Caucasian, 21% Hispanic and 10% either Native American, African American or Asian.

In 1980, the Parks, Recreation and Library Department's South
Phoenix Youth Center was opened next to a high school. The Center
was built in response to requests from teenagers who said they
needed a safe place to hang out. This Center offered a "one-stop-
shop" for youth recreational and social services.

In 1985, residents from West Phoenix expressed concern over the
lack of structured activities for teens and the emergence of juvenile
delinquency activity in their area. The Department responded by
drawing upon the philosophy, approaches, and programs that had
been developed at the South Phoenix Youth Center, and expanded
this type of service to become a mobile outreach service providing
recreational, educational, social, and cultural programs for teens at
outreach sites such as malls, schools, and park sites at which there
was no regular programming. This program was named The City
Streets Program.

By 1990 The City Streets concept had spread to all areas of the
city. In 1991 the Department further confirmed its commitment to
youth by identifying youth at-risk as a priority for the next decade.
In response to this charge and input provided through a citywide
youth conference, a Youth At-Risk Task Force was convened to
research and evaluate the Department's youth programs and services.

The Task Force recommended that youth services be increased throughout Phoenix with special programming emphasis for at-risk youth.

In July 1993 the Department centralized many youth programming resources and created the City Streets/At-Risk Youth Division. The Division initially was designed to provide administrative and specialized support services for staff and to explore community resources to create partnerships for expanded programs and services. The Division is still currently providing this support, but has taken on many additional programs, coordinating and supervising direct services for youth. From its initial staff of five, the Division has grown to a full-time staff of 32.

The Division's goal statement reads:

> The Department is committed to providing youth services in a safe and nondiscriminatory environment. Further, the Department strives to maintain open communication with youth and agencies and to provide linkages and needed referral information for services not provided by the Department.

For programming purposes, youth are divided into five age groups: 1–5, 6–12, 13–15, 16–18, and 19–21 years old. The Department seeks to identify the needs of each of these age groups and respond with appropriate programming.

At-risk youth come from all backgrounds, races, and areas of the city. They are youth who are, or have the potential to be, influenced negatively by familial, environmental, peer, and/or social factors that deter their positive mental and social development. These factors may include:

- substance abuse;
- lack of educational opportunities;
- child abuse;
- poor peer relationships;
- behavior/discipline problems;
- low self-esteem;
- lack of positive role models;
- dysfunctional home environment;
- lack of positive leisure activities;

* economic deprivation;
* unsafe school/neighborhood environment; and
* early sexual activity.

The Division's Philosophy

Prevention is the building block for sponsoring quality youth recreational, cultural, and educational services. According to Jim Colley, Director of the Phoenix Parks, Recreation, and Library Department:

> We in the Park and Recreation profession have always
> taken pride in the enrichment we bring to people's lives.
> The role of recreation is evolving, as is the environment
> of our youth, due to the social changes occurring in
> today's world.

The city of Phoenix realizes the importance of recreation and the many benefits it has to offer: leadership opportunities; ethnic and cultural harmony; environmental education; physical fitness; positive self-esteem and self-image; and, most important, the opportunity to reduce the antisocial, juvenile delinquent behavior prevalent among many youth (see Exhibit 6A, pages 72–73).

Jim Colley stated:

> My staff say we are becoming counselors and social
> workers. That's fine, I believe we should be. My phi-
> losophy is that if a young man comes in on drugs or a
> young woman comes in who is pregnant, we have to
> help. Young ladies come to my female staff and say 'I'm
> pregnant, will you come home with me and help me talk
> to my mom.' They are scared, so of course we help. We
> often adopt these kids. We respond as best we can to
> whatever they need. I would not have a problem with
> my Department being called a Department of Commu-
> nity Services.
>
> Our job is to make young people whole in any way we
> can, and offering wholesome recreation activities is only
> one aspect of that. It's a way of reaching them. It gives
> us an opportunity to help them straighten out other parts

Exhibit 6A

"It's Not Fun To Be a Good Kid"

Jack is 14 years old and has been in a gang since he was 11 years old. His dad died from an overdose of drugs, his mother is a waitress and works two jobs. His older sister is on drugs. Jack has snorted so much cocaine that the membrane in his nose is almost destroyed. Jim Colley, Department Director, describes his personal experiences with Jack:

> My staff took Jack on a camping trip on the San Juan River with a mixed group, half of whom were young, hard-core gang members and the other half were disabled young people. At first Jack was standoffish. He was hard to get to know, but he gradually bonded with one of our staff members. He began to communicate. Sitting on the banks of the river, he said it was the first time he could remember sitting relaxed and comfortable without the fear of some-body shooting him.
>
> When the group returned, the staff introduced me to Jack. We hired him part time in one of our centers. Last semester he got all A's in high school. We have held his hand. One of my staff invites Jack along when she goes on a date with her boyfriend to a movie or to dinner. I take him out to dinner occasionally and bought him some clothes for Christmas.
>
> I say to him, 'If I had been subjected to what you have been subjected to, then I would belong to a gang if there was one in my town.' I tell him, 'You have got people committed to getting you out. Use your leadership skills and help others get out from the gangs.' When you look at all the things that he has done, you can understand why he said, 'It's not fun to be a good kid.' He has been on both sides of drive-by shootings; done all kinds of illegal things; so to keep him interested you've got to have some things that are high-risk and challenging.
>
> We had a reunion of the 70 kids that we have taken on San Juan River trips over a weekend. I couldn't believe what I was seeing. The way Jack and other gang members helped the disabled kids was amazing. They took a 14-year-old, who was in a wheelchair and could not walk, and put him

Exhibit 6A (continued)

on their backs and went hiking in the woods. I saw hard-core gang members help paraplegics go to the rest rooms, and say to my staff, 'It feels so good to be helping someone.'

The problem is that when those kids go back into their home environment in Phoenix, they go back to the old lifestyle. We expose them to good things; they buy into it; then we put them back into their old bad scene. My concern all the time in these situations is how do we follow through. We aren't doing that well enough, but I don't know what we can do to improve, given the limited resources we have.

One day the staff member who has been closest to Jack came into my office crying. She said, 'we may have lost Jack. He got into a big fight with his mother so Jack is on the streets right now. He hasn't been in to pick up his pay checks. He called in.' My staff member said '"Jim will be disappointed," and Jack said "I don't want him to know." I'm confident that unless the kid gets back to his gang or the police pick him up, he will be back to us.'

A few months later Jack returned from the streets. He has since reapplied to participate in the tattoo removal program; he is back working with the internship program and is attending summer school. Jack knows that he messed up and wants to make up for it. He also has noticed how some staff do not provide him the support he received before he left, and feels that those that do not support him are not 'legit.' Jack will continue to need staff and family support in making life decisions and setting goals. Staff will continue to support Jack as long as necessary. Staff also discuss consequences for actions, goal setting, following through with commitments, and decision-making skills with Jack. He has not yet discussed where he was during his hiatus from the program; staff feel that discussion will be forthcoming when he feels he can trust us again.

of their lives that are not good. You have to do this work
one case at a time. If you talk about doing it by the
masses or in general terms, it will fail. Follow-through
is critical and that is our limiting factor. We don't have
the manpower or money to follow through at the level
we should.

Resources

To supplement the city's resources, the division has secured federal,
state, and private foundation grants. To facilitate the grant writing
process, a full-time grant researcher and coordinator were hired in
spring 1994. In the first full year, the Division submitted 25 applications for funds, of which 15 were successful, yielding almost $1
million in additional resources.

To support this grant application work, a resource library of data
and statistical findings related to youth has been developed. Programs funded by outside sources request applicants to demonstrate
identifiable causes, existence of need, and/or current trends relating
to the proposal issue. Community assessments and community
readiness plans are also being collected. This library ensures these
data are readily available to be included in grant proposals.

The city's Golf Enterprise Fund also generates approximately
$150,000 per year for at-risk youth programs. In 1993, despite vig-
orous opposition from golfers, the Phoenix City Council agreed to
take 25¢ for each round of golf played at the city's five golf courses
and direct it to specific youth programs. Other recreation activities
which generate revenue such as athletic leagues or adult classes
could not as easily be used for this purpose. Approximately $50,000
of the golf money is used for a junior golf program for at-risk youth,
but the remainder is used elsewhere.

Programs

Juvenile Curfew Program

In 1992 gang-related homicides and other gang-related crimes, including drive-by shootings, increased six-fold over 1990. In response to the increasing number of youth affected by violent crime,
Phoenix started enforcement of the Juvenile Curfew Ordinance, the
Juvenile Gun Law Ordinance, and the Juvenile Liquor Law Ordinance,

which were previously passed but not widely enforced. Initially, the Juvenile Curfew Program was enforced in one section of the city on a trial basis for under-16 youth and youth 16–18 who were on the streets between 10 p.m. and 5 a.m. and, midnight and 5 a.m. respectively. Groups in that section who thought they were being singled out by the police department opposed this enforcement. However, the curfew was so successful that council members from other parts of the city wanted it implemented in their area, and the opposition disappeared. Public meetings were held across the city and there was overwhelming support for the curfew.

The Juvenile Curfew program is jointly operated by the Police and Parks, Recreation and Library Departments. Four recreation centers are open all night as screening stations, one in each quadrant of the city. Each is staffed by two police officers and two recreation leaders. Youth caught violating the curfew are transported by police officers to one of the recreation centers. Parents and/or guardians are notified and youth undergo a 35-minute processing by police which includes checking for a criminal history and detecting signs of substance abuse or health problems. Youth are issued a citation, photographed and then turned over to the recreation leaders while awaiting their parents. If no parent or guardian can be contacted or if the parent or guardian fails to pick up the juveniles, they may be placed with Child Protective Services or taken to the local Juvenile Court Center.

The police and recreation staff work well together. Recreation staff are particularly helpful in facilitating and communicating with youth who often distrust or dislike the police. Unfortunately, the Juvenile Courts caseload dramatically increased by about 5,000 per year. To alleviate the overload, the city introduced a diversion program through which a citation can be dismissed if violators and their parents attend and complete a parenting education class. If they complete the class, the citation is dropped. Youth who do not go through the diversion program and cannot pay the citation are referred to the Park, Recreation and Library Department to perform community service at selected park sites, libraries, mountain parks, and community centers. Over 1,500 such youth were referred to the Department in the first six months of the program.

A counseling component addresses common issues including substance abuse, lack of job opportunities, lack of job skills, teen pregnancy, teen parenting, school dropouts, prostitution, lack of parental support, homeless youth, and nonpositive recreation activities.

The Division recognized that picking up the curfew violators, charging them, and sending them home again was not efficient since all their other problems remained. The Juvenile Courts had a counseling system, but it was so overwhelmed that it was 30 days or more before a follow-up phone call was made. Thus, the recreation staff in the four centers took over this task. They became the follow-up agency responsible for getting the youth back into school, seeing a drug counselor, entering a GED program or arranging whatever other services were needed. The goal is to give the youth some hope and point them in a direction which may enable them to address their problems. Unfortunately, with approximately 100 youth passing through the Juvenile Curfew Program per week, follow-up cannot be inclusive enough to follow up on all cases on a long-term basis.

In the first 11 months of the curfew program, police statistics revealed a 10.4% reduction in juvenile arrests for violent crimes such as homicide, sexual assault, robbery and aggravated assault. During that same period adult crimes, citywide, increased 6.7% while overall juvenile crime increased only one-half of one percent.

Tattoo Removal Program

The Division has been successful in persuading some youth to leave gangs, but the existence of tattoos on their arms, hands, neck, or face makes progress difficult. These insignia make it hard to find employment, to avoid fights in school, and to convince people that they have left a gang.

Doctors typically charge between $500 and $1,000 for the laser removal process which leaves no scarring of the skin tissue. The laser equipment costs almost $100,000 and removal requires between two and six treatments depending on the size of the tattoo and ink color.

The X-Tattoo program grew out of a discussion between a Phoenix businessman and a former gang member who were on a rafting excursion together. He learned of programs in San Jose, Dallas, and Chicago which removed tattoos from youth in exchange for community service. He then raised $8,000 to start the program in an office in a recreation center. As of February 1995 there were 75 youth enrolled in the program with 60 on a waiting list.

Collaboration with the Police Activities League

For many years the Police Department operated Police Activities League (PAL) Centers, but never collaborated with Park and Recreation, and vice versa. PAL has recreation centers that would close when, for example, officers and youth participants would go off-site on field trips to sporting contests. In addition, the number of youth who could participate in off-site trips was limited by a lack of transportation.

In July of 1994, with Arizona Supreme Court Crime Reduction Funds, the Park, Recreation and Library Department offered to assist within the PAL Centers, thus providing staff to offer structured, supervised programs on a regular basis. This began a collaboration which provided three part-time recreation leaders, working for 25 hours per week in PAL Centers in Central and South Phoenix.

Mobile Unit Partnership Program

The City Streets Mobile Unit Partnership was developed in 1992 in collaboration with the Arizona Cactus Pine Girl Scouts Association which was seeking to provide direct outreach services.

A renovated bookmobile brings employment, recreation, education, and social services to otherwise underserved communities. Activities and services reflect the needs and demands of site participants, and are adapted from existing Department and Girl Scout programs. Inside the mobile unit are computers, Ping-Pong tables, foosball tables, library books, and other recreation resources. It visits five school sites during their lunch period and, in the evenings, five unstaffed park sites that have reported problems. In one week the mobile unit serves approximately 1,000 youth citywide.

Youth Sports Program—Public Housing

Through a 1994 $125,000 Youth Sports Grant from the U.S. Department of Housing and Urban Development (HUD), recreation services were expanded in five public housing sites. The Youth Sports Program seeks to reduce drugs, gangs, and violence by educating and empowering youth through recreational, social, and educational programs. The Park, Recreation and Libraries Department, working with the city Housing Department offers intramural sports leagues, youth development workshops, sports development clinics, youth employment opportunities, cultural awareness activities, and citywide district sports. A teen council assists in programming and outreach. The intent is to encourage positive, drug-free, lifestyle choices that will have a long-term positive impact.

Recreation Internship Program

The people needed to lead at-risk youth programs have to be individuals with whom youth can identify. Often this requires training people on the job. University programs do not have curricula which are geared to developing at-risk youth program leaders. This means reverting back to the old apprenticeship system of recruiting people (often former gang members or former athletes) and setting up a program to train them.

The recreation internship program assigns youth, ages 14–19, to a mentor who will work with them as they progress through a series of experiences. Workshops are offered where they learn skills like CPR and first aid, how to fill out a job application, and how to interview for a job. Recreation programming and leadership skills such as how to run special events, sports leagues and typical recreation operations are also taught.

Teen Councils and Forums

Teen councils foster youth empowerment, ownership and responsibility for their recreational and social activities. Their popularity has grown tremendously in the Department. From the original teen council established in 1980 at the South Phoenix Youth Center there are now over 25 councils throughout the City.

Youth representatives from recreation centers, schools, or park sites meet weekly or bimonthly to plan activities, trips, special events, educational development, and agendas with trained professional recreation staff. Teen council members elect their officers and representatives.

Local teen councils have led to the development of a citywide Youth Advisory Board. Through a partnership with the local United Way and Nestle's Corporation, a Teen Council Outreach Program has been formulated.

Three programs which have developed because of input from the Teen Councils are Wuzz-Up Teens, Youth Forums, and an annual

Teen Conference. Wuzz-Up Teens is the name chosen by youth for a quarterly newsletter and a cable television program used by the department to communicate with teens.

The Division, in collaboration with the Human Services Department, the Neighborhood Services Department, Equal Opportunity Department and the Police Department, planned, developed, implemented, evaluated, and reported on a series of youth forums held in each city council district. Youth were provided with the opportunity to present issues, concerns, programs, and services to each city council member. The forums were held in community centers, libraries and schools.

The annual Teen Conference consists of a day-long program of workshops. It brings together teen councils from across the city, gives them leadership experience, and usually attracts around 200 youth participants.

Chapter 7
The Real Deal:
The Evolution of Seattle, Washington's, At-Risk Youth Program

Presenters:
Reco Bembry
  Teen Programs Coordinator, *and*
Al Tufono
  Senior Recreation Specialist, City of Seattle Department of Parks and Recreation

Background

The 1980s marked an unprecedented surge in violent juvenile crimes, due in part to a transition by young people from drug *use* to the profitable and highly competitive drug *trafficking* market. Traditional youth recreation programs and approaches became irrelevant because they were not aligned with the current behavior and circumstances of the participants.

A new mayor was elected in Seattle at the end of the 1980s and at every public meeting he attended he was asked, "What are you going to do about gangs?" Seattle had a reputation of being America's most livable city. Although known for its high quality of life, this image was being tarnished by the gang problem. The public, political officials, and businesses were all applying pressure to the bureaucratic system to address the gang problem. Reco Bembry, Seattle Teen Programs Coordinator, noted, "It was clear the solution had not been found yet, so the community and government were open to new ideas."

In 1989 a consortium of recreation professionals in the city was established as the "Seattle Team for Youth." In addition, a Mayor's task force was formed comprised of the heads of city departments which deal with youth. The Department of Parks and Recreation analyzed crime statistics provided by the Police Department and determined that the four major categories of serious crimes (i.e., homicide, rape, robbery, and aggravated assault) involving youth ages 16 and younger, as either victims or offenders, reached their peak in the afternoon between the time school let out until midnight. Between midnight and 6 a.m. the percentages were relatively low. As a result, the department chose to focus the efforts on the afternoon and evening period, and became part of a joint planning team to initiate The Late Night Recreation Program. Forty-three thousand dollars in Federal support was received to launch the program based on a collaborative team proposal written by staff from Juvenile Rehabilitation, the school system, Parks and Recreation, and personnel.

An important first step was to bring representatives of at-risk youth to the table to determine program content. From the start, the program embraced more than basketball. Activities of interest to specific cultural groups, such as Asians and Pacific Islanders, were incorporated. Donations of computers from businesses were solicited as part of the plan to incorporate an educational component.

The Late Night Recreation Program began at two community centers: Garfield and Rainier. Each Friday and Saturday night 400 youth were involved in activities in these high-risk areas until 1 a.m. instead of being out on the streets. The Police Department collected statistics from the census tracts which were determined to be within the zones of influence of the two centers. Data were collected from the period March 1, 1990, to November 30, 1990, and pertained to the number of arrests of youth, teens, and young adults ages 13–23 for the following crimes committed in the two areas: murder, rape, robbery, aggravated assault, residential burglary, nonresidential burglary, motor thefts and assaults. When compared to the same period the previous year, crime in these zones was reduced by approximately 30%.

Crime reduction could not be solely attributed to the Late Night Recreation Program because a concerted effort in these two urban areas was also made by several other agencies to implement a crime prevention program, Drug-Free Zones, and an increase in the number of police officers in the area.

Initial success was sufficient to win political support to expand the Late Night Program to other sites and to add many other dimensions to the overall at-risk youth program and expand the operating budget to its current level of $508,000. This additional support has been gained by responding to what is politically important: reducing crime by 30%, funding 70 jobs each year for at-risk youth without any government subsidy, and acquiring enough community support to get a bond issue passed to build five more community centers.

Philosophy

The staff associated with the at-risk youth programs in Seattle does not talk of recreation. Rather they talk of the re-creation of human life. This is a powerful way of communicating to elected officials and taxpayers what is being done in these programs. Reco Bembry who is the teen programs coordinator states:

> The way we think about teens influences how they act. We always try to describe them in positive terms. The adjectives we use to describe kids should be positive: creative, imaginative, fun, excitable, curious, etc. It isn't the kids who are the problem, it is the environment to which they are exposed. It's an at-risk environment, and we need to provide hope, a lifeline, a way out of that environment. Gangs aren't bad, it's the things that they do which are bad. There are no positive social outlets in the high-risk environment in which these kids live. We have to offer that.

> Everything we do rests on five building blocks: Trust, Self-Esteem, Consistency, Respect and Integrity. These are the values our staff seeks to instill in the youth by the way we act towards them, and the way we expect them to respond to us. They come to our programs because we give them reinforcement for positive behavior.

> We don't really go out and find at-risk kids and pull them in by the hand [for an exception, see Exhibit 7A, page 84]. What we do is to create opportunities which will encourage them to come and find us. We have to have something they want. If you know what they want and provide it, they are going to show up. Word-of-mouth gets around.

> If you rescue one kid, he or she influences others. Your influence is leveraged. Take it one kid at a time, then that influence is multiplied among their peers. Our job is to instill the five building blocks in one person, and get him or her to commit to doing this with one other

person. We have to teach them the building blocks and
teach them in such a way that they will teach others.

Exhibit 7A

A Beacon in a Time of Trouble*

On the night the Los Angeles police officers charged with
beating Rodney King were acquitted there were substantial
protests in Seattle. Reco Bembry and James King, who
supervised the youth program at the Garfield Center, were
watching the news that night when they saw some familiar
faces involved in the protest on the city's Capitol Hill.

    The men mobilized a group of youths and police who
drew signs saying "Late Night Program." They plastered the
signs on the side of a Metro Bus, headed for Capitol Hill and
picked up about 35 youths, who Bembry said, were fed up
with the protests.

    "In that case we took the alternative to the kids. Some-
times you can't wait for the kids to come to you," King said.
"We are trying to create heroes, not zeros," he added.

*Mayor Norm Rice characterized the Late Night Recreation Program as "a beacon
in a time of trouble."

Staffing

To lead at-risk programs, the Department looks for role models with
whom the kids will identify. The role models will often be former
gang members or former athletes. Hiring people who have lived in
an environment where there are gangs, who have experienced what it
feels like to be in a gang and what it feels like to get out of a gang is
important. The people hired had the opportunity to get out and,
therefore, are interested in creating similar opportunities for others.
Al Tufono, who directs the *Together for Teens* program, is a good
example. He was a former gang member, who got out and became a
star player on the University of Washington championship football
team. He subsequently coached with the team. In addition, he is a
Pacific Islander and is, therefore, particularly effective in communicating with that target group.

Program leaders have to show a passion for the work and commitment to it. Reco Bembry notes, "It is about going beyond the paycheck. They can't pay us enough to do what we do." Often the program leaders have not attended college because they do not meet the required academic standards, and few colleges are prepared to change the standards to meet their needs. Hence, the staffing model is often an apprenticeship program through which staff are trained on the job. After they have been on the job for a couple of years, staff may be encouraged to go to college to improve their academic credentials and skills.

The Department pays program leaders between $10.50 and $15 an hour. This is a high-profile, difficult job involving mentoring and conflict resolution. Paying people at this relatively high level means the Department expects a relatively high level of performance.

Programs

Late Night Recreation Program

The Late Night Program has now expanded to include a total of five Community Centers and two middle schools. The centers have extended hours from 10 p.m. to 1 a.m. on Friday night and 8 p.m. to 1 a.m. on Saturday night. Although designed for youth between 17 and 21 years of age, the program has attracted youth as young as nine and young adults up to age 23. In 1991, the weekly average attendance was 1,600 teens; currently the centers are serving about 2,500 teens per week. Special events draw 300 to 400 youths.

The Late Night Recreation Program provides:

(1) educational services such as tutoring, computer and teen parenting programs;
(2) intercultural activities such as ethnic dancing and bead making;
(3) athletic activities such as basketball, football, volleyball, gymnastics and several other sports;
(4) adults, leaders and role models who care about and listen to the young people; and
(5) a positive alternative to life on the street.

Special events have ranged from outdoor excursions to a talent search, as well as a trip to San Francisco. On the San Francisco trip some teens participated in a regional basketball tournament, while others created and performed a show at a sports banquet. They all participated in a Drug and Alcohol Resistance and Education (D.A.R.E.) seminar. The trip was made possible by the Parks and Recreation Department, the Seattle Housing Authority and many local businesses. A "Make It Big Talent Search," sponsored by Parks and Recreation, The Bon Marche, and The Seattle Center, was also held. This was a big hit and provided youth with an opportunity to break into the entertainment industry.

Teen Advisory Council

The Teen Advisory Council is a group of young people, ages 16–21, who meet every other week from 4:30 to 6 p.m. to plan, organize, and help implement activities such as dances and special events. The council serves in an advisory capacity by recommending desired activities and programs. Council members are from different communities throughout the city and are recommended by recreation staff to serve on the council.

Every teenager wants a safe place where the doors are always open and they feel like they are welcome. Young people are tired of adults making decisions that affect their lives. The Advisory Council plans activities and dances for teens that are safe and fun. The council members also deal with issues and topics that affect the communities and neighborhoods they represent. Teen council members feel that their input will keep some young people off the streets and therefore decrease the chances of gang violence and drug abuse. The expectations and responsibilities of teen council members are listed in Exhibit 7B.

Transportation

To enable youth to get to the Late Night Program, the Department has an arrangement with Metro, the local transportation company. Metro provides two buses and drivers for the Late Night Program. Youth who do not have access to this special transportation or their own transportation are given free passes on regular Metro routes so they can get to the centers.

In addition to Friday and Saturday night activities, Late Night continually develops new activities and special events. The newest Late Night Centers were implemented in neighborhoods with high

EXHIBIT 7B

Teen Advisory Council Goal, Roles and Responsibilities

Goal:

to involve youth in planning for youth programs to better provide activities and resources for youth.

Roles:

- to find activities for youth to enjoy;
- to attract youth and increase participation in programs;
- to communicate with the public to increase awareness and participation;
- to raise funds for youth projects; and
- to serve as a youth advisory group to the citywide teen programming unit.

Responsibilities:

- attendance at all meetings, two absences permitted;
- must attend all special events, one absence permitted;
- undivided attention at meetings, insightful input and participation;
- willingness to work volunteer hours;
- complete any task assigned to you;
- be on time (two tardies is the same as one absence); and
- call in when unavailable to attend a meeting or event.

To be on the Teen Council is a privilege, and these responsibilities must be followed to remain on the council.

Asian gang populations. According to Reco Bembry, "Late Night is the hottest teen program on the west coast. The proof is that the program is constantly growing. Twenty-four other cities have started programs of their own modeled after ours in Seattle." Further evidence is the unsolicited testimonials of the program participants such as that quoted in the news clipping extract shown in Exhibit 7C, page 88.

Exhibit 7C

This is better than hangin' around

> 'This has been a dyn-o-mite evening,' a tough-
> looking 16-year-old called out at Reco. 'All fun
> and no fighting, man,' he said, coming as near to
> gushing as his street-wise years would allow. He
> was so impressed that he thrust a handful of bills
> toward Reco. 'Me and my homeys liked it so
> much—no fighting, no problems—that we want
> to support this program, so take this money,' he
> ordered. Reco tactfully refused the help but
> thanked him for the offer and bid him to return
> often.

That incident happened one night at the Department's Late
Night Recreation Program. It is testimony to the impact the
program is having on young people in Seattle's Central Area
and Rainier Valley.

Seattle Post Dispatch (May 6, 1992) p. A-10.

Security

Two uniformed police officers are on duty at each site. The role of
the police in this situation is not primarily that of a cop; rather, it is
that of a public employee whose job is to safeguard life and property.
The presence of the police gives participants a chance to meet police
on a one-to-one basis. These encounters help overcome youth's
suspicions of police and authority and also help the police understand the kids. At three of the centers, all those entering the site are
handwand searched. At the other centers, the staff feel confident that
this is not needed.

Costs Versus Benefits

The cost of the Late Night Recreation Program is $84,000 per year.
But as Reco Bembry notes, "Part of the problem of doing a cost

benefit analysis of the program is that you cannot measure what didn't happen. We save lives, but how can you measure a shooting that didn't occur because the kid was in this program?" One way of doing this may be to calculate the cost of particular crimes and the costs of charging and incarcerating guilty individuals. An overall cost savings could be calculated based on decreasing crime statistics in neighborhoods in which programs are operating.

Inner City Outings

The Inner City Outing program provides wilderness activities for inner-city youth who would not normally have access to experiences in the mountain and wilderness areas of Washington state. The wilderness belongs to all, yet many are unable to experience the outdoors because of socioeconomic constraints such as a lack of transportation and the cost of the basic equipment. The mission statement of this program is to "work with multiethnic youth to create an environment for community leadership and empowerment." Its specific goals are to:

(1) teach leadership, self-esteem and survival skills for the wilderness that translate into achievements and survival in the urban environment;
(2) provide a retreat from everyday stress to facilitate basic skills needed to attain their "dreams;"
(3) provide wilderness activities and environmental education; and
(4) facilitate understanding of options for life goals and lifestyles.

The wilderness skills that these youth learn translate into achievements in their urban lives as well. Taking young people out of their routine inner-city surroundings gives them a chance to see life with a new perspective, a new curiosity, and reminds them that there are opportunities open to them that they might not have experienced. Trips offer young people a chance to retreat from the everyday stresses of life in the inner-city, to discover the importance of preservation of the environment, to learn and actually practice survival and leadership skills, to develop friendships with peers, and to build mentoring relationships with adult role models.

Together For Teens

Together for Teens is directed primarily at reaching Asian and Pacific Islander groups. These target populations are often referred to as the traditionally underserved in Seattle. This summer teen activity program for Seattle's at-risk youth operates at three sites in the city. Its goals are to:

(1) provide safe, upbeat and positive alternative programs and activities for teens throughout the summer;

(2) encourage cultural diversity and understanding by increasing participation from new refugee, new immigrant and Asian and Pacific Islander populations; and

(3) empower teens to get involved in the program planning process.

Four types of activities are offered through this program:

(1) multicultural activities such as ethnic dancing, cooking and athletic events;

(2) educational services such as computers, tutoring, and teen awareness workshops;

(3) YO! Hott Shotts entrepreneur job training program; and

(4) drop-in sports activities, including basketball, volleyball, rattanball, and Ping Pong.

YO! Hott Shotts

The YO! Hott Shotts program is sponsored by Starbucks Espresso Company and meets the critical need for more youth employment opportunities. This entrepreneurial program is intended to inspire at-risk youth to take an interest in business and self-direction. Ten young people work with Starbucks, learning how to make espresso, market the products, organize daily cart operations, track sales, and other essential aspects of running an espresso operation.

Youth trainees are recruited and referred from community-based agencies and organizations that work with at-risk youth. Interested young people complete an application and interview process. The selected trainees undertake 100 hours of basic training and an additional 150 hours of management training. Some training components

---

Exhibit 7D

1993 YO! Hott Shotts

Certified Youth Baristas' Comments:

"It was really fun and I learned a lot."
                    Kang Chong—16 years old

"If there was no YO! Hott Shotts program I'd probably be
    just hangin' out."   Rosie Laronal—15 years old

"This is a pretty cool program."
                    Robert Kitiona—16 years old

"Can I come back next year and be in the program?"
                    Stephanie Lee—17 years old

"I know how to make all the espresso drinks and Italian
    sodas."   Monique Jones—17 years old

---

include learning the characteristics of an exemplary employee, discovering what it takes to make the best café lattes and Italian sodas, what it takes to achieve success in the espresso business, computer skills, inventory control, ordering, public relations, and customer service.

When the training is completed, the youth trainees become certified "baristas." Each barista is awarded a certificate signed by the mayor describing his or her accomplishments, and receives recommendation letters from Starbucks and Seattle Parks and Recreation. The YO! Hott Shotts Certification Program assists in job placement and provides the young baristas with marketable skills and solid references when they apply for future jobs.

Reactions from some participants in the program are shown in Exhibit 7D. The Department regards this program as a demonstration program to illustrate to businesses the types of partnerships that can be created. It is anticipated that its success will cause other businesses to cooperate in similar ventures.

Jobs With Concessionaires

To further encourage job opportunities, the Parks and Recreation
Department includes in their concessionaire specifications, a requirement that concessionaires hire and train one or more at-risk youth.
While the net result may be a lower revenue bid for the department,
the trade-off of providing youth with job training is considered
worthwhile.

9teen Talk

The department links with Channel 9 to coproduce a 30-minute
television talk show which provides a unique venue for teens to
express their thoughts and opinions on issues that directly affect their
lives, but about which they often feel powerless. Program content
includes problem solving, dealing with criticism and rejection, conflict resolution, transferable life skills, and developing a process of
setting and achieving goals, as they relate to each topic. *9teen Talk*
provides a controlled yet innovative environment through which
youth can develop the discipline, confidence, motivation, and technical skills necessary to achieve a competitive edge in a changing high-
tech job market. Youth involved in the "behind the scenes" production aspects of *9teen Talk* gain valuable experience and technical
knowledge in television production.

Adult involvement in the television program provides mentors
and role models. Youth service providers serve as panelists on the
shows to respond to youth questions and concerns. Program directors, camera operators, and other technical staff train participants in
entry-level technical skills. In return, the adults benefit from an
opportunity to learn more about youth needs and opinions, thereby
improving their ability to provide needed agency services.

Entrepreneurship is emphasized by helping youth develop a
strong work ethic and marketable employment skills. The audiovi-
sual productions provide a platform for program participants to express themselves creatively, develop social skills, and enhance and
strengthen self-esteem.

9teen Talk is also incorporating the city's high schools as show
venues. Schools provide support in a variety of ways including
educators and counselors as panelists. Schools also provide a diverse
audience base for the shows.

Hang Time: Collaboration with the Ackerly Youth Foundation

Over 60,000 youth statewide participate in the very popular Hang
Time program which includes basketball skills instruction, academic
incentives and—the big draw—direct interaction with Seattle Super-
sonic players. The program is one of many supported by the Ackerly
Youth Foundation, established in 1993 by Barry and Ginger Ackerly,
owners of the Supersonics (see Exhibit 7E).

Sonics players participate in summer Hoops Camps, teaching
basketball fundamentals and life skills and rewarding kids who stay

---

Exhibit 7E

Mission Statement:

> To provide at-risk youths with positive influences
> and recreational activities as alternatives to violent
> actions.

The Ackerley Youth Foundation was formed by Barry and Ginger
Ackerley in the fall of 1993 with the goal of supporting Seattle's
at-risk youth through the resources of Ackerley Communications,
Inc.

The idea for the foundation grew out of a conversation the
Ackerleys had with Seattle Mayor Norm Rice on ways to prevent
youth violence in the city. The Ackerleys also drew upon the
many positive experiences they shared with children who participated in the Seattle SuperSonics' community relations programs.
Children's enthusiasm for positive interaction can be seen in the
success of the Sonics basketball camps held each summer. The
Hoops Camps provide kids with the opportunity to learn basketball fundamentals and life skills from SuperSonics players, while
rewarding kids who stay off drugs and in school with Sonics
tickets and giveaways. The success of this program, which after
four years has grown to 60,000 kids participating statewide,
prompted the formation of the Ackerley Youth Foundation.

The Ackerley Youth Foundation will utilize the resources of
all local companies of Ackerley Communications, Inc.: Ackerley
Outdoor Advertising, The Seattle SuperSonics, radio stations
KJR-AM/KLTX-FM, and television station KVOS in Bellingham.

off drugs and in school with Sonics tickets and giveaways. An annual Stay-in-School Jam honors middle-school students who have achieved 95% attendance for the semester. This program, which targets twelve schools in the Seattle School District, features all twelve Sonics players, Coach George Karl and his staff. A mascot dunk competition, giveaways for the students, and special entertainment are also included as part of the Hang Time program.

In addition to support for special events, the Ackerley Foundation has supported recreation programs and activities by purchasing vans to transport youth to and from community centers, refurbishing several basketball courts, and purchasing a variety of athletic equipment for recreation centers throughout Seattle. The Foundation also supports ten recreation leader positions to help develop and coordinate recreation activities for youth.

The Foundation refurbished three basketball courts in the Seattle area in the 1993-1994 basketball season and provided a variety of athletic equipment including basketballs, footballs, soccer balls, T-shirts, uniforms, caps, and other items to a number of community centers throughout Seattle. In addition, the Ackerley Youth Foundation funds other recreational activities such as arts and crafts projects, and provides nutritional snacks and beverages for the youth at each community center.

The Foundation coordinates Family Nights at five community centers hosted by a Seattle SuperSonics player and his family. The admittance ticket for kids enables them to bring a parent or guardian with them to participate in this family event. Sonics players share experiences and life skills, and kids are treated to NBA video entertainment, refreshments, and a mini-basketball clinic.

Section III
Organizing the Community

Chapter 8
Youth Summits: Exploring Collaboration to Maximize Opportunities
for At-Risk Youth in Portland, Oregon

Presenter:
David A. Jordon
   Youth At-Risk Coordinator, City of Portland

> While retaining our uniqueness and autonomy, we in the
> field of recreation, who share the same values and goals,
> can accomplish more by working together than we can
> on our own. This is the chance for us to demonstrate the
> full value of who we are and what we can do. Our youth
> are at-risk, and our society is at a loss. Up to this point,
> we've been fighting a nuclear war with conventional
> weapons. The first addition to our arsenal must be a new
> way of thinking...we must learn to work together. Be-
> cause society needs help with its youth. And we have a
> piece of the solution. (Charles Jordan, Director, Portland
> Parks and Recreation)

Background

In 1992 the Portland Parks and Recreation Department began using
youth summits to bring together youth-serving agencies in order to
shape an agenda to serve the needs of at-risk youth. In this era of
diminishing resources, collaboration between recreation providers
and others in the community is essential if the role of recreation is to
be maximized to its full potential. Since the first summit, other
summits have been held focusing on the needs of particular areas of
Portland. This has helped focus attention on services at the neighborhood level.

In his keynote address to the first summit, Portland Parks and
Recreation Director Charles Jordan told representatives of Portland's
youth-serving organizations, that funding providers increasingly
insist upon collaboration between service providers before they will

consider the worthiness of any recreation program. "Therefore," Jordan concluded, "it is imperative for us to be proactive and proceed toward real collaboration, i.e., working towards shared decision making, shared resources, and a shared mission."

In support of Jordan's statement, Willie Stoudamire, a director of the Mallory Christian Church's "People Are Beautiful" program, noted that collaboration gives their program more legitimacy in the community. "Traditional funders tend to just gloss over us," said Stoudamire. "But if we're in a group effort, they pay attention."

From the funder's perspective, Don Ballenger, a Senior Vice President with United Way, explained why his agency was trying to encourage collaborative efforts:

> The single youth care provider can't effectively serve its clients anymore. The problems are just too overwhelming. So if agencies can demonstrate that they are working together, they get a much more favorable review.

Focus on Prevention

Jordan also recognized the need to reposition the role of recreation in the community. While maintaining its function of providing "fun and games," recreation must also portray itself as a powerful tool in

---

Exhibit 8A

There was a certain river and many human beings were in it struggling to get to shore. Some succeeded; some were pulled ashore by kindhearted people on the banks. But many were carried down the stream and drowned. It is no doubt a wise thing; it is nobler that under those conditions charitable people devote themselves to helping the victims out of the water. But... it would be better if some of those kindly people on the shore engaged in rescue work, would go up the stream and find out who was pushing the people into it.

Tom Johnson
Mayor (1901-1909)
Cleveland, Ohio

providing at-risk youth with positive alternatives in their lives. This is the key to winning support for recreation in a society that remains unconvinced about the merits of preventative programs. According to Jordan:

> The mission of the recreation field is to demonstrate that we are more than just fun and games. Allowing ourselves to be relegated to just fun and games has weakened our competitive position at budget time. We are big brothers and big sisters. We are the nurses, the chauffeurs. We feed them. We pick them up. We patch them up. We are their role models; we are their friends. We play multiple roles in parks and recreation, and that is why the responsibility is so awesome. But it is also a tremendous opportunity, and we recognize that.

So far, the funding scale is heavily weighted towards dealing with the symptoms rather than the causes. Los Angeles currently spends $25 million a year on school security. Detroit spends $4 million, and New York spends $75 million a year. That's enough money to hire 2,000 more teachers or to buy books for 537,000 students. "Now you tell *me* where the emphasis lies," says Jordan.

> Society may want to get tough on crime, but society does not seem prepared to say that prevention is more effective than rehabilitation. Prevention and rehabilitation—we need them both. However, I contend that the only permanent, affordable, and sustainable solution is to be found in prevention.

Exhibit 8B

The [Summit] meeting broadened my appreciation for the vitally important role that recreation can play in the lives of families and our communities. In that light, Portland Parks and Recreation stands as a key building block to providing and facilitating current and future opportunities.

Stanley D. Peterson, Director
Youth Gangs Program

Each young person has to travel down a road of choices. One road leads to higher self-esteem and leadership, values, and support; the other to violence, destruction, hate, and fear. Each of those roads brings the young person in contact with the larger community, one in a positive manner, one in a negative manner. Even those who end up in the juvenile justice or criminal justice system eventually end up at the beginning of the road of choices again. Along with education, employment, family, and other supportive, positive influences in a person's life, recreation has a role to play in helping lead young people down the positive path of choices.

Summit Procedures

Long-Range Goals Identified

During a typical summit, attendees break into small groups to explore the concept of collaboration. Each group is asked to establish its common ground, what can be accomplished by working together, how to make collaboration work, and what the next step should be in making this concept a reality. At the first summit in 1992 the groups identified three primary long-term goals:

(1) to ensure that every youth who wants it has access to affordable recreation opportunities regardless of his or her finances, cultural background, or ability;
(2) to reinforce the role of recreation in improving public safety through prevention; and
(3) to have a stronger, united voice in maximizing limited resources.

Recognizing that collaboration needs both form and direction, the recreation providers also identified critical tasks needed to ensure success. These included:

(a) focusing on increased networking and public relations; and
(b) developing a mechanism for evaluating the effectiveness of their programs.

Networking

The goal of networking is to work more closely together to provide a safety net to ensure that every child is served by someone, whether this be the park and recreation department, the Boy Scouts, or whoever. Knowing which providers offer what programs and activities and to identify roadblocks that prevent them from offering more is essential for success. At the summit, delegates laid the groundwork for creating a *resource needs* and *resources-to-share data base* among organizations with information on facilities, funding, transportation, participants, volunteers/mentors, and training.

This system has led to increased opportunities for children in their community. For example, one program group wanted to develop a computer learning program for youth in a specific area of the city. Luckily, within a one block radius, a program that had 15 computers was already available. Networking enabled these two providers to come together to better serve the youth in that community. In another instance, one group might have a gymnasium, while another group has an arts-and-crafts room. The group with the gymnasium wants to add an arts-and-crafts program. Rather than build new facilities, access to existing facilities is provided.

Public Relations

Another issue of importance to summit participants was how to improve communication with the public. In identifying the best methods to reach every child and family with information on available recreational opportunities, the group discussed two strategies:

Exhibit 8C

Sometimes we need a reality check. I work with teen mothers. And sometimes I forget to think if what I'm doing is really helping them. I need to walk in the shoes of these moms. I need to let them speak for me.

Cheryl Chatman
Portland Public Schools
Monroe Program

---

(1) the development of a *multiprovider activity guide* or brochure which provides information on activities, as well as the appropriate provider to contact; and

(2) the organization of an annual *Recreation Fair* for children and their families with representatives from all recreation providers on hand to talk about their programs.

Evaluating Effectiveness

Finally, summit participants recognized that in order for their efforts to be taken seriously, procedures had to be developed for evaluating the effectiveness of their programs. To meet their short-term goals, recreation providers require information on who is being served, what their needs are, and whether those needs are being met. This information also forms the basis for a long-term evaluation of what

---

Exhibit 8D

Transportation is our highest priority. Some of these kids never get away from where they're living. Taking them to the waterfront is like taking them to Heaven... and it's less than two miles away. But we just don't have the transportation to do it very often.

Dr. Dapo Sobomehin
Operation E.A.S.Y.

There is no limit to what you can accomplish if you do not care who gets the credit.

Through a collaboration between Campfire Boys and Girls and Portland Parks and Recreation, we were able to take 13 teen mothers on a two-night camping trip. What happened up there was more wonderful than I can explain. They bonded with each other. They learned they could rely upon themselves. Only two of the girls had ever been camping before.

Anna Street, Director
PIVOT

---

role recreation plays in providing positive differences in the lives of participating young people. Evaluation provides the statistical evidence necessary to compete effectively for the ever-shrinking pool of funding resources.

However, setting up a system for documenting the impact of such a broad array of services throughout a large city is likely to be extremely costly and time-consuming. Therefore, summit participants decided to focus their study on the North, Northeast and Southeast sections of the city. This would enable them to tap into an already-existing data gathering system set up by "The Leaders' Roundtable," a team of civic, private and business leaders committed to the goal of 100% high school graduation in the adopted area by the year 1996. By adding their own questions to the Leaders' Roundtable questionnaire, summit participants were able to gather the information they needed to document their own endeavors.

Collaborating to Deal with Immediate Needs

Summit participants also focused on partnerships to maximize resources. They agreed that regular meetings should be established to build trust and teamwork principles, and that a good starting point for these meetings would be tackling the most immediate challenges: funding, transportation, and volunteers.

In response to such immediate needs, Portland Parks and Recreation Director Jordan committed to organizing a second meeting for recreation providers within six weeks, with transportation being the first issue covered. Two suggestions were to be discussed at that meeting:

(a) using the limited financial resources of the Portland Parks and Recreation Youth Trust Fund to leverage additional support for buses and vans; and

(b) establishing communication with foundation representatives and mass transit agencies (both of whom would be invited to attend).

Many members of the group had a successful collaborative experience as a result of the Summer Partnership Program. An official from the Oregon Museum of Science and Industry explained how collaboration with Portland Parks and Recreation gave his fundraising efforts added impetus:

As a result of the meeting, a seed was planted on how to
get more for our money. Using $1,000 provided by
Portland Parks and Recreation as leverage, I was able to
go to five other organizations and ask them for matching
funds, ultimately turning the original $1,000 into $5,000.
It really gave us legitimacy to be able to say we were
working with Portland Parks and Recreation on this.

Clearly, recreation providers working together can accomplish
more than any single agency ever could. But to engage their fullest
potential also requires collaboration with others in the community
(see Exhibit 8E).

The Youth Summits have begun an important dialogue
about ways local government and human service agencies can work together to better serve at-risk youth. I
applaud this important first step. It will make a real
difference in the lives of our children. Because when
government and the community can combine their resources, we become a powerful force for social change.
(Earl Blumenauer, Portland City Council Member)

Identifying Other Resources for Collaboration

To really make a difference in the lives of young people will
mean reaching beyond recreation providers and working with others
in the community to maximize resources. These "others" include
businesses, foundations, corporations, schools, government agencies,
and individuals. This not only maximizes program opportunities and
enables more children to be reached, but it also enables the needs of
the whole child to be better served.

When the corporate community saw that service providers were
working collectively together, they were more willing to invest dollars because they knew those dollars would be well-spent. Thus,
Nike Corporation provided funding for an education program, basketball court, and play area at a program that serves young people
who are kicked out of school. Instead of staying home, it is mandatory that the youth participate in the program. The program helps
them keep up with their studies and avoid the negative impact of
being at home with nothing to do.

Exhibit 8E

Ways that collaborations help communities identify gaps in current services and cooperate to fill the gaps:

- expand available services by cooperative programming and joint fundraising and grant programs;
- provide better services to clients through interagency communication about client needs, referral programs, and client case management;
- develop a greater understanding of client and community needs by seeing the whole picture;
- share similar concerns while being enriched by diverse perspectives that different members from varied backgrounds bring to the collaboration;
- reduce interagency conflicts and tensions by squarely addressing issues of competition and "turf;"
- improve communication with organizations within the community and, through those organizations, to larger segments of the community;
- mobilize action to affect needed changes through collective advocacy;
- achieve greater visibility with decision makers, the media, and the community;
- enhance staff skill levels by sharing information and organizing joint training programs;
- conserve resources by avoiding unnecessary duplication of services; and
- decrease costs through collective buying programs and other collective cost containment opportunities.

In another case, AT&T Wireless Services has provided 14 free cellular telephones to members of neighborhood response teams to speed up the response time for dealing with crisis situations involving area youth. In addition, over the past two years, AT&T Wireless Services has completely refurbished the Black Education Center's interior and exterior, and has renovated and landscaped the Columbia Children's Aboretum.

Collaboration is not the answer for every situation. An organization by itself can often plan and implement an activity more expediently than a group of organizations can. However, in many contexts individual organizations acting alone may lack the resources and the clout to produce the desired results.

Collaborations are more effective at developing an understanding of the communitywide implications of problems and solutions. They are more able to mobilize large segments of the community to effect change. A group effort can bring together diverse opinions and develop a program, an activity, or a campaign that will be supported by many organizations.

Funding for Collaborative Efforts

One of the means of providing the city's share of funding for some of the collaborative efforts that have emerged from the Summits is the Portland Parks and Youth Trust Fund. The Fund derives its money from a 50¢ fee for each round of golf played at one of the four city-owned golf courses. This raises between a quarter of a million and $300,000 a year, which is earmarked specifically for youth at-risk programs throughout the city of Portland. An additional fee of $1 per round of golf for nonresidents also raises close to $375,000 to help fund after-school programs. This money is leveraged by partners' contributions to the many collaborative projects in which the Parks and Recreation Department is involved.

Ongoing Efforts

The process of meeting with agencies and having summits is ongoing. The Coordinator of Youth Services meets with service providers in the various sections of the community several times a year, and with particular service providers as often as once a month. The Youth Trust Fund acts a catalyst for insuring community involvement and collaboration. Access to funding is only available to programs that involve more than one agency. This principle also applies to Parks and Recreation Department programs.

Chapter 9
Urban Initiatives:
A University/Community Partnership
in North Philadelphia, Pennsylvania

Presenter:
Delores M. Andy
     Associate Professor, Temple University, Philadelphia, Pennsylvania

Background

The Center for Public Policy Urban Initiatives at Temple University
is building a partnership between a North Philadelphia community,
the City of Philadelphia, and the university. The project is funded by
a $582,563 grant from the U.S. Department of Education and an
additional $193,198 in matching funds contributed from a variety of
participants, most notably the Beech Corporation, and Habitat for
Humanity. The Recreation component received approximately
$134,000 for three years, much of it used to award community
grants. The project was designed to complement and expand ongoing technical, training, and evaluation assistance to the Cecil B.
Moore community as part of Temple University's urban mission.

The central theme of Urban Initiatives is *community empowerment*. Rehabilitation of the physical and social landscape is achieved
by linking the analytic, problem-solving, and educational resources
of Temple University with a broad-based coalition of agencies seeking to improve the quality of life in the Cecil B. Moore area of North
Philadelphia. The three-year effort is aimed at:

(1) working with the local residents and civic and municipal
    leadership toward the social and physical betterment of the
    community;
(2) providing technology transfer to community-based organiza-
    tion and business interests so continuation of these develop-
    mental efforts can be institutionalized within the community,
    thus enabling the community to be less reliant on external
    assistance;

(3) creating viable demonstration projects which involve all part-
     ners, and which leave tangible impacts on the community; and
(4) elaborating on the role which the urban university should be
     playing in urban neighborhoods by designing curricula and
     involving students in urban policy analysis and community
     design projects.

The Cecil B. Moore community is located in North Central
Philadelphia and three contiguous census tracts. The area displays
the signs of urban decay found in many urban centers: crumbling
houses, abandoned autos, overgrown and littered lots, cracked side-
walks, and potholes, as well as an array of social disorganization and
public health safety problems.

The total population of the area is 12,094, with a slightly higher
number of females (6,309) than males (5,785). Over 90% of residents are African American. Close to one-third (32%) of residents
are under 18 years of age. There is also a fairly significant elderly
population, with 15% of residents over 65 years of age. Many children under 16 are being raised by grandmothers.

The target area includes 6,287 housing units. Over one-third of
the housing units are unoccupied, abandoned, and blighted. Many of
the houses are actually owned or supervised by the city of Philadelphia. One-third of the units are single unit attached or rowhouses.
Most of the housing units are valued at less than $15,000. Half of
the rental units lease for less than $250 a month.

Recreation opportunities are limited in the target community.
Many of the recreation facilities are open only a few hours a week
and, when open, are staffed with temporary or patronage employees.
Most of the recreation centers are old, poorly maintained and in need
of capital improvements. Teen violence, vandalism, and theft impact
negatively on recreational programs and community participation.
City and department budget constraints, job freezes, public safety,
and public health priorities limit opportunities to provide or create
programs to meet the special needs of at-risk youth living in the
target area.

Program Objectives

Urban Initiatives has five major objectives:

(1) to assist in the social and economic development of the community by designing and implementing programs to increase
community organization, share community information, develop mentoring programs, and train a number of community
residents in community organization and leadership skills;

(2) to increase public safety, particularly in public places, by planning for and implementing a police "mini-station" in the target
community;

(3) to improve the physical landscape and land use in the target
community through collaboration of academic and technical
assistance, and "projects" conducted in collaboration with the
Beech Corporation and Habitat for Humanity;

(4) to design, provide, and support recreational opportunities
planned by and for the community; and

(5) to increase education and training opportunities for community
leaders, local business persons, and community residents.

Each of the objectives is intended to contribute directly to stabiliza-
tion of the community, while at the same time providing a vehicle for
community organization and self-determination.

Key Players

A *Community Advisory Board* was established to better coordinate
the project and provide a linkage with community and governmental
representatives. The Recreation Networking Advisory Committee
(RNAC), consisting of 12 community residents who live in the Cecil
B. Moore neighborhood, was established to determine guidelines and
approve funding for recreation proposals and monitor the services
rendered. Many of the members are long-time community activists.
The committee meets monthly to establish criteria and guidelines for
administrating grants and to monitor them. The RNAC also advises
the Sport Management and Leisure Studies faculty at Temple University on potential opportunities for fieldwork and intern placement.

The RNAC is staffed by one coordinator and a doctoral student
majoring in sport and recreation administration. The coordinator is
supervised by a faculty member, familiar with the Cecil B. Moore

target area, its problems and needs. The coordinator is responsible for planning RNAC meetings and activities, developing a calendar of events for the service/learning projects, compiling data for the resource directory, providing technical assistance; monitoring and evaluating activities, program development, and supporting and cooperating with other Urban Initiatives project coordinators.

The second group of key players is the *Principal Investigators Working Group*. This group meets to discuss project efforts, activities, and outcomes. The group has fostered a closer relationship among internal Temple University faculty and staff, and helped to forge an academic coalition, which has resulted in joint programming among several project elements and the creation of project Community Forums.

The Recreation Program Content

Specific objectives of the recreation component are as follows:

(1) award community grants for recreation programs;
(2) implement a service/learning program led by Temple University students in the Cecil B. Moore community;
(3) coordinate development of a community resource directory;
(4) support the Recreation Networking Advisory Committee;
(5) provide resource consultation to the community;
(6) provide additional training for the adult population;
(7) promote socialization networks; and
(8) monitor community grants.

Community Grants

The Recreation Networking Advisory Committee evaluates applications for grants from community groups seeking to offer programs in the target area. Some of the community grants, which range from $500 to $2,000, targeted for at-risk youth are as follows:

(1) *Aloha Tutorial Camp* —Founded and conducted by a resident from the Cecil B. Moore community, the camp is based at Smith Memorial Playground in East Fairmount Park. This day camp emphasizes education, providing remediation and reinforcement in math and reading through recreation activities. Campers experience a variety of activities including rhythmic

activities and field trips, and lunch and snacks are provided. Over 90 neighborhood children, ages 3–10 years participate.

(2) *Martin Luther King Flag Football Team*—Fifty adolescents, 14 and under, participate in a sport program that focuses on teaching teamwork, self-discipline, responsibility, and respect for others, while developing sport skills. All coaches are volunteers from the neighborhood. Funds provide uniforms, equipment, and awards.

(3) *Girl Scouts of Greater Philadelphia Extended Family Program*—This program targets troop activities for girls living in homeless shelters. Troop leaders and volunteers are recruited from the neighborhood. During the summer, the girls attend a day camp in suburban Philadelphia.

(4) *Police Explorer Scouts*—The local police district community relations officer directs and supervises youth from the neighborhood to perform community service at recreational events. Funds were used to purchase two-way radios.

(5) *The North Philadelphia Senior Center at North City Congress*—The Intergenerational Choir was organized to bring together neighborhood youths and senior citizens living in the Cecil B. Moore neighborhood. Funds are used to purchase sheet music and provide light refreshments after choir rehearsals. The choir entertains at nursing homes and special events during the year.

(6) *Heritage Community Study Buddy Program*—A need to focus on academic preparation through recreation is the hallmark of this program. Study Buddy provides community volunteers and tutors for neighborhood children. Funds are used to purchase school supplies and equipment.

(7) *Boy Scouts of Philadelphia, Liberty Council*—Funds are used to support a Boy Scout Troop and a Cub Pack at a neighborhood church. By purchasing camping and other scout equipment for the troop, Boy Scout membership fees, and subscriptions to *Boys Life Magazine,* scouts are given an opportunity to attend summer camp. Equipment is shared with other Cecil B. Moore Boy Scout troops to maximize participation by other boys from the neighborhood.

(8) *North Philadelphia Partnership's Youth Ambassador Corps*—Approximately 75 boys and girls are trained to improve ambassadorial skills such as public speaking, knowledge of their

community and its relationship with other neighborhoods, and the history of North Philadelphia, including its community activists who made a difference. Once trained, they serve as tour guides and become a part of a conservation effort cleaning and landscaping vacant lots.

(9) *Mt. Lebanon Community Baptist Church*—This organization founded by church elders uses grant funds to support recreation and education programs for youth in the target community.

(10) *Sabree Youth Corps*—A community service organization, using veterans and neighborhood volunteers, Sabree trains youth at-risk in marching and singing drill teams. The corps performs at community special events, neighborhood playstreets, and drill team competition.

Service/Learning Projects

Twenty students, all sports/recreation management and therapeutic recreation majors, provide social and recreation programs at a neighborhood nursing home, John Wanamaker Junior High School, and the North Philadelphia YMCA. In addition, the students conduct a spring and a fall clean-up-fix-up day at the neighborhood recreation center. They also organize a warm clothing drive for adults, infants, and children. The students organize a canned goods drive and volunteer with the Recreation Networking Advisory Committee.

Chapter 10
Winton Hills Teen Violence Prevention
in Cincinnati, Ohio

Presenter:
Ronald W. Chase
> Director, Cincinnati Recreation Commission

Background

In 1991 the mayor established the Youth Steering Committee which was composed of Directors from the Recreation Commission, the Department of Health and Safety—the Employment, Training, and Human Services Divisions—and members from the Citizens' Committee on Youth and the Cincinnati Human Relations Commission. The Committee launched an agenda of extensive planning and research to develop a coordinated system of services to deal with youth issues in Cincinnati. The mayor felt that a coordinated plan of action was needed to help avoid serious and widespread incidents of violence that were occurring in Cincinnati.

The Committee identified the root cause of the detrimental behavior of youth ages 13–21 as historical disenfranchisement, poverty, discrimination, inadequate education and skill levels, damaged self-esteem, and thwarted aspirations. More adequate healthcare, education opportunities, improved economic development of communities, better delivery of human services, and fairer treatment in the criminal justice and legal systems were identified as areas where services and approaches needed to be improved.

Back on the Block Program

To help bring about improvement in the situation for young people, the Committee encouraged representatives of communities and existing service agencies to engage in a "process of closing the gaps in service delivery and improving the negative conditions of the urban population." The Youth Steering Committee determined that a program to take services to the streets and decentralize control away from city hall was needed. *Back on the Block* (BOB) was a ten-week summer program, but its initial success led to year-round implementation as funds became available.

Twelve of the 52 neighborhoods in the city were targeted for attention based on their high levels of poverty, number of single heads of household, and incidence of crime. To achieve the goals of the program, the Youth Steering Committee which was chaired by the Director of the Recreation Commission recommended that several structural elements be put in place, including establishing lead agencies, community oriented policing, community youth support teams, community relations monitors, recreation programs, and a summer youth employment program.

Lead Agencies

A *lead agency* was designated from existing social service organizations that operated in each targeted community. These agencies were charged with bringing together all social service agencies, community groups, and interested citizens to address at-risk youth needs. A list of lead agencies and their target communities is shown in Exhibit 10A. The responsibilities of each lead agency are to:

- convene regular meetings (at least once a week) to disseminate information and identify "hot spots;"
- manage the process of neighborhood collaboration;
- identify neighborhood projects and/or services for youth;
- develop referral services for youth;
- identify and increase volunteer involvement; and
- identify families with problems, and work to secure needed services.

Each lead agency was also to distribute funds allocated for programs and activities within its targeted community. To assist lead agencies in the referral process, the Cincinnati Recreation Commission put together a "Social Service Directory," which lists major services available in the community, e.g., drug and alcohol rehabilitation, day care, counseling, shelter, food and clothing support. Initially, the BOB operated during the summer period, and each lead agency was given $5,000 from the United Way to help develop local services for youth.

Exhibit 10A

List of Target Communities and Lead Agencies

Target Communities:	*Lead Agencies:*
Heinold	Cincinnati Union Bethel
Winton Hills	Cincinnati Union Bethel/ Terrace Guild
Bond Hill	Coalition of Neighborhoods
Over-the-Rhine	Emanual Community Center
Evanston	Human Involvement Project
Lower Price Hill	Santa Maria Community Services
West End	Seven Hills Neighborhood Houses
South Fairmont	Urban Appalachian Council
Avondale	Victory Neighborhood Services
Walnut Hills	Victory Neighborhood Services
Northside	Working in the Neighborhoods
Madisonville	YMCA Madisonville Branch

Community-Oriented Policing

A second structural element, Community Oriented Policing (COP), was established by the police department. Neighborhood officers increased their contact with residents through foot patrols in the neighborhoods and established direct communications with community leaders and businesses to help identify problem areas within each target community. The COP officers also participate in youth activities and BOB events.

Community Youth Support Teams

The city also established Community Youth Support Teams which consist of representatives of the Cincinnati Recreation Commission (CRC), the Cincinnati Human Relations Commission (CHRC), Citizens' Committee on Youth (CCY), the United Way and Community Chest, social service agencies, COP officers, and community and youth representatives. A support team was assigned to each of five geographical areas. Each team has a supervisor who reports to the

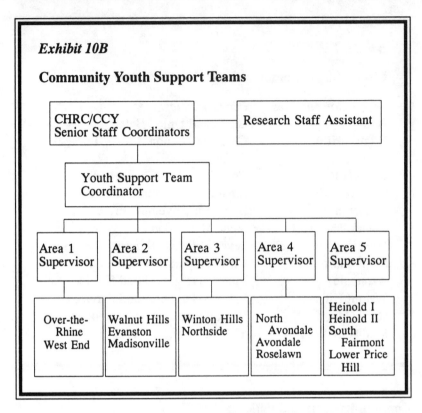

Exhibit 10B

Community Youth Support Teams

overall Youth Support Team Coordinator and the Coordinator reports directly to the CHRC/CCY Senior Staff Coordinators (see Exhibit 10B).

The Youth Support Teams work out of social service agency facilities, recreation centers, or youth service bureaus. Youth Support Teams operate 32 hours per week on a flexible schedule depending on the needs of the community. The primary duties of the Youth Support Teams are to:

(a) act as a liaison between lead agencies, community councils, youth and social service agencies, neighborhood residents, and COP officers;

(b) provide referrals to various social service agencies for at-risk youth who need assistance; and

(c) monitor community events and recreation services.

Community Relations Monitors and Crisis Response Teams

A fourth structural element was the establishment of Community Relations Monitors (CRMs) and Crisis Response Teams. Monitors are trained in conflict resolution, mediation and other community involvement skills. The CRM Teams respond at the request of a social service organization or the police to monitor events and to help diffuse explosive situations. The effort is designed to keep situations from escalating and avoid formal involvement of the police. As a backup, a Crisis Response Team comprised of experts from a variety of agencies, was formed to respond to particularly critical incidents.

Expanded Recreation Programs

The Recreation Commission expanded its programs in the targeted areas to include:

(a) mayor's summer concerts which feature young local talent, but also have headliners;
(b) expanded hours at the recreation centers;
(c) neighborhood basketball shoot out (three-on-three) in 30 locations which attracts 3,000 participants; and
(d) tennis programs, which include Arthur Ashe's National Junior Tennis Program, and a special urban tennis camp.

Youth Employment

A Summer Youth Employment Program was established under the sponsorship of the Citizens' Committee on Youth and Youth Employment Services (YES). Through their efforts, approximately 2,500 youth find summer jobs during the summer. In addition, the Recreation Commission has an extensive aquatic training program to train at-risk youth as lifeguards and also hires at-risk youth to work in the recreation centers. An overview of how these structured entities interrelate is shown in Exhibit 10C, page 118. The police division is shown on the chart as the last line of defense to which the city can turn if everything else fails.

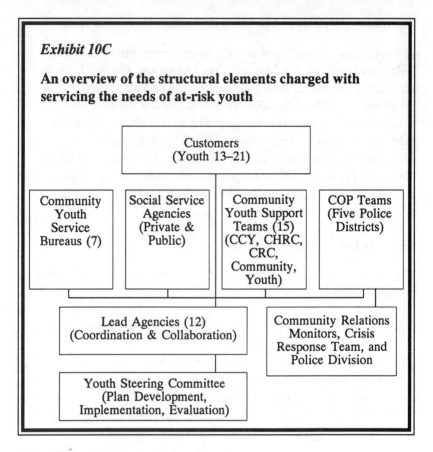

Exhibit 10C

An overview of the structural elements charged with servicing the needs of at-risk youth

Customers
(Youth 13–21)

| Community Youth Service Bureaus (7) | Social Service Agencies (Private & Public) | Community Youth Support Teams (15) (CCY, CHRC, CRC, Community, Youth) | COP Teams (Five Police Districts) |

Lead Agencies (12)
(Coordination & Collaboration)

Community Relations Monitors, Crisis Response Team, and Police Division

Youth Steering Committee
(Plan Development, Implementation, Evaluation)

The Winton Hills Program

Fortunately, the intricate system of coordinated service agencies and response teams was in place when a crisis emerged in Winton Hills. The area was the scene of a massive drug raid led by the FBI in July 1992. The tensions and problems were exacerbated when, on January 4, 1993, three men jumped from a van and gunned down a 20-year-old at a crowded intersection. A newspaper reporter and photographer were shot at on January 5 while investigating the shooting. These highly visible incidents and the day-to-day violence and drug dealing galvanized the community and city leaders to address the problems of the Winton Hills community.

The Winton Hills community is composed of three distinct neighborhoods containing public housing units managed by a metropolitan housing authority. The community is plagued by the common problems of violence associated with poor living conditions, poverty, drugs, and loss of hope among the residents. It is composed of approximately 6,800 residents (88% African American) with almost 70% below the poverty level. Forty-five percent of the family units are headed by single parents with children less than four years old.

Immediately following the shooting incidents, the Mayor of Cincinnati called a community meeting in the Winton Hills Community Center, operated by the Cincinnati Recreation Commission, to hear the concerns and recommendations of community residents related to the violence issues. As an outgrowth of that meeting, the City Council took immediate action to provide a $50,000, one-time emergency grant to the Recreation Commission to establish recreation programs which would alleviate the impact of the ongoing street violence in the community.

Objectives

Objectives of the Recreation Commission's Winton Hills program were:

(1) through a grass-roots collaborative process identify specific recreation and social-service type programs desired by community residents, with an emphasis on services to teens and young adults;

(2) as part of this collaborative effort, identify and bring to the table all individuals, agencies, city departments, and private supporters to address the problems and to arrive at solutions; and

(3) utilize the one-time funding allocation to provide programs and services not currently offered at the community center.

Key Players

Under the leadership of the Director of Recreation, a series of consensus building sessions were held at the Winton Hills Community Center which included community council representatives, teenagers, volunteers, United Way funded agencies, the Police Division, the Health Department, the Citizen's Committee on Youth, the Human Services Department, the Cincinnati Human Relations Commission, Recreation Commission staff, sports associations, churches, and the Metropolitan Housing Authority, among others. After three meetings, a plan of action evolved that used the recreation center as the focal point for recreational, educational and social services for youth and young adults in the community. The plan called for tutoring, drug awareness and increased athletic programs, expanded weekend center hours, midnight basketball programs, drill teams, girls' sports, boxing, educational field trips, sewing classes, and other activities.

Program Content

The target population of the project included the youth and young adults ages 13–21. The recreation center was the focal part of many of the planned programs. The center consists of a major gymnasium, an indoor roller-skating rink, a fitness room, arts and crafts room, multipurpose room and a room allocated for tutoring which incorporates a resource library.

The consensus building process resulted in allocating the $50,000 grant to fund expanded weekend operating hours, girls' basketball programs including a skills development camp, registration fees for youth football teams, a community reunion and block party, midnight basketball programs, a girls' drill team with uniforms, field trips, sewing program, boxing, skating parties, drug awareness, tutoring programs and self-enhancement programs. A fitness room was developed in what was formerly a large storage room. An ongoing program entitled Future Leaders, which was designed to create greater self-esteem among the community teens, received much needed audiovisual equipment.

Social service agencies contributed staff and volunteers to either specifically conduct programs such as drug awareness and tutoring, or to augment the efforts of community center staff. The Health Department of the city provided self-awareness programs.

The Cincinnati Metropolitan Housing Authority partnered with the Recreation Commission to sponsor a 20-week midnight basketball program for teens and young adults which averages 350 participants on Friday and Saturday evenings. The Police Department stepped up its Community Oriented Policing efforts in the community with officers walking the beat, visiting the recreation center and generally creating a more positive bond with community residents.

Finally, volunteer residents played a key role in recruiting and linking young people with the community center staff and volunteer leaders. Their leadership resulted in an enhanced level of trust between loosely knit gangs. Adult volunteers acted as point people in informing the community about the variety of program opportunities available at the center.

Program Outcomes

The one-time infusion of $50,000 was leveraged with volunteer contributions, enhancements of existing programs, federal grants (for programs like midnight basketball), foundation funding and social agency efforts, so that approximately $100,000 worth of program services could be delivered. Agencies focused on the mission as opposed to "who gets the credit." Ron Chase, Director of the Recreation Commission, stated:

> Don't worry about who takes the credit. That's a bottom line. The one thing I have been trying to tear down, even in our own Department, is this idea that we have to take credit for things when they occur. I'd rather give credit, quite frankly, to other agencies that come on board and work with us because that encourages them to cooperate.... We all know intrinsically we've had success, even though we can't specifically measure it. The neighborhoods help us tremendously because they come out at budget time in a big way and yell and scream at the city council when they think about cutting our budget.

An immeasurable but obvious outcome of this program was the cooperative and collaborative spirit which emanated from the program effort. This remains an integral part of the service delivery system within the Winton Hills community.

According to police statistics, a crime reduction of 31% occurred within the first six months of implementing the prevention programs. Incidents of crime in the Winton Hills community dropped from 174 in the first six months of 1992 to 119 incidents in the first six months of 1993. An additional $30,000 operating funds was allocated by the Recreation Commission as a direct result of the crime prevention program.

The total involvement of community representatives, social service agencies, and various city departments working in concert with police officers assigned to the Winton Hills community has resulted in a successful process of taking back the community from the drug dealers and the criminal element who previously had the residents living in fear and with little hope for the future.

Chapter 11
Project Hope
in Scottsdale, Arizona

Presenter:
Daul Valenzuela
   Recreation Manager, Human Services Division, Scottsdale,
   Arizona

Background

Scottsdale, Arizona, is not immune to the problems which make the lives of our nation's youth and families challenging, difficult and sometimes desperate. Concerns expressed at annual youth town hall meetings, local parent councils, and school youth forums, along with police statistics on the number of emerging gangs and amount of graffiti in the parks, led the community to conclude that part of the problem was the amount of idle time experienced by young people during nonschool hours.

Although an affluent community, Scottsdale's fastest-growing population is the poor. In 1980 only 3.5% of the population lived below the poverty level. By 1990 the poverty rate had jumped to 5.9%. With the city rapidly expanding in population (1990: 130,069; 1995: 165,430 estimated), the number of people living below the poverty level is also rapidly increasing. The problems associated with economic deprivation (e.g., delinquency, teen pregnancy, school failure, drug and alcohol abuse, teen violence) are all a growing source of concern. In 1994 referrals for violent crimes increased 53%, and documented gang members increased by 51% over the previous year. These problems were not confined to low-income families.

Risk factors associated with transitions, mobility, low neighborhood attachment and community disorganization also occur in Scottsdale. Rapid growth is attracting an ethnically diverse mix of young adults and families searching for economic opportunity. The promise of relocation is often met with disappointment as entry level employment, with inadequate or nonexistent healthcare benefits, fails to provide the compensation needed to economically sustain individuals and families. Scottsdale's new citizens often leave behind traditional support systems.

The 1993 Maricopa County Needs Assessment found that 34% of respondents in Scottsdale had no family, and 11% reported no friends in the area, or no friends at all. Ten percent said they shared their residence in the past year with someone who could not afford their own housing, and 10% said they were displaced within the past three years. The survey also identified barriers to receiving social services in Scottsdale: 61% did not know where to find a particular service, 36% could not afford service, 28% were ineligible for nonfinancial reasons, and 26% had family/personal objections to seeking services.

Without family or friends to temper the effects of unrealized dreams and frustrations, the likelihood of problem behaviors increases. In 1994 Scottsdale's Police Crisis Intervention Team recorded an increase of 15% in domestic violence calls, an 18% increase in family relations problems, a 23% increase in requests for suicide counseling, an 18% increase in sexual abuse interventions, a 21% increase in child abuse calls, and a 27% increase in contacts for runaways.

Further, the city reports a 44% increase in juvenile crime since 1989; in 1992 juveniles made up 26% of all those arrested in Scottsdale. In 1993 and 1994 Scottsdale citizens ranked crime, drugs and gangs as their highest and second highest priority concerns. In 1993, 61% of Scottsdale high school students believed there were gang members in their schools, 54% said they knew gang members and 74% said they knew someone who had brought a weapon of some kind to school. There were 93 births to teens in Scottsdale in 1993 and 433 high school dropouts in 1993. The 1991-92 dropout rate for Scottsdale School District was 34th out of 105 districts in the state. Illegal drug activity is also a problem. A survey of high school students reported that 36% used marijuana, 17% said they had used hallucinogens and smaller percentages reported having used narcotics, cocaine and methamphetamines. A 1993 survey of Scottsdale high school students showed rates of substance abuse at least as high as state and national rates. Fifty-two percent of high school students had used alcohol within the last 30 days compared to 43% statewide in 1991. Thirty-two percent of high school students reported smoking cigarettes compared to a national average of 29%.

Program Description

Program Goals

With the above issues in mind, Project Hope was created to provide a holistic set of services to meet the recreational, employment, educational, and other social service needs of youth in Scottsdale. Thus, the teen program in Scottsdale is an investment in renewing the spirit and restoring hope in today's youth. Although Scottsdale had a lot of beautiful parks and an array of programs, no programs existed in 1990 for middle schoolers or teens.

The goal of Project Hope is:

> To provide a variety of safe supervised places for middle-school and high-school-aged youth to gather, feel a sense of belonging and ownership, interact with positive role models and be empowered through learning social and instrumental skills to become healthy productive young adults.

As a result of participating in the program, participants are expected to:

(a) increase self-esteem among teens participating regularly;
(b) improve self-discipline, decision-making and leadership skills;
(c) increase positive interpersonal relationships;
(d) increase knowledge of issues affecting youth;
(e) facilitate the development and/or maintenance of positive, functional life and leisure skills; and
(f) increase knowledge and skills in creating and using sources of help when needed.

To achieve these outcomes, Project Hope seeks to work collaboratively with other community institutions to create shared prevention strategies that serve as vehicles for strengthening protective factors which diminish the risk factors causing adolescent behavior problems in Scottsdale.

To help measure success in meeting its goals, outcome targets were set:

(1) a communitywide collaboration will be developed, consisting of youth, adults and service providers with a shared vision of the positive development of youth and families in Scottsdale (formed in June 1993);

(2) risk and protective factors unique to Scottsdale will be identified through a comprehensive risk and resource assessment, based on Hawkins and Catalano's Communities That Care Model for risk-focused prevention (completed in June 1995);

(3) a comprehensive Prevention Plan will be completed, approved by community leaders and implemented through a system of task forces within Scottsdale's community collaborative (completed in December 1995); and

(4) benchmarks (i.e., statistical indicators) will be created by community leaders and members of the community collaborative from risk factors identified in the community risk assessment, and updated annually to measure change against the baseline data. Correlation between reduction of risk factors and reduction of problem adolescent behaviors will determine the degree to which the program has met its goal (completed in December 1995).

Program Content

Project Hope consists of a number of program elements, each of which came about through a unique set of collaborative arrangements.

Middle School Madness: In spring 1990, the Scottsdale Parents Council approached the city with its concern that there was nothing for middle-school-aged children to do in the summer months. While there were no budgeted funds available, staff from Scottsdale Recreation, Scottsdale Boys and Girls Clubs and Scottsdale Parents Council pooled resources and created a series of special events for middle schoolers. An eight-week program, Middle School Madness, has been funded by the city at one of its Community Centers during subsequent summers since 1991 for $10,000. The program is now called *The Zone* and serves middle- and high-school-aged teens.

In the fall of 1991 a recreation leader began a teen outreach program in another of Scottsdale's community parks adjacent to a high school. Initially, the program focused on having food and volleyball once a week in the park and using this activity as the basis for establishing positive relationships with a caring recreation leader. This was followed by efforts to create a gathering place the teens could make their own inside the community center.

Youth Intervention Unit: In 1993 the city's mayor and council approved the launching of a $500,000 youth intervention unit. Further, they approved funds for two full-time positions for teen recreation programmers in two of the four city community centers. A year later an additional full-time position was created for a third community center teen programmer and the YMCA agreed to take ownership of teen programming in the fourth center.

LINKS: In 1993 two years of community visioning efforts (including a youth forum representing students from all of Scottsdale's middle and high schools, a community leader's summit on changes taking place in Scottsdale, and a long-term youth visioning committee composed of service providers) culminated in the formation of a community collaboration. It was called LINKS, and was composed of youth and adults interested in creating a safe, healthy and productive community.

As a participant and leader in these visioning efforts and the LINKS collaborative, Scottsdale Recreation Division created interdisciplinary partnerships to meet adolescent needs. Further, the Division has maximized limited resources during nonschool hours in all four of its community/neighborhood centers. Existing recreation resources have been reallocated to create teen programs, and new resources have been added to create full-time adult leadership based on the principle that the single most important factor in reaching healthy adulthood is a positive relationship with a caring adult.

Job Skills: Scottsdale Youth and Family Services provides *job skills, employment opportunities and behavioral health services* with teens in consultation with recreation leaders at teen centers instead of limiting services to their central offices. Scottsdale Prevention Institute conducts leadership, cognitive and social skill building training with youth and staff, while assisting in the creation and refinement of a research instrument with Arizona State University, the YMCA, and Boys and Girls Clubs, to measure the effectiveness of programs with teens. Scottsdale Police are changing teens' perceptions by participating with teens in recreation activities.

Other programs have also been created: The Youth Leader Program is a one-to-one mentoring experience between youth and city employees that exposes youth to career choices and the world of work and involves them as contributing members of their community. In 1994, 110 teens were recognized at the end of the summer program for contributing over 12,000 hours of voluntary service. Those who elected to do so earned high-school credit.

Education Support Program: As a result of the alarming number of high-school dropouts, the high-school principal, recreation manager, and other city and school staff, created an *alternate classroom* at one community center and a *GED class* was instituted at a second center. Funded initially by Scottsdale Concerned Citizens and the school district, the alternate classroom is now funded by a state grant through the school district. The GED class conducted by Rio Salado Community College continues with both adult and teen participants.

The need for *homework assistance* was met by recruiting an Honors Society from Arizona State University to provide volunteer tutoring. In its second year of operation, Friends of the Library, through the local United Way agency, funds a coordinator for the program. Another center's tutoring staff is funded by an annual allocation by the local Setroma Club.

Other Programs: *Teen Councils* have been formed at each center to involve youth in leadership skill building opportunities and facilitate planning and operation of their own programs. Fundraising and service projects, with the assistance of parent groups, are another integral component.

Other program components facilitating outcomes include having participants actively involved in all phases of recreation programming (e.g., planning, conducting and evaluating); introducing a free-food component provided by Waste Not, a nonprofit organization that delivers Scottsdale restaurant food to areas of need in the community; annual awards ceremony for recognition of skills learned and goals reached; guest speakers and theme presentations focusing on specific youth issues, e.g., sexuality, teen rights and responsibilities; citywide grass roots basketball league in conjunction with the YMCA and Boys and Girls Club, cultural activities that promote self-identity and pride, e.g., photo art project and exhibit at Center for the Arts, several murals and other community building activities.

A unique aspect of the program is the park reinstatement program which involves a behavior contract created with kids who previously might have been kicked out of the parks for misbehaving.

These youth are now referred to an outreach counsellor to develop a behavioral contract on the basis of which they are readmitted to the program.

Staffing and Scheduling

Staffing varies for the different teen programs. The city's teen programs located at its three community centers are staffed with a full-time teen programmer and part-time staff to maintain a 1:20 ratio. The 1:20 ratio helps justify the budget and provides a useful benchmark when requests for additional funding are made.

Program hours vary from one center to the next. For example, at the center adjacent to the high school, hours are 2 to 6 p.m. Monday through Friday during the school year. Hours at another center are 3 to 10 p.m. Monday through Friday with middle schoolers coming after school and high schoolers coming after 5 p.m. The third center is open in the evening hours Thursday through Sunday. Teens are involved in setting hours at all three centers.

The YMCA and Boys and Girls Club use a similar mix of full-time and part-time staff with three programs offered at their sites and one at the city's neighborhood center. The YMCA has one program one night a week and another program the other five evenings of the week. The Boys and Girls Club program is two evenings a week at both locations. Staff at these programs not only report to a full-time community center coordinator at their individual locations but also meet and plan on a regular basis through the formation of a teen programmers' cross sectional team. This group's meetings often expand to include representatives of the Boys and Girls Club and YMCA, Youth and Family Outreach Counselors, and staff from other agencies.

The Youth and Family Outreach Counselor has recently been assigned to a newly formed team composed of community center coordinators in charge of park and recreation staff in each of their respective areas. The team reports directly to the Parks and Recreation Director. This frees up the former supervisor, a recreation manager to perform training, neighborhood enhancement development and expansion work with the LINKS community collaborative to promote integrated prevention strategies and enhance youth and family services coordination, marketing and evaluation.

Staffing for the five middle school programs is coordinated by a full-time recreation leader who selects, trains and supervises part-time coaches, instructors for specialty classes and leaders for clubs at each of the middle school locations. Each middle school provides a staff person who serves as school liaison to the after-school program. Activities are held twice per week after school, from 3:30 to 5:30 p.m.

Marketing

The teen programs in the community centers, Boys and Girls Clubs and YMCA are free and attract youth from their immediate neighborhoods. While the Community Service's quarterly program guide lists all programs offered to all ages and is delivered to each household in Scottsdale, it is not read by many teens. Word of mouth, teen staff "working" the school and the neighborhood, student newsletters and PTO newsletters seem to be the most effective vehicles for reaching teens rather than the traditional flyer or media release.

The middle-school programs charge a fee to help cover part of the program cost. Programs are well-attended in more affluent neighborhoods; however, programs in less affluent areas have experienced numbers considerably below capacity. The formation of an advisory council for these programs is underway with an initial goal of finding ways to increase participation.

Financing and Resource Allocation

The three community center teen programs and the five middle-school programs are primarily funded from general revenue generated by the city of Scottsdale. Programs are supplemented considerably by in-kind services and cash donations from other key player agencies in Scottsdale. A limited breakdown of program staffing and costs follows:

Middle School Program annual budget: $122,800
    Staffing: 1.4 FTE full-time, 3.7 part-time
Community Center Teen Programs annual budget: $100,000
    Staffing: 3.75 FTE full-time, 1.75 part-time

Measurement of Program Outcomes

The number of safe, supervised places teens can gather has grown
from none to twelve in the past five years. Two each are operated by
the YMCA and Boys and Girls Clubs and serve an average of 30 to
40 teens per week per location. Three city community centers serve
an average of 160 teens per day with over 350 registered participants. Five middle schools are serving over 500 students after
school with intramural sports, classes and clubs. The latter is a new
program funded by the city and supported by the Scottsdale School
District as a result of extensive research and lobbying of the Mayor
and Council and Scottsdale School Board by the Scottsdale Parents
Council, the same organization that approached the city five years
ago about middle school students.

The primary vehicle for measuring the effectiveness of commu-
nity centers, YMCA, and Boys and Girls Club teen programs is a
participant pretest/posttest instrument developed collaboratively with
Scottsdale Prevention Institute, Scottsdale Recreation, Boys and
Girls Club, YMCA and the Arizona State University West Recreation
Program.

The pretest/posttest is designed to measure perceptions both at
the beginning and end of a school year teen program that will provide indications of changes in teen behavior and attitudes. It has
already proven to be an effective vehicle for determining which
programs have the greatest impact on improving participant perceptions. Future program planning is based on what is gained through
the insights provided by this information.

Participant and parent surveys, along with feedback from adult
leaders, service providers and other involved parties, are other vehicles used to measure program outcomes.

Chapter 12
Youth 2000: The Challenge of Changing Mentalities
in Montreal, Quebec, Canada

Presenter:
Pierre Morin
Superintendent, Montreal Sports and Recreation

Background

In 1989 the city of Montreal's Recreation and Community Development Department began to evaluate the effectiveness of its youth programs. Three main factors led to this evaluation. First, over a period of approximately ten years there had been a successful campaign promoting the "taking charge" of recreational activities by local community groups in city neighborhoods. A consequence of this was that activities had evolved based on a "user-pays" philosophy. Further, activities were often selected because of the ease with which they could be organized and supervised by volunteers. One result of this philosophy was that fewer programs were available for spontaneous participation by teenagers at no charge. In addition, this group was often excluded from any significant access to municipal sponsored leisure programs.

Second, in those few instances where local groups or administrators attempted to offer activities for youth, there were consistent problems involving:

- inadequate resources for the acquisition of equipment;
- criticism and complaints from other clients, as well as from some municipal employees;
- lack of continuity of employees resulting from inadequate remuneration; and
- lack of coordination between community, social service, and governmental agencies and programs, each with its own methods, mandates, and priorities.

Third, an increase in youth violence led municipal authorities to be concerned that significant numbers were not making constructive use of their free time. Many of the problematic youth seemed to be isolated from their peers and difficult to involve in current services.

The Department commissioned a study to address these concerns while simultaneously launching a brainstorming and concept development process among its senior managers. The consultants who did the study noted:

> The majority of young people go through adolescence without venturing into delinquency or other antisocial behaviors. However, in public opinion, it appears that adolescence is related more closely to a pathology than to one of the most fertile phases in the life of an individual; adolescence and delinquency seem to be two terms which have become complementary.

The study noted, among other things:

- media present the most alarming situations of youth: gangs, drugs, violence, prostitution, dishonesty;
- after West Germany, Quebec ranks second in the world in suicide rate among young people;
- youth are portrayed in advertising as thoughtless and irresponsible consumers: fast food, heavy metal music, shocking clothes;
- youth are often associated only with problems within the educational system, such as dropping out and absenteeism; and
- recreation programs offered or supported by municipalities have been deserted by 13- to 17-year-olds, who are generally less interested in structured activities.

Following the study, an analysis indicated that lack of interest was only part of the reason why teenagers were not involved in recreation programs. They were often deliberately excluded from programs, because they were disruptive or because providing recreation activities which this age group would find interesting was relatively costly.

Since they were not politically organized enough to insist on services, nor economically able to support provision of their own programs, 13- to 17-year-old youth were generally excluded from services. Action was needed to reestablish the constructive involvement of these young people in their communities.

To this end, a working group composed of the superintendents of the nine recreation administrative districts of the city was set up to develop means for reaching nonparticipating teenagers. Recreation programs were viewed as important vehicles for working with teens. The working group cited the *Catalogue of Benefits of Parks and Recreation* (Balmer, 1991) published by the Canadian Parks and Recreation Association which concluded:

> Impact studies done with individuals indicate that the practice of recreational activities promotes physical and mental well-being, creative expression, and the stimulation and the development of the person. More specifically, the practice of recreational activities by youth promotes the development of moral values and constitutes a valid alternative to counter self-destructive behaviors such as substance abuse and suicide.

The working group proposed that a multifaceted approach should be implemented over a five year period by:

(1) adapting traditional programming;
(2) maintaining existing teen clubs;
(3) establishing specific agreements with school boards to establish after-school activities;
(4) establishing intervention programs for young people in housing projects; and
(5) developing the Youth 2000 program.

Youth 2000 Guidelines and Key Concepts

In 1989 and 1990 the working group produced basic specifications for a new type of intervention—Youth 2000. The objectives of this approach were to:

(1) reach 13- to 17-year-old youth and provide them with permanence and continuity in their pursuit of recreational activities;
(2) give young people control of and responsibility for their free-time recreation;

(3) encourage development and personal fulfillment of participants through the quality of supervision and support, and through a program which respects young people's needs and supports them in making and carrying out decisions;

(4) develop partnerships with other organizations to help carry out the program;

(5) encourage access to other Recreation Department programs, such as indoor skating rinks, pools, cultural centers, and libraries; and

(6) facilitate the intervention of social service organizations.

Key Concepts

Youth 2000 depends on a dynamic partnership of municipal government together with the voluntary and private sectors, to manage and carry out the Youth 2000 project in 24 different neighborhoods. Twenty-seven organizations were included such as: neighborhood recreation committees, youth centers, sports and cultural associations, community centers, and youth houses (known as *Maisons de Jeunes* in French, which are youth drop-in centers offering social services and leisure activities). Partners were selected by local implementation committees based on the following criteria:

(1) a willingness to make a formal commitment to respect the objectives of the program,

(2) an ability to ensure access to space exclusively available for the program,

(3) the existence of activities which were available to 13- to 17-year-old youth, and

(4) the capacity to involve additional clientele.

After evaluating needs, opportunities, available expertise and resources, each committee recommended a location for a Youth 2000 project and identified the local organization which would be best suited to sponsor and manage the project. A key example of Youth 2000 was captured in the following observation:

Learning to be autonomous requires that young people take part in the decision-making process, particularly in the areas which concern them directly. It also requires

that young people have a place, or are able to occupy a
space where their behavior is not constantly questioned,
and where they can deal on an equal basis with others.
This is a precondition for them to identify with a neighborhood and to participate in its improvement.

Rather than proposing a schedule of activities based on a conventional program, teenagers are assisted in their efforts to develop
and carry out activities which they have proposed. Youth 2000 is
based on the principle that programming is by and for youth:

BY: implies direct involvement of young people between 13 and 17 years of age in the organization of their
recreation and in the decision-making process; and

FOR: implies encouraging the acquisition of skills
which promote personal development and which lead
participants to become increasingly responsible.

Emphasis is placed on the capacity of young people to take initiative, be creative, and display organizational and managerial abilities. The process is facilitated through the involvement of adult
"animators" who make participants feel welcome and facilitate participant involvement, while also encouraging youth to be in charge of
their own activities. The animator becomes a significant role model,
a resource person, and a source of expertise and counseling.

Operating Procedures

Exclusive Access to Facilities: Each of the 24 Youth 2000 projects
in Montreal occupies exclusive facilities. The projects are situated in
places such as recreation centers, church basements, and park chalets.
   Accessibility: Most activities are offered free of charge, with a
few special projects sponsored on a self-financing basis.
   Schedule: Facilities are accessible and activities are offered at
least five days per week; a minimum of three hours per day; a minimum of 30 hours a week for a minimum of 48 weeks per year.
   Supervision and Support: For participants there is an average
of two animators per project with a ratio of one animator per 15
teenagers. Each of the nine administrative districts of the city has a

youth coordinator whose efforts are further supported by the district management team, and by a resource person in the Department who coordinates planning, development of guidelines, and consultation and evaluation processes.

Since 1990, 15,000 teenagers (67% male; 55% ages 15-17) have participated in the program. Seventy-five percent of projects have a multicultural character, thus reflecting the demographics of their neighborhoods.

Changing Mentalities: The Challenges of Youth 2000

Youth 2000 presents a number of important challenges.

(1) Young people who are users of recreational services resist an approach which requires them to make personal commitments and sacrifices.

It is important to accept young people as they are and then gradually help them learn to fit in, get involved, and take charge of their own activities. Because this process can take a long time, a high degree of competence and the stability of the animator is key to the program's success.

(2) Some parents are concerned about sending their teenagers to a program where the supervision is unconventional.

Unconventional supervision and support enables teenagers to have a variety of experiences and promotes increased levels of self-discovery and personal development. At the same time, the teenagers are also looking for role models whom they feel may be appropriate to follow.

(3) Some adults in the neighborhood feel that the local trouble-makers have taken over.

Although not always successful, in many situations setting up open house activities and developing communication with neighborhood residents has helped to modify the negative perception held about youth programs. Coordination and collaboration with other organizations in the neighborhood has also played an important role in alleviating concerns.

(4) Skepticism from organizations that are introduced to new ways of working in partnership with the city may result.

Innovation is required of the partner organizations. Selection of sponsor organizations, negotiation of contractual agreements, and clear definitions of objectives have helped change the role of the city from "paternalism" to "partnership."

(5) Some partners believe that working with a protocol is too formal an approach.

Evaluation of each project is done by measuring outcomes against goals. Goals are developed in collaboration with the Youth Coordinator of each district, and reflect the realities of each neighborhood while respecting the general guidelines and objectives of the program.

(6) Often civil servants and bureaucrats resist change.

Acceptance of new methods requiring significant modifications to established organizational behavior and procedures has been achieved, but not without some conflict. The program has provoked change in certain fundamental values held by some employees in their work situations. Some placed a negative interpretation on the arrival of so called "youth specialists," and the assumption of responsibilities by partners which had traditionally been the employees' domain.

Although the program is intended to support and improve youth intervention, certain interests saw it as representing a loss of their personal power, since they were no longer the sole frontline experts. They resented their loss of hierarchical control. However, after five years of experience with the program in many local areas, the approach is largely, though not completely, accepted.

(7) Sometimes a municipal structure can cause excessive administrative delays.

In the first phases of the program, the municipal structure demonstrated a clear commitment to change. For example, in the first months of operation, over $250,000 worth of

equipment was acquired through an adapted purchasing procedure. In spite of this, habitual tendencies predominated which
caused delays in the acquisition of equipment, as well as in
hiring animators and activity specialists. Since the expression
of needs by teenagers is often spontaneous, unnecessary delays
lead to a loss of motivation or interest and frustration. To
resolve these problems the partner organizations and the city
developed improved operating procedures.

Conclusions

Many of the participants have become youth "animators" in their
own neighborhoods. In addition, many participants sit on the boards
of directors of their own group or of other community organizations.
Some projects have had an important impact in reducing interracial
gang fights or in decreasing criminal acts committed by youth. In
1992 the city of Montreal received the Willis Award for Excellence
from the Canadian Association of Municipal Administrators in recognition of its "exceptional initiative and creativity in municipal
programming."

Youth 2000 has had a significant impact on a large number of
young Montrealers and on the perception which young people have
of municipal services. Nevertheless, two important challenges remain. The first lies in evaluating the precise impacts of this type of
program. Aside from the participation statistics, and the number of
activities or hours of service, better information needs to be provided
on the positive impact of the program. The second challenge lies in
further involvement of partners (e.g., municipal, community, educational, and institutional) in developing additional intervention strategies for, with, and adapted to youth.

References

Balmer, K. (1991). *Catalogue of the benefits of parks and recre-
    ation.* Ottawa, ON: Canadian Parks and Recreation Association.

Section IV
It's a Matter of Time

Chapter 13
A.P.P.L.E.: At-risk Programs Promoting Leisure Education
in North Miami, Florida

Presenters:
Jean H. Fountain
  Director, *and*
Jim Stamborski
  Superintendent, City of North Miami Parks and Recreation

Background

According to the 1990 Census, few communities in the United States
have changed their demographic profile in the past decade as much
as North Miami. In 1980 less than 13% of the city of North Miami's
population (42,554) was under 15 years of age. By 1990, the population had grown to 50,000, and the 15 and under population was now
20%. In addition, since 1980, the African-American population has
grown 377% primarily as a result of the migration of Caribbean
peoples to Dade County and specifically to the North Miami area.

This rapid increase in the number of youth and the expansion of
diversity has had a major impact on leisure programming. Established recreation programs which were developed when the community was almost entirely white and middle class suddenly became
irrelevant as they failed to meet the needs of newly arrived residents
from other countries. This alienation was felt particularly by teenagers and other at-risk youth, some of whom even under ideal conditions may experience self-doubt and low self-esteem.

Due to population increases, the four central-city neighborhoods
now contain the majority of city residents. Major characteristics of
these neighborhoods are:

• a declining median age which is attributable to death or depar-
  ture of older residents and to the migration of younger residents;

- greater racial and ethnic diversity due to expanding numbers of African-American and Caribbean peoples, and Cuban and Central/South American Hispanics; and
- lower per capita household income due not only to people being employed mainly in low-pay service and labor jobs but also to the fact that there are more people per household.

The idea of community organized recreation programming is alien to most foreign-born youth, especially Haitian children. In Haiti, sports and recreation opportunities are organized by churches, schools, and private clubs. In Haiti there are no park and recreation departments, so many children are not aware that the city of North Miami has a Parks and Recreation Department which offers them recreational and cultural activities. Further, anything associated with a governmental agency, no matter how innocuous, is viewed with suspicion. Children in North Miami are desperate for a place to play and they need someone to teach them not only about sports, but also American culture.

The majority of Parks and Recreational facilities are located in historic population centers that are distant from the growth neighborhoods. Many of these facilities were designed for different users with traditional "American" interests. Shifts in programming are inhibited by the existing design of facilities. Many youth athletic facilities are located far from emerging population centers. In addition, recreation centers that formerly focused on older adults will have to shift their focus to younger children, youth, and families.

Program Description

Rationale

In 1992 a pilot after-school program for teenagers funded by the city council was developed in the central business district. Since then, a number of additional free leisure activity programs for youth ages 8–15 years have been financially supported by the city. The overall program is entitled "At-risk Programs Promoting Leisure Education" or "A.P.P.L.E."

The central area is one of the major business districts of the city as well as the location of a middle and high school. When school recessed in the afternoon, teenage students swarmed into thoroughfares, businesses, and shops to hang out, wait for rides, and visit.

The area does not have a recreation center or an available park site for young people to utilize immediately after school, so businesses, convenience stores, the public library, and street corners were the preferred sites for teenage group gatherings. As a result, businesses were disrupted and many citizens were afraid to go into the area.

A.P.P.L.E was an effort to diffuse the situation. The success of the pilot program was instrumental in the expansion of after-school activity programs at all five elementary schools, and the development of the North Miami Middle School mentor program, the citywide Golden A.P.P.L.E. Reward Program, and the Recreation Police Leader Program.

Objectives

(1) to provide North Miami's youth with positive alternatives to hanging out on city streets, in city businesses, and on vacant school grounds, by offering structured leisure programs that provide positive role models with whom students can relate;

(2) to develop collaborative efforts between the city's public agencies which provide support and leadership to youth; and

(3) to offer leisure programs that will contribute to reducing youth crime and antisocial behavior.

Key Players

The A.P.P.L.E. programs are a joint effort between the city of North Miami City Council, the city's Parks and Recreation and police departments, and the Dade County School District. The funding required to support the A.P.P.L.E. program is shown in Exhibit 13A, page 146.

Program Content

Pilot Middle After-school A.P.P.L.E. Program: Funded by the Parks and Recreation Department, the middle-school pilot program began in 1992 and consisted of intramural sports, guest appearances by sports figures, general games, modeling, art, and other lifetime activities, all of which were free to participants. Program planning was undertaken by representatives from the Parks and Recreation Department, the police department, and middle school administration. The program was led by strong, personable, "professional"

Exhibit 13A

North Miami Budget For A.P.P.L.E. (1993-1994)

A. A.P.P.L.E. Program Coordinator (ten months) $17,538

B. Middle After-school A.P.P.L.E. Program (one site)
    Salaries $10,460
    Supplies   1,026
    Special Events   1,560
                                                          13,046

C. Elementary After-school A.P.P.L.E. Program (five sites)
    Salaries $59,047
    Supplies   6,460
    Uniforms   349
                                                          65,856

D. Mentor Program Awards   1,500

E. Golden A.P.P.L.E. Program (five sites)
    Salaries $2,532
    Buses   6,250
    Supplies   1,500
    Special Events   11,250
                                                          21,532

F. Recreation Police Program
    Salaries (two officers) $58,816
    Equipment and Vehicles   10,418
                                                          69,234

                              Total Cost: $188,706

recreation leaders and police officers. Opportunity for casual conversation and interaction with leaders by the students was built into the program structure. A former Miami Dolphin football player was hired to direct daily activities which added a considerable amount of credibility to the program in the minds of the participants. After one month of activity, the Middle After-school Program was described by all officials involved as a tremendous success and plans were made to expand the program.

Elementary After-school A.P.P.L.E. Program: In 1993 the success of the middle-school program led to the development of elementary-school programs designed to address the problem of vacant school yards and the high number of latchkey children. A free after-school pilot program for fifth and sixth grade students was established at the two largest elementary schools. The program format centered around intraschool athletic competition that encouraged fellowship, social interaction, and cooperation. The programs were organized through meetings held with principals and physical education teachers at the respective schools and the recreation program staff. The program's success was instrumental in securing additional funding in 1994 to expand into the other three city elementary schools and to grades three and four.

North Miami Middle-school Mentor Program: In 1993 the city and the North Miami Middle School established a mentor program. Middle-school students are paired with city employees, who volunteer a few hours each week, to help students develop self-esteem and a knowledge of the working world.

Mentors work with the same student for an entire school year. On two-hour field trips, mentors and students go together to local areas of interest, such as Greenwich Film Studios; the Miami Dolphins training camp; other professional sports facilities; local radio, television and recording studios; and local universities. While the field trips themselves are interesting, the time spent traveling to and from the activity provides a valuable opportunity for mentor and youth to communicate.

The majority of time spent between mentor and youth is one-on-one. The mentors provide a resource for the young people in a nonconfrontational, objective setting. Early meetings between participants usually are filled with questions, but as time goes by confidence and understanding replace fear and uncertainty.

A program such as this will succeed only if top management makes a commitment to allow employees time to participate. Most of the youth come from homes with one parent, or are living with a grandparent or relative. They are good kids, but they are prone to influences from the streets and are in need of guidance and a friendly ear. By helping these children at this critical time in their lives, the employees can make a difference.

Golden A.P.P.L.E. Program: In January 1995 the city launched the Golden A.P.P.L.E. Program in all five elementary schools. The program is designed to provide tangible rewards to students for excellence in behavior and leadership. Students are given the opportunity to participate in free special events such as trips to professional sports games, ice skating, miniature golf, zoo trips, airboat rides, musical productions, and nature trips. Selection criteria for participation in the Golden A.P.P.L.E. Program is based on positive student attitudes demonstrated by being helpful, considerate, and polite in relationships with others. The school administrators in each individual school select six students each week to participate in the weekly field trip. The selection procedure is determined by the individual school. Selection of children whose families do not have the resources to attend local attractions is particularly encouraged. Recreation staff and school teachers chaperon the activities.

Recreation Police Leader Program: In 1994 the City received a police-hiring supplement grant from the U.S. Department of Justice. The money was used to fund additional police officers, two of whom are known as Recreation Police Leaders (RPLs). Officers are assigned to specific sectors of the city with the general mandate to reduce crime and antisocial behavior. The grant application was developed by recreation staff and resulted from meetings between the police, parks and recreation, and planning departments. The application plan stressed interdepartmental cooperation in combating crime and antisocial behavior in the city's parks.

Two police officers, one assigned to the east side of the city and one assigned to the west side, patrol park and school playgrounds in comfortable workout clothing, with a police department staff shirt, badge, and firearm. The officers engage in interactive recreation activities with teenagers such as basketball, softball, shooting pool, or Ping-Pong. They function as planners, organizers, and facilitators drawing in teens to active and passive activities at the recreation sites. The RPLs work closely with recreation staff already in place at the parks to curb antisocial and criminal behavior within the parks and a quarter-mile radius around the parks. RPLs also function as resources for teens who need referrals to social services to deal with abusive parents, teen pregnancy, and health and school problems.

RPLs have helped alleviate the level of physical and verbal abuse directed at recreation employees. The RPLs are used to supplement and assist in enforcing the rules recreation staff are obliged to enforce for the safety of all park patrons. Since recreation staff at the parks are virtually defenseless when a crime occurs, they must call the police. By the time the police arrive, the perpetrators are usually gone, because they realize that it takes time for staff to get to a telephone and have the police respond.

The program allows the RPLs to perform low-profile police work in a relaxed setting, thus enabling officers to relate to teens more as a big brother or friend than as a formal police authority. Recreation personnel and the RPLs assist each other in sharing information and intelligence about teens at-risk and in trouble, or about known or rumored criminal activity occurring in and around park facilities. Information is gathered through informal and formal networks. Conversely, if habitual teen offenders come to a recreation facility, they will be more easily identified. RPLs also visit the parents of teens who are trouble in the facility to discuss behavior management.

The final strategic objective of the RPL program is to supply tangible incentives for positive constructive behaviors exhibited in the parks and the community. Rewards are given for the number of hours a teen helps around the park facility, and intangibles such as a better attitude toward staff, quitting smoking, or not carrying a weapon. Rewards are graduated and include fast-food vouchers, movie passes, Miami Heat tickets, clothes, and basketball shoes.

Marketing

The Parks and Recreation Department distributes seasonal program books by mail to all city residents. Brochures are also available at all park facilities, local businesses, and offices. Individual activity flyers outlining program details are distributed in local schools. The city's public relations firm has successfully promoted celebrity appearances, interagency cooperation, and special events on television, radio, and in print.

A Recreation Needs Assessment Study identified that communication barriers are an inhibitor to the program's success. While the city uses traditional methods of program publicity, the community's cultural diversity means that established methods of communication are not effective in communicating with all citizens. In some cases the new populations have language difficulties. In other cases, the study's respondents indicated a distrust and dislike of "government" propaganda. Therefore, successful promotion of the city's A.P.P.L.E. programs has relied heavily on personal contact by the recreation staff, school officials, and satisfied youngsters who have discovered the benefits of positive leisure activity and tell their peers about it.

Measurement of Program Outcomes

For the middle-school program, 20–75 students participate daily and 200–300 students over the academic year are exposed to a variety of recreational experiences such as free swimming lessons, bowling, trips to the University of Miami basketball games, intercity flag football games, and free Karate lessons. The program has dramatically reduced the number of police problems around the middle school and the number of police calls to nearby businesses. In the adjacent city park, gang activity, vandalism, and fights between students have been similarly substantially reduced. By providing positive role models, there are constant reminders and reinforcement of the value of staying off drugs, away from gangs, and developing confidence and self-esteem.

Since school budget cuts have eliminated physical education programs and after-school athletic programs, the Elementary After-school A.P.P.L.E. Program supplies latchkey students with a place to go after school. Three hundred students have a supervised playground staffed by teachers whom they know and respect, greatly reducing gang and vandalism problems on the school sites immediately after school. One principal summarized the positive outcomes of the program by explaining that she had several students who completely reversed poor academic and behavioral problems. The principal attributed the reversal to positive reinforcement generated by the athletic programs conducted by her staff who have been hired as recreation department employees.

The North Miami Mentor Program has resulted in a number of the students making personal and academic adjustments that could be measured in demonstrated achievements such as: improved decision-making and conflict-resolution skills, increased career awareness, self-esteem, and goal-setting skills.

Chapter 14
Youth After-hours Program
in Longview and Kelso, Washington

Presenters:
Gloria Morehouse
    Director of Membership, Pacific Peaks Girl Scout Council, *and*
Kristin Renzema
    Teen Coordinator, Longview Parks and Recreation

Background

In the fall of 1992 a Longview police officer noted that nearly 18% of Longview's distress police calls came from the Highlands neighborhood that surrounds St. Helen's Elementary School. The highest number of calls came between 3 and 6 p.m. What was most alarming was that youth were often involved, either as the victims or the perpetrators. The officer questioned why these youth were not engaged in structured afternoon activities, and she contacted the Kelso Superintendent of Schools to see what might be done. This area of the city comprises less than 5% of the city, but it contains one-fifth of the under-18 population.

From this initial contact—and the subsequent efforts of community leaders, school administrators, law enforcement officials, and youth organizations—sprang the Youth After-hours Program. Project staff determined that two factors kept low-income youth from participating in activities offered by more traditional programs: the cost of materials, and the availability of adult volunteers. Many parents, for example, could not afford to buy scout uniforms. Youth also needed consistent positive activities and interaction with adult role models.

The Youth After-hours Program is an after-school program offered at two elementary schools in Longview and Kelso, Washington. Both schools are located in high-crime, high-risk neighborhoods. Many families and children are experiencing financial distress, substance abuse, violence and other abuse (i.e., physical, emotional and sexual). Approximately 40–45% of the parents in these two neighborhoods have not completed high school. Eighty-five percent of the kids are on the free lunch program.

The challenges facing Wallace Elementary School in Kelso and St. Helen's Elementary School in Longview caused both schools to elect to operate on a modified academic calendar. This approach involves shortening the summer break to six weeks and creating additional breaks throughout the year. The principals at both schools feel that their school should be the hub of the neighborhood and that community collaboration can be a catalyst for changing students' lives. This philosophy undergirds the Youth After-hours Program (see Exhibit 14A).

Exhibit 14A

Children who feel attached to their school and neighbor-hood tend to be more likely to go to classes and to suc-ceed there. If not, they'll find something else to be attached to, such as a gang or peers that may be a nega-tive influence.

—Ramona Leber, Cowlitz Substance Abuse Coalition Coordinator

Program

Beginning in the fall of 1992 a coalition of community leaders, school administrators, law enforcement, and youth development organizations began to work together to identify the needs of this highly at-risk population. The group concluded that the best way to meet the needs of these children was to provide free, positive after-school activities. The youth organizations agreed to work together to provide a program every day after school until 5:30 p.m. The Cowlitz Substance Abuse Coalition acted as lead agency for the project. Each participating organization that offered programs was able to keep its identity. The agreement signed by the participating organizations is shown in Exhibit 14B.

Each agency provided life-skill, hands-on activities two to three times per week, and the parks and recreation departments provided activities every day. This system allows agencies to provide activities in which they specialize while avoiding reinventing programs and services that community departments are already offering. Most

Exhibit 14B

Youth After-Hours Program—
Interagency Memorandum of Understanding

It is understood by the undersigned agency that they will
participate in the cooperative Youth After-hours Program,
coordinated by the Cowlitz Substance Abuse Coalition, offered at Wallace Elementary School in Kelso, and/or St.
Helen's Elementary School in Longview, State of Washington,
under the conditions listed below. This program is designed to
offer youth development program opportunities to children in
a daily after-school setting at the school building.

It is recognized that each agency independently enters
into this program opportunity and that its own agency rules,
regulations and policies dictate its program delivery and
assure the safety of children that will participate. It is recognized that each agency will participate with promotion of
cooperative communication among and between participating
agencies. Each agency commits a representative to serve on
the Steering Committee which will meet regularly to manage
and evaluate the program.

Conditions of Participation:
As a participating agency in the Youth After-hours Program
our agency will:

- provide program activities as agreed upon by the Steering
  Committee;
- provide adequate supervision as defined by agency;
- provide health and safety procedures as necessary by
  agency;
- complete facility agreement as required by the Longview
  and Kelso School Districts and assure opening, closing
  and care of room as outlined in the districts' rules and by
  their direction;
- provide necessary insurance documentation (Certificate of
  Insurance) as required for facility usage;
- provide program supplies as necessary to carry out agency
  program unless separate arrangements have been made to
  use school equipment;

Exhibit 14B (continued)

- participate as appropriate in the coordinating meetings of the Steering Committee to be scheduled as necessary;
- understand that the program being delivered is to support and enhance the role of the school districts in meeting the needs of children and respect the regulations regarding their participation in the federally funded feeding program;
- understand that the role of the Cowlitz Substance Abuse Coalition is that of facilitating communication between agencies participating and assisting with obtaining and managing program funds;
- submit appropriate requests or reports for expenditure of program funds, within established budget guidelines and properly documented, on a monthly basis to the Coordinator of the Cowlitz Substance Abuse Coalition for approval and submission to the fiscal agent;
- agree that United Way of Cowlitz County is authorized to act as fiscal agent for the Youth After-hours Program; and
- provide at least 90 days notice of intent to terminate participation in the program.

Any participating agency/program failing to comply with the aforementioned conditions may be subject to review and/or sanctions from the Steering Committee.

_____   _____
Agency Name   Authorized Signature—Position

_____   _____
Date   Authorized Signature—Position

of the youth organizations involved use adult volunteers to work with youth. However, it is difficult to find volunteers who would commit to an ongoing program for the entire school year. Thus, it was decided to have paid staff members conduct the activities. This ensured consistent, positive role models and helped establish trust.

To fund this program for the 1993-94 program year for two schools approximately $66,000 was needed. The Cowlitz Substance Abuse Coalition wrote grant applications to business, industry, and service groups. In response, Weyerhaeuser Company Foundation became the major funding source (with a three-year commitment), along with assistance from the Ben B. Cheney Foundation. The three-year commitment from Weyerhaeuser was critical to the program's success because it provided funding for a time period sufficient for the program to demonstrate its viability. Several local service clubs also contributed from $500 to $10,000 each.

Although only 35% of the budget had been committed at the beginning of the school year, the youth organizations began the program in August 1993. A parent or guardian had to complete a registration form. Children could attend as frequently as they wished (e.g., every day, once a week, twice a month). At the start of each day, every child had to sign in and wear a name tag. Registration and the name tag procedure helped resolve issues such as who was authorized to pick up the child at the end of the day. In addition, children could not leave the program early if the registration form indicated that a parent would not be at home. The program is currently using picture ID tags to help identify children and to separate children who are participating in the program from those who are just involved in free play on the school grounds.

After signing in, children receive a snack and choose which activities to participate in for the day. On a typical afternoon children participate in two different activities with two different agencies. Hands-on activities that have been offered include: clowning, rocketry, photography, drama, music, dance, creative arts, cooking, math, science, recycling, environmental education, sports, cooperative games, wood science, and cultural awareness. Every other Friday, participants go swimming at the YMCA.

The program tries to maintain a 1:15 staff-to-child ratio. For the program to have continuity, each school has a site coordinator (a community college work-study student) who prepares the school site, briefs staff, deals with student behavior issues, supervises staff, and serves as a liaison to the parents and the school principal. The site coordinators are critical to the success of the program. For example, if a child has a discipline problem, the program leader can call in the coordinator to help deal with it, rather than disrupt the flow of the program. Site coordinators also decide what goes into the monthly parent newsletter, and they undertake special projects, like holiday parties or family nights.

In 1994-95 the program averaged 110 participants per day with over 250 students registered. Because management of the program is so time-consuming for the coordinator of the Cowlitz Substance Abuse Coalition and the chair of the Steering Committee, the budget included funds to hire a program coordinator. In addition, the 1994-95 budget of $111,179 includes two site coordinators, increased staffing costs, YMCA reimbursement, and funds to evaluate the program—all costs that were not included in the budget for the previous year. Partial funding has been provided again by the Weyerhaeuser Company Foundation. Additional funding will be sought from United Way, Longview Community College Work-Study program, local service clubs, Ben B. Cheney Foundation, and other foundations.

Program Objectives

Local risk assessment studies utilizing data collected through public meetings, key informant interviews, and surveys indicate that most children in the two target neighborhoods (Wallace and St. Helen's) are affected by one or more risk factors in everyday life. While the Youth After-hours Program affects some risk factors, it is primarily designed to enhance certain protective factors to counterbalance the risks these children face daily.

The program is designed to build resiliency in children by providing them:

(1) secure and stable relationships with caring peers and adults;
(2) safe and attractive places to relax and be with their friends;
(3) opportunities to develop life skills; and
(4) achievement, recognition, a sense of belonging, a sense of purpose, goal setting, and self-esteem.

The program is seen as more than fun and games; the goal is to teach the participants such skills as how to communicate, make decisions, and solve problems.

Cooperating Agencies

The youth serving agencies providing activities at Youth After-hours include: Camp Fire Boys and Girls, Pacific Peaks Girl Scouts Council,

Boy Scouts of America, Longview Parks and Recreation Department, Kelso Parks and Recreation Department, W.S.U. Cooperative Extension/4-H, and the YMCA of Southwest Washington. Each of these agencies sends a representative to monthly steering committee meetings. The program is managed by the coordinator of the Cowlitz Substance Abuse Coalition and the chair of the Steering Committee. Also involved in the Steering Committee are Longview and Kelso School districts. The United Way of Cowlitz County serves as fiscal manager of the program. One official noted, "These organizations never had a reason to get together before. Fortunately, they left the turf issues behind."

Program Evaluation/Outcome Indicators

- In 1993-94, the program had 350 participants registered at Wallace and 231 participants registered at St. Helen's. This represents approximately two-thirds of the two schools' population.
- Over 18,000 child days of service were provided.

An evaluation was completed in June 1994 using written surveys of staff (19), parents (14), and focus group interviews of participants (73) with the following results.

School staff stated:

- the Youth After-hours Program (per the principal at St. Helen's) is a contributing factor to a decrease in the number of office referrals;
- the program has a positive influence on school day attendance because children want to go to Youth After-hours, but they must attend school in order to do so;
- students seem happier at school;
- children who earlier did not want to go home at the end of the day, now have something to which to look forward;
- students are excited to go to the after-school program, so it is a great motivator for getting work done during school time, because they don't want to miss after-school activities; and
- the program keeps kids off the streets, out of abusive homes, and puts them in a safe environment.

Parents commented:

- they have a difficult time convincing their children to come home after school, because they enjoy the program so much;
- they use participation in the program as an incentive in behavior management;
- 58% of parents surveyed rated quality and choice of activities as "super;"
- 42% of parents surveyed stated they had seen an improvement in the behavior of their child as a result of the program; and
- 82% felt that recognition of their children's accomplishments was important and well-done.

Participants commented:

- 58% of students rated the overall program as "great" or "very good" (See Exhibit 14C).

Exhibit 14C

Third grader David says he likes the program and comes every day. "It sure beats staying home alone watching TV, which was boring and sometimes made me mad. Since the program started, I'm not mad!"

The program offers staff the opportunity to counsel individuals (some as young as third grade) into participating in the program rather than becoming involved in gangs. A few have left the program to join gangs and then returned after direct contact with a site coordinator.

In 1994 the program received several awards including the Governor's FACE IT award for prevention, and the Community Leadership Award from the Washington Association of School Administrators. According to Larry Wilgus, Director of Student Services with Kelso School District, and the person who nominated the program for the award:

The program is truly a harbinger for communitywide cooperation in the future as we all strive to meet the needs of increasingly needy students.

Chapter 15
Multiple Strategies for Reaching
At-Risk Youth
Used by the Madison, Wisconsin, School-Community
Recreation Department

Presenter:
Robert P. Humke
  Director, Madison, Wisconsin, School-Community Recreation
  Department

Background

Under provision of enabling legislation created by the state of Wisconsin in 1911, community recreation services have been provided by the Madison School District since 1926. Public park lands, facilities, and services are provided by the city of Madison through a municipal parks division.

In November 1982 the Madison School-Community Recreation Department (MSCR) published its *Action Plan for the 1980s: Perspectives on Programs, Projections for Progress* which included the following mission statement:

(1) to provide year-round recreation opportunities which are accessible to all residents of the Madison Metropolitan School District, responding to expressed interests and making maximum use of all available resources in the school district;

(2) to educate community citizens, with emphasis on children and youth of school age, on the value of learning and practicing lifetime leisure skills and appreciations; and

(3) to serve as a community resource and catalyst for recreation services: providing referral information, organizational expertise and planning with other agencies, organizations and citizen groups in order to more fully meet the recreational needs of all community residents.

Goals and objectives were developed to help achieve this mission. Two update reports were published in 1985 and 1988, and included information on goal and objective achievement.

In the early 1990s it became clear that the city (population approximately 200,000) and school district were becoming more urban in character. The school district had 25% minority enrollment, with 58% of African Americans, 55% of Asians, and 43% of Hispanics classified as low-income. Of 57 census tracts in the city, seven had between 23% and 30% below the poverty level, and another seven had between 11% and 18% below the poverty level.

MSCR staff and department advisory committee members held planning retreats to identify what came to be known as the *MSCR 2000 Mission Focus*. This statement indicates that MSCR will:

(1) *focus* its resources on improving services to school-age youth, families, low-income, minority, and disabled residents, while maintaining quality adult programs;

(2) *expand* outreach and service as a recreation resource and catalyst to individuals, groups, and organizations; and

(3) *maintain* a tradition of excellence that meets community needs and expectations.

With the support of the advisory committee and board of education, program, service, and budget priorities were reordered to reflect the emphasis of the 2000 Mission Focus. Some administrative staff reorganization was necessary. Programs and services aimed primarily at reaching at-risk youth have been dramatically expanded since 1990. Key strategies for increasing success in serving target neighborhoods and constituencies were identified and successfully implemented through the programs, services, and operational procedures employed by the department.

Identification of Program Strategies

The following strategies were identified to help achieve the overall goals outlined in the 2000 Mission Focus.

School-based Programs: MSCR staff have good access to schools and students. Emphasis is primarily on programming in the 29 elementary and ten middle schools, with less emphasis on the four public high schools. Support of school principals is the key to success; they assist with access to "minority achievement funds" and various participation incentives.

Neighborhood-Based Programs: Neighborhoods with high concentrations of low-income youth are targeted. Parks, schools, and neighborhood and community centers are utilized for a wide variety of programs. Efforts are under way to create more "ownership" of programs by neighborhood associations and other citizen groups.

Culturally Responsive Activities: Programs are adapted in response to interests expressed by young people. After-school clubs, sports, music, and other cultural arts reflect the background of the clientele, as well as provide opportunities for them to learn about lifelong activities outside of their everyday experiences.

Accessible Services: Accessibility is enhanced by the school board's "no hassle" fee waiver policy, transportation to programs and to special program events, and the provision of one-to-one participation assistance for youth with special needs who may have emotional, physical, or mental disabilities.

Employment and Training of Neighborhood Residents: MSCR has made a practice of hiring and training residents of low-income neighborhoods to work in local programs. In some cases they constitute 75% of the staff. This provides good part-time employment opportunities and helps program participants immediately identify with program leaders.

Outreach Services: Besides targeted mailings and "directed word-of-mouth" communication, MSCR employs two regular part-time outreach workers who identify needy families through school social workers and other sources with follow-up phone calls or visits. These outreach workers encourage registration and ongoing participation through the use of fee waivers, provision of transportation, and other creative aids. The Outreach Subcommittee of the department's 15-member citizen advisory committee reviews and enhances MSCR's outreach efforts to target populations.

Collaboration and Partnerships: All MSCR programs for at-risk youth involve a high degree of interagency collaboration and/or partnerships with other governmental, civic, not-for-profit, businesses, and corporations. The department places a high priority on establishing and maintaining professional and interpersonal relationships with other community leaders who strive to improve services for at-risk youth.

New Funding Sources: MSCR's 1982 Action Plan officially endorsed an increased level of community fundraising, but not until 1990 did these efforts dramatically increase, especially in support of programs that fit the MSCR 2000 Mission Focus. In fiscal 1993-94, over $175,000 was raised from individuals, corporations and businesses, foundations, civic organizations, and other governmental entities. For the 1994-95 fiscal year, the goal was $750,000. There has also been increased federal grant support for at-risk youth programs.

Key Programs Employing the Strategies

After-school Recreation: Efforts are being made to expand the number of elementary schools providing clubs, sports, arts, and special events, with emphasis on schools with high numbers of at-risk youth. All ten middle schools have recreation counselors who employ school staff to lead clubs and intramural sports. Principals typically provide late buses to get kids back home. Elementary-school program attendance is 50 to 150 a day; most middle schoolers sign up for one or more activities during the year.

AmeriCorps: A U.S. Justice Department grant (AmeriCorps) to the city of Madison focuses on at-risk youth and provides 30 low-income adults from three target neighborhoods full-time work in schools and recreation programs.

Art Cart: MSCR's mobile summer free arts program is operated collaboratively with the Madison Art Center and stops for one or two days in low-income neighborhoods. It also visits summer day-care groups serving younger at-risk kids. Approximately 2,500 youth are served through its programs.

Basketball Clinics: Saturday morning basketball clinics are offered during the winter. Over 300 youth are bused to one of the two program locations.

CASPER: An after-school program is offered for homeless children who reside at the Salvation Army shelter. School and MSCR staff jointly plan and run the program which serves 30–80 young people a day.

Kids Day Out: On several teacher in-service/conference days each year MSCR, in collaboration with other agencies, provides sports, arts, and environmental education. Professional performers also entertain the youth. From 100 to 300 youth participate at each site, and some programs are underwritten by corporate sponsors.

Midnight Basketball: About 70 at-risk young men, 90% African American, participate in a summer league which incorporates a mandatory group counseling program. Role model coaches, including representatives of the police and fire departments and local corporations, provide leadership (see Exhibits 15A and 15B, pages 166-168).

Playgrounds (Supervised): A citywide summer playground program at 25 to 30 locations is provided. From 20 to 75 children per day are actively involved in sports and games, crafts, and many special events. In 1995 a "Super Center" program was initiated which provided all-day supervision, sports and swim instruction.

Safe Haven: Federal "Weed and Seed" funds provide extensive after-school and summer programs at three elementary schools serving at-risk students. Some of the funds are also used to subcontract with other agencies having centers in high-risk neighborhoods. Daily participation ranges from 40 to over 100 neighborhood youth.

Saturday Recreation: Morning drop-in programs at schools in high-risk neighborhoods serve 20–50 young people each session at each site during the coldest winter months. Asian Hmong children participate extensively at one location.

Sports Camps: Three summer programs each serve 40–60 youth in high-risk neighborhoods. Emphasis is on sports skill instruction, but the attendees also participate in special events and field trips.

Swim Instruction: MSCR's "Grow Our Own" minority aquatics staff development program employs low-income neighborhood adults who register kids for Saturday instruction and then bring them (20–30 per session) by bus to an indoor high-school pool. In the summer, free and reduced-rate group instruction is scheduled for kids from neighborhood centers and MSCR's programs serving at-risk youth.

Youth Connection: Dane County Youth Connection, Inc. is a nonprofit teen program affiliated with MSCR, headquartered at MSCR's Downtown Arts and Activities Center. Youth Connection serves hundreds of high school age youth per month, including many low-income, minority, and "punk" youth utilizing countywide multicultural teen council, addiction support groups, weekend dances, cable TV discussion shows and other activities.

Exhibit 15A

Madison Midnight Basketball Program

Purpose
The purpose of the Madison Midnight Basketball Program is to reach young, at-risk minority males, provide them with role models, and connect them to existing community services. The objectives are twofold: (1) to provide league-format basketball activities on Friday and Saturday nights, especially in the summer, when the target group of young men are most at-risk of drug and alcohol involvement which may lead to involvement in criminal activities; and (2) to successfully link these young men to educational, vocational, and treatment programs which may increase their self-sufficiency and well-being. Through playing basketball, players are encouraged to learn to work together to develop and implement strategies, analyze situations, look out for others, increase leadership ability, discover personal strengths, and gain positive attention from their families and friends. Off-duty police officers are employed as security for each game night.

Recruitment Criteria
League activity begins in May when an open player recruitment process is initiated by the team coaches. To be accepted the player must be between the ages of 19 and 29, live within the targeted neighborhoods (i.e., Allied, Bayview, Broadway-Simpson, Darbo-Worthington, Kennedy Heights, Northport, South Madison, Vera Court, Wexford Ridge), and have played less than two years of organized posthigh school basketball.

Coaches and Team Development
The teams are developed primarily by street-smart African-American coaches who lead the young men into the summer workshops to meet counselors and role models from community agencies. The coach's role is pivotal: he develops the strengths of the players, builds team cooperation, and through this role, is granted authority to enforce the league rules and pull the players into line if they lose their focus. Additional requirements for all players are: (1) no antisocial activities, and (2) no contact with the criminal justice system.

Exhibit 15A (Continued)

Summer Workshops
Each program participant is required to attend formal workshops focusing on stress management, dealing with alcohol and drug abuse issues, education and employment. The 40-minute sessions are intensive, confrontational, and instructional.

Paul R. Soglin, the Mayor of Madison, stated:

> We are constantly striving to improve living conditions in our vulnerable neighborhoods, both for individuals and the community at-large. Midnight Basketball targets a population of young men who are substantially at-risk for substance abuse, criminal involvement, and unemployment, and who are often neglected in our services planning. The program's commitment to provide workshops on education and employment as well as substance abuse, combined with recreational basketball, offers an effective way to challenge and assist these young men to move forward in a positive way. We are particularly pleased that the program has generated support from the business community and service clubs.

Richard K. Williams, Madison Chief of Police, commented:

> The Madison Police Department supports and endorses Midnight Basketball as a successful and needed program in our city. Midnight Basketball offers positive programs for young men from our community during hours which they could easily become involved in less productive activities. Through these programs young men learn values which help them become productive citizens and role models in the community.

Exhibit 15B

One year ago, Ronald was unemployed and unsure of his next move in life. After moving to Madison in 1990, Ronald enrolled in the University of Wisconsin, but then decided he didn't want to attend school there. Last week, Ronald started his second semester at Madison Area Technical College (MATC) and is studying to become an industrial engineer.

The reason for his turnabout? Ronald was one of 71 young men who played in Madison's first midnight basketball league last summer. "I'm trying to move forward and do a lot of positive things," said Ronald, 20, a Chicago native who lives on Madison's near West Side.

Besides Ronald, at least three other league participants are attending MATC part time and another three have started earning their General Educational Development (GED) diplomas elsewhere. Ronald and Vince, 21, are both enrolled in MATC's General Studies program and playing on MATC's basketball team, the Trojans.

According to the program leaders and a former MATC basketball coach, "Nearly all of the league participants praised the workshops and some have even heeded the advice. It exceeded our expectations."

Measurement of Outcomes

While MSCR has yet to implement a department-wide program evaluation system, there are many indicators, along with concrete data, that indicate strategy and program success. These include:

- dramatic increases in participation by at-risk youth;
- positive feedback from participants, parents, community leaders (including school board members), and agency representatives;
- dramatic increases in employment of minority and high-risk neighborhood residents;
- increased skills by program participants, e.g., aquatics, sports, social, artistic; and
- increases in number and frequency of other agencies (e.g., governmental, social service) which seek collaborative arrangements with MSCR.

The program staff have cooperated with a University of Wisconsin-Madison research team in the development of several studies of the after-school program. One of the studies indicated that third graders in formal on-site after-school programs when compared to others not in such settings:

- earned better grades and conduct ratings;
- got along better with peers;
- spent more time on studies and enrichment activities;
- shared more activities with adults and peers; and
- spent less time watching television and playing outdoors with peers without supervision.

Other studies are planned for the future.

Chapter 16
The Sunnyvale Teen Express Program (STEP)
in Sunnyvale, California

Presenters:
John Christian
  Director
Kelvin Fountano
  Recreation Program Coordinator; *and*
John Lawrence
  Recreation Supervisor, Recreation and Parks Department,
  Sunnyvale, California

Background

Effective programming for youth and teens has been identified in
Sunnyvale, California, (population 120,000) as a high priority for the
Parks and Recreation Department in the 1990s. The radical shifts in
family structure in recent years (related in many cases to divorce,
remarriage, and economic recession) are elements of social change
which have significantly affected children and teens. For example,
the 1990 census estimates that 19% of the households with children
in Sunnyvale are headed by a single parent, and of those, 80% are
single mothers. Even for those households with two parents, many
of which may represent blended families, 66% have both parents
working outside the home. It is also significant that 6% of
Sunnyvale's children overall, and 16% of the children of single
mothers, live below the official poverty level.

Program Description

In the fall of 1993, the Sunnyvale city council took action on two
policy documents which provide a framework for the provision of
services for middle-school and high-school youth in the city. These
documents provided the conceptual guidelines for the Sunnyvale
Teen Express Program (STEP) and the Columbia Neighborhood

Service Center which is currently under construction. The four objectives for the overall program are to:

(1) Provide coordinated services to those youth already identified. A group of 50 high-risk youth and their families will be targeted, including preteenagers and teenagers who have been involved with the criminal justice system, school truancy, gang activity, and/or substance abuse, as well as youth from abusive or deprived home environments.

(2) Increase middle-school performance by coordinating educational, health, and social services to students and community members. The goals are to (a) increase student performance by 5% on standardized achievement tests; (b) reduce absences by 20%; (c) reduce disciplinary referrals by 10%; and (d) increase parent contacts by 10%.

(3) Provide rehabilitation, predelinquency, neighborhood education, leisure services, youth employment, and neighborhood volunteer services. This would reduce the FBI crime rate by 5% and help maintain an annual juvenile offender recidivism rate of 4% or less.

(4) Promote leadership and training opportunities through youth involvement in the advisory and program planning process of youth and teen services.

STEP and Columbia Neighborhood Service Center

To bring STEP and Columbia Neighborhood Service Center to fruition required a collaborative effort between the Sunnyvale city council, the office of the city manager and several city departments; Sunnyvale area youth, teens, and their parents; community residents; Sunnyvale school district; social service organizations; local court and probating agencies; Stanford University; Advanced Micro Devices; and AGFA Film Corporation.

Program Planning

Sunnyvale Parks and Recreation Department has a long history of providing recreation services, staff support, facility support, and funding to the Sunnyvale school district. However, most of these youth and teen services focused on noontime and special event programming. Research, surveys, community input, and staff recommendations clearly outlined a need for after-school programs. In 1992 STEP was introduced, offering Sunnyvale area youth and teens fun and exciting activities in sports, leisure services, recreation, community services, job training, employment placement, volunteer opportunities, and teen alternative programs. STEP now offers over 75 after-school and summer programs on a year-round basis. The after-school programs are scheduled from 3:30 to 5:30 p.m. each day at two middle-school sites. Field trips are scheduled to coincide with teachers' in-service training days. The elements which comprise STEP are shown in Exhibit 16A.

The Columbia Neighborhood Center concept was developed in response to two different situations. The first was the financial inability of a local school district to provide a middle-school gymnasium. The second was the desire of the city to provide a neighborhood

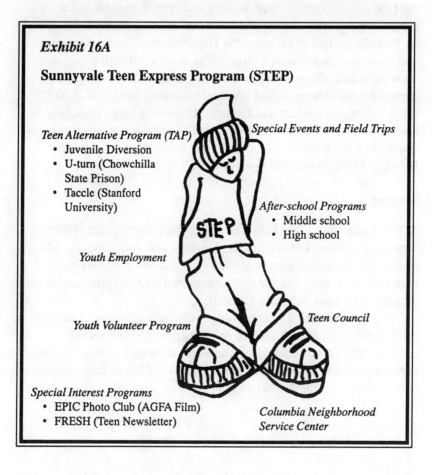

Exhibit 16A

Sunnyvale Teen Express Program (STEP)

Teen Alternative Program (TAP)
• Juvenile Diversion
• U-turn (Chowchilla State Prison)
• Taccle (Stanford University)

Special Events and Field Trips

Youth Employment

After-school Programs
• Middle school
• High school

STEP

Youth Volunteer Program

Teen Council

Special Interest Programs
• EPIC Photo Club (AGFA Film)
• FRESH (Teen Newsletter)

Columbia Neighborhood Service Center

center which would meet the long-term goals of improving the performance of students at Columbia Middle School while reducing the crime rate in the neighborhood. Accomplishment of these goals is through the coordinated delivery of a broad array of community services including educational, health, social, recreation, and public safety services. These services meet the needs of middle-school youth in the nonschool hours as well as providing services to support and enhance youths' educational performance and meeting their social service needs. In addition, services are offered to provide the balance of the neighborhood residents with social, recreational, and educational opportunities.

Some of the services currently being offered at existing school facilities include: classrooms, libraries, computer centers, multipurpose rooms, and swimming pools. Construction of Columbia's Neighborhood Center will provide a health center including two medical exam rooms, private waiting and reception area, and a records storage area; three soundproof counseling rooms to be shared by juvenile probation services, the Department of Social Services, and education counselors; a large lobby area; a job listing and interview area; and office space for the site manager, case manager, and recreation and school district physical education staff; and locker rooms. The gymnasium will feature a basketball court, bleachers to hold approximately 1,000 people, space for two crosscourt basketball courts, and three volleyball courts or six badminton courts. The Neighborhood Center will open in late 1996.

Staffing

STEP is supervised by a full-time recreation program coordinator who reports directly to the Sports, Aquatics and Teen Division Manager. Four recreation specialists and five recreation leaders work part time or on-call. Staff are also supported with program and coordination by a Teen Advisory Council.

The Neighborhood Center will largely be operated with existing staff: either city, school district, or repositioned social service agency staff. Overseeing of the center requires two additional positions: a site director and clerical staff person. Cost of the overhead will be shared by the district and the city.

Marketing

Most STEP after-school and field trip programs are fee-based with fee waiver and scholarship programs available for those who qualify. Nonfee programs such as noontime activities, late night basketball, and a special teen project through Stanford University are available year-round. Local newspaper agencies, Sunnyvale's cable channel, school newspapers, and daily school bulletin announcements are effective marketing strategies. The STEP Program also publishes a free monthly teen newsletter (FRESH) which is mailed directly to the homes. FRESH has a mailing list of over 700 middle-school and high-school teens. Registration tables and a display area are located on-site at each school; flyers and posters are displayed throughout each campus; registration brochures are printed for each eight-week session; and staff are assigned to each school to continually distribute flyers and promote activities.

The Neighborhood Center has received considerable press coverage. A series of neighborhood meetings and school presentations were scheduled over a three-month period. Ongoing marketing efforts will continue through the completion of the Columbia project and beyond.

Financing and Resource Acquisition

The STEP Program budget was $26,704 in fiscal year 1994-95. The cost for constructing the Columbia Service Center is approximately $3.3 million of which Advanced Micro Devices will cover $1 million. The annual operating cost is projected to be $287,000 ($95,000 for facility maintenance and $192,000 in staffing costs). These costs will be shared by the city and Sunnyvale school district. Anticipated revenues from leisure services in the service center are $34,000.

Measurement of Program Outcomes

Identifying the need and importance of an after-school and weekend youth and teen program was based on months of program evaluations, surveys, data research, and staff and community input. Collaborative agencies all agree that this planning was crucial for success. Long-term performance measures such as improved achievement on standardized tests and reduced crime rates are currently being monitored. Immediate impact was apparent through higher job placement rates, higher teen program registrations, less vandalism on school sites during in-service days and vacations, participant retention, and parental involvement. Additionally, through the field trip program, many participants visited area amusements sites and state landmarks for the first time. Many students who were unable to participate on school varsity teams because of academic or economic restrictions were able to play in city sponsored leagues. The completion of the Neighborhood Center will allow these and future programs to expand.

Chapter 17
The Good Life Mentoring Project
in Metropolitan Dade County, Florida

Presenter:
Jack Kardys
>Executive Assistant to the Director, Metropolitan Dade County
>Park and Recreation Department

Background

In January 1993 Metropolitan Dade County Park and Recreation
Department was joined by the Greater Miami Chamber of Com-
merce, the City of Miami, Dade County Public Schools, and Florida
International University in endorsing implementation of the Good
Life Mentoring Program. Doctors Laura Blitzer and Robert Wolff of
Florida International University designed and wrote a *Program
Manual* (1993) for the program. The following information is taken
in whole or in part from the manual.

The initial Good Life Mentoring Program concept grew from a
conversation between internationally renowned tennis players Arthur
Ashe and Butch Buchholz about their own favorable experiences
with sports and the people who had positively impacted their lives.
Both Ashe and Buchholz were concerned that many school-age children in Dade County were not receiving exposure to the opportunities they had experienced in their youth.

Estimations suggested that 3,000–5,000 youth ages 11–24 were
involved with one of over 80 active gangs identified in the area. Of
these youth, 75% came from single-parent households, 91% had
prior arrest records, and 80% were high-school dropouts. An alarm-
ingly high number of these youth (94%) reported they were bored
with nowhere to go and nothing to do. They filled their time by
turning to drugs and gangs. Given the costs to society of incarceration and healthcare, prevention programs were seen as a sound investment. Prevention as opposed to punishment makes more sense
when you factor in the following cost figures. The state of Florida
spends $40,000 per year to maintain just one youth at a correctional
facility, but it costs less than $7,000 yearly to provide that same

youth with intensive community-based programs. According to the Florida Prevention Association, for every $1 spent on preventive measures, such as preschool education and recreational services, more than $15 is saved in future healthcare and criminal justice costs.

Ashe and Buchholz believed that the energies of urban at-risk youth could be redirected with a comprehensive sports program, heavily endowed with aspiring mentors who would serve as successful role models. Butch Buchholz took this idea to the Deputy Director of Metro-Dade Park and Recreation and to the Executive Vice President of Sun Bank who is also Chairman of the Sports Council of the Greater Miami Chamber of Commerce. They worked collaboratively and involved others to further refine and develop the original idea.

From its inception, the Good Life Mentoring Program has emphasized collaboration. Its Board of Directors represents many of the affected, potentially affected, and concerned organizations of Dade County. The program's major participants include:

- Greater Miami Chamber of Commerce
- Dade County Public Schools
- Metro-Dade Park and Recreation Department
- City of Miami Park and Recreation Department
- Miami Police Department
- Florida International University
- YMCA of Greater Miami
- Greater Miami Services Corps
- Professional Sports Organizations:
  - Miami Dolphins
  - Doral-Ryder Open Golf Tournament
  - Lipton Tennis Tournament
  - Miami Heat
  - Florida Marlins
  - Toyota Grand Prix

Each of these organizations has contributed expertise, personnel, and/or resources to help address the needs of at-risk youth through the Good Life program.

Program Description

The Role of Schools

The program's major goal is to identify a pool of high school athletes and other students interested in volunteering as mentors who are willing to serve as positive role models and tutors for pre-high-school at-risk youth. The program targets youth from elementary and middle schools which serve as feeder schools for the high schools which supply the mentors.

Prehigh-school youth are involved in educational and recreational extracurricular activities that will help them develop new school-related interests while reversing the trends that propel them toward behaviors of social irresponsibility and poor school habits. The high-school athletes and other students who volunteer to instruct, supervise, and coach their pre-high-school counterparts develop leadership skills. Both groups are involved in year-round sports and academic programs at park and recreation facilities located near each school. The ultimate goal is to involve 400 volunteer students at each of the high schools and a total of 2,000 students from the elementary feeder schools.

The Role of the Park and Recreation Department

The park and recreation staff's primary responsibility is to assist in the development, facilitation, and operation of sports programs for the pre-high-school youth. Good Life Mentoring sport cycles have been developed for the parks system and include flag football, volleyball, soccer, basketball, swimming, tennis, track and field, baseball and softball, bowling, badminton, wrestling, water polo, diving, and golf. Recognition awards are utilized to reward participation, improvement, and success both during and at the end of each sport cycle. The park and recreation department and public schools are in the process of developing arts programs through their drama and art departments.

Program Objectives

The goals of the Good Life program are:

(1) to provide opportunities for individual and group development (mentoring skills);
(2) to demonstrate a willingness to accept and respect individual differences and the need to address them through accepted program goals (tolerance for diversity);
(3) to acknowledge the beliefs, goals and assumptions of all who participate in the program and integrate those beliefs in accepted program goals (empowerment);
(4) to demonstrate a long-term commitment to the program through a willingness to revisit and possibly change existing program goals, thereby making the program self-renewing (commitment);
(5) to maintain strong communication links with all participating organizations and stakeholders (interdependence);
(6) to establish geographic service regions using selected high schools as hubs of operation;
(7) to contact, establish, monitor, and maintain centers of operation at six selected high schools with plans to engage other schools as time and resources permit;
(8) to utilize the services of professionals associated with public schools, park and recreation departments, and other agencies and a local university to maintain these centers of operation;
(9) to establish a volunteer mentoring program involving professional athletes, university, and high-school students (including athletes and artists) to work with pre-high-school youth;
(10) to establish a business, school, and community partnership that will encourage the participation of corporations and their employees, school faculty and staff and other community organizations and their personnel in the Good Life project; and
(11) to develop a system of evaluation that will assess program goals and objectives, centralized goals and objectives, outcomes measures for all participants, long-term effects of treatments, and an analysis of costs and benefits.

Early Accomplishments

Dade County Public Schools have helped organize centralized committees at the six high schools included in the program. Programs have been implemented at three schools. These committees have involved administrators from the high schools and feeder schools, teachers and coaches, park and recreation personnel, parents, students and student athletes, business and community representatives, extracurricular club members, guidance personnel, and police officers. In-service training was conducted for counselors in each of the pilot schools to assist in development of the student mentoring program. Workshops for coaches, the development of mentoring techniques, and Summer Peer Counseling courses have been planned. Sports, self-esteem classes and academic tutoring programs have been developed to promote and supplement the sports-park program.

The Greater Miami Chamber of Commerce has developed a network of private, public, and not-for-profit agencies which provide volunteers to train, coach, mentor, umpire, and prepare both youth participants and mentors to accomplish program goals. The Chamber also participates in fundraising activities to support the program.

The program is currently operating at three school sites, with approximately 150 youth participating at each site daily. A total of 12 leaders have been hired; four work at each site. A budget of $350,000 funds the program. The Good Life Mentoring Program runs year-round, after school from September through May, and all day during the summer months.

Principals in the local schools coordinate monthly meetings between the police, community-based organizations, Optimist Clubs, YMCA, the Boys Clubs, and area businesses to provide services in a local area with the school serving as the hub. In some cases, this responsibility is delegated to the school athletic director.

Preliminary Evaluation Results

Interviews with program administrators and participants indicate that the aims, goals, and objectives of the Good Life program are valued and appreciated by the surrounding communities. Several sites have taken the Good Life message of "youth helping youth" and personalized it in such a way that the program is now a "fixture" in the community. The program is most successful in those schools where there is a strong commitment by the school administration. Support from feeder schools, and surrounding park and recreation staff, is also critical for success. Some sites reported difficulties with transportation, personnel, and financial issues. Leader hiring and retention is difficult, due to the salary level of $18,000 and an inadequate benefits package. The issue is being addressed by hiring qualified youth mentors and helping them view this type of work as a viable career option.

The Good Life program is still in its infancy and is growing slowly. Although support from community agencies is significant, there is no particular plan in place at this time that addresses how best to allocate available resources. The development of such a plan is essential as contacts and support increase.

Those who have participated in the Good Life program feel positive about their involvement. This is particularly evident among the high-school mentors and the feeder school students. The mentors expressed some surprise at how well they have been received by the mentored youth. They feel they have gained the respect and admiration of the younger youth and are proud to report that they are "looked up to." The self-esteem issues that are being addressed on both sides of the mentoring relationship are significant.

References

Blitzer, L. E. & Wolff, R. M. (1993). *The Good Life Mentoring Project Program manual: A guide for developing, implementing, and evaluating a localized Good Life program with the assistance of established community agencies.* Department of Health, Physical Education and Recreation, Florida International University, Miami, Florida.

Chapter 18
The Recreation Plus Program
in Houston, Texas

Presenter:
Petty Hunter
  Assistant Director, City of Houston Parks and Recreation Division

Background

With a population of 1,631,766, Houston is the largest city in Texas. Twenty-eight percent of the city is African American, 28% Hispanic, 25% Caucasian, and 19% other races. Youth crime is a major problem. Much to society's disappointment, many crimes are being committed by very young boys and girls, either as individuals or as members of a gang. The crimes range from skipping school to selling and buying drugs to murder. Youth in the community have been as concerned about these issues as have adult residents. For example, the Recreation Plus Program, Houston's current effort to provide a response to these conditions, started when Houston children told Mayor Bob Lanier in November 1993 that they wanted the Department of Parks and Recreation to do something about crimes that were being committed against youth by youth. The youth did not have the answers, but they said, "Mayor, it's your responsibility." As a result, the Recreation Plus Program was proposed to provide enhanced programming at 31 selected Community Centers throughout the city.

Program Description

The goal of the Recreation Plus Program is to offer children free, supervised, entertaining, and educational activities in an effort to focus their time in a positive and productive manner. Although it is aimed primarily at youth 12–18 years of age, the program will also help youth 6–11 and young adults 19–26. The program provides for an average of 36 additional hours per week at each of the 31 recreation centers.

Objectives

(1) Provide a greater opportunity for teen interaction and enrichment, allowing for positive influence and support from role model members of the community in a recreation and leisure setting.
(2) Address the idle time of youth at-risk.
(3) Promote prevention and provide idle youth with needed alternatives to the negative impacts of crime, drug-use, and gang activity.
(4) Involve all the potential stakeholders in each community in shaping the respective community's strategy. Key contributors such as schools, residents, law enforcement, religious institutions, businesses, community agencies, government, and residents' organizations are included in the planning.

Program Structure

In December 1993 the program was launched at nine sites—one in each of the council districts. Advisory councils were established consisting of a cross-section of the community including citizens, educators, religious leaders, and youth, who came together to analyze each community's needs and to identify some immediate solutions that could be implemented. In January 1994, Recreation Plus was extended to another ten sites, and in February, the total was increased to 31. Security, program quality, equipment, and operating hours were common issues that needed to be addressed at each site.

Participants are given a laminated registration card, which is presented each time they enter the building. Attendance rosters are filed and monitored by site. A master report is formulated and presented each month to track performance.

Youth programs developed at each of these facilities are community-based in nature and include tutorials; self-esteem building; teen enrichment; cultural enrichment including drama, art and music experiences; and youth sports. The community-based programs were formulated with input from each neighborhood. By extending hours at the recreation centers, the parks and recreation department is able to provide enhanced programs for youth for various age groups to enjoy. The new hours also allow greater involvement by parents which encourages role modeling and support.

To initiate the program, 75 university students majoring in education and physical education were hired as program staff. A summit of youth service providers was held. As a result, over a thousand agencies have come forward to provide assistance. This has led to the creation of some 60 partnerships.

An additional 12,000 participants are being reached annually through the Recreation Plus Program. The involvement of citizens and partners such as the Police Activities League (PAL), the Boys Club, the YMCA and YWCA, Girl and Boy Scouts, churches, schools and corporate sponsors and two additional staff persons at each site have all enhanced the program. In addition, parents are recruited to chaperon, coach, speak to groups, and assist in other capacities.

Activity Areas

The department provides:

(a) Educational programs including speakers and visual aids that encourage youth to feel good about themselves and to build self-esteem.

(b) Meaningful and rewarding activities through community service projects that enhance the lives of youth and citizens in the community.

(c) After-school study time and one-on-one tutorial assistance to youth having problems with school work.

(d) Programs, activities, and other events to keep at-risk youth involved after regular school hours and on weekends. Typically, these youth lack the talent to become members of a school sports program, and are not likely to volunteer for any activities. Equipment, supplies, and uniforms are given to each participant to help develop a sense of belonging, order, and structure.

(e) Coaches who are either recreation personnel or volunteers have been certified by the National Youth Sports Coaches Association (NYSCA). Coaches are responsible for providing a roster and arranging practice schedules for each team; formulating rules for all participants to follow; and ensuring that all youth learn the fundamentals of each sport. Recreation staff are responsible for officiating games as needed.

(f) Contract security at each Recreation Plus Program facility. A uniformed security guard is on duty through the late evenings until closing time.

Chapter 19
Project Phoenix
in Raleigh, North Carolina

Presenter:
Carol P. Langley
    CLP, Education Development Supervisor, Raleigh Parks and
    Recreation Department

Background

Raleigh, with a 1994 population of almost 240,000, is the state capital of North Carolina. From 1980 to 1990, Raleigh's population grew faster than any other major North Carolina city. Its annual average increase of over 4% during this period was three times the state average. Raleigh's population is 71% Caucasian, 27% African American, and 2% other races. The average unemployment rate is only 4%, with an average per capita income of $16,896 and median family income of $42,212.

In 1994 *Money* magazine voted Raleigh as the "best place to live in America." *Fortune* magazine has also voted Raleigh as one of the "best cities for business in America." Another recent survey called Raleigh one of the safest places to live in the United States.

However, there is another side to Raleigh, as there is to most cities. The accolades do not consider:

- a mother in Chavis Heights, one of several public housing areas, who was afraid for her children to play outside because of stray bullets;
- the little, fourth grader who carries a beeper on his hip so he can be like his big brother who makes good money selling drugs;
- the 15-year-old trying to decide if it is worth the hassle of staying in school because she is pregnant; or
- the well-to-do mother of a son shot to death at a local high school.

While these issues impact citizens throughout Raleigh, special concern was voiced by residents and community leaders from several of Raleigh's public housing neighborhoods. In June 1989 they met with the Mayor, some members of the city council, city administrators, and the executive director of the Raleigh Housing Authority to discuss the developing drug problem in certain areas of the city.

In July the city manager spearheaded development of a comprehensive strategy for the fight against drugs, taking into consideration ideas and suggestions made by concerned residents. The city worked with several other public and private agencies to develop a comprehensive strategy to fight drug sales and use in Raleigh's neighborhoods. This comprehensive plan was named Project Phoenix.

The major programmatic elements focused on law enforcement, federal housing penalties for drug use, street lighting of public areas, neighborhood clean up, counseling services for employment and substance abuse problems, family and youth recreation, and education and tutoring.

Program Description

The Raleigh Parks and Recreation Department was asked to play a major, proactive role in Project Phoenix by offering lifelong education and leisure opportunities to at-risk youth and families. Utilizing available facilities and expertise, the department developed a curriculum of extended after-school and summer programs.

Participating Agencies

Project Phoenix was implemented through the combined efforts and resources of several public and private action groups. Effective mobilization of the Raleigh community at-large, as exhibited by a shared approach to leadership, was crucial for a comprehensive attack on the sale of drugs and on the conditions which are conducive to drug use. The public and private organizations involved in Project Phoenix were:

- North Carolina Drug Cabinet
- Drug Action of Wake County
- Citizens and neighborhood groups
- Various private businesses
- Raleigh Police Department
- Raleigh Parks and Recreation Department

- Raleigh Housing Authority
- Raleigh Human Resources Department
- Raleigh Public Works Department
- Raleigh Transportation Department

Goals and Objectives

Project Phoenix was designed to stop the sale and use of drugs in problem areas throughout the city. The objective of Raleigh's Parks and Recreation Department in this effort was to provide youth with resources, accurate information, and training in subjects such as communication, positive peer pressure, and self-esteem building. The mission for the department's role in Project Phoenix follows:

> When we work with children, we have the potential to create changes that are not only recreational, but empowering, challenging, and educational to the individual and his or her future quality of life. We are building enduring relationships with each child and providing the experience to realize there are important, interesting, exciting opportunities going on beyond what is familiar and comfortable. This important challenge is not only an opportunity, but our obligation to all generations.

Program Content

In September 1989 family-oriented recreation programs began to be offered at facilities within the targeted communities and as part of field trips away from the communities. Activities included a family fun day, musical performances, skits, magic shows, improvisational theater, and storytelling. Family trips were planned for such places as the North Carolina State Fair, Pullen Park, Lake Wheeler, and the North Carolina Zoo. These activities provided a structured environment for the use of leisure time.

Special programs were planned specifically for the youth population to provide attractive alternatives to those who might otherwise get involved with alcohol and drugs. As the lead agency for the youth program, the department planned a range of activities, trips, and classes that would appeal to youth ages 8–18. Programs included the following:

- Field trips to area college athletic events.
- A summer basketball league to improve skills in working together as a team.
- Activities and/or athletic events offered on a scheduled basis such as flag football. Tournaments for volleyball, badminton, soccer, and Ping Pong. Also, pool tournaments, video game and card game tournaments were held.
- Movie nights twice a month at each of the targeted areas.
- Arts and cultural enrichment classes on topics such as porcelain jewelry, Christmas ceramics, and dance movement. Other offerings included jazz camp, video camp, and choral camp.
- Teen dances held at each of the targeted areas.

The goal of Project Phoenix was to provide targeted youth with appropriate programs for positive growth. However, the staff quickly discovered that these types of programs were needed throughout Raleigh since all youth were at-risk.

> Raleigh Parks and Recreation has accepted the challenge
> of the growing numbers of high-risk youth, latchkey
> kids, children from single-parent homes, and indeed all
> of our youth. Through the education component, we are
> seizing the opportunity to be a positive force in their
> lives in an attempt to help all our city's youth.

In the summer of 1990 the education component expanded and was provided free of charge at 31 sites for eight weeks throughout the city in various parks and schools. The program was called "SPARC in the PARK"—Summer Program with Academics and Recreation for Children. The program took a leisure education approach:

> Leisure education is a process through which students
> can learn and practice life skills such as: decision making, planning, problem solving, accessing transportation,
> using community center resources, and developing activity initiation and assertiveness skills. The goal is to
> become more independent in community life during
> leisure hours.

Each site served approximately 75–125 children. Traditional recreation activities such as arts, crafts, and sports were offered alongside programs in reading, math, civics, health, nature, history, fitness, violence prevention, life skills, and science. Activities enabled the children to have fun, but did not follow the traditional park and recreation "fun-and-games" approach.

Some of the staff were teachers who ensured the appropriateness and quality of the programs. However, preference for many positions was given to college students, because they bring a high level of enthusiasm to the program and interact well with children. The program began with a reading program Radical RAP (Reading At Parks) and evolved over the years to involve a myriad of activities including:

Radical RAP (Reading at the Park) is a noncompetitive motivational reading program for elementary-aged children. The program focuses on getting children excited about reading by building their confidence and helping them explore quality literature in a new way. Radical RAP integrates storytelling, role playing, arts, and singing into the fundamentals of reading. An education specialist, or "Radical Rapper," visits each site once a week for an hour and 45 minutes.

Math Magic is a learning program geared towards making math fun and challenging. This program attempts to create success in math by building each child's confidence. An education specialist, or "Math Magician," visits each site once a week. Children are presented with math as it would appear in everyday situations in the hope that the transfer of knowledge from their school books to everyday life will become clearer. An administrator commented, "At first I thought, 'Math on the playground?' But, it worked! It really did, and the children have great fun with it."

P.E.A.C.E. (Politics, Equality, Action, and Citizenship for Everyone) is an awareness program designed to teach children to be responsible citizens. Careers, ecology, multiculturalism, and the responsibilities of being a citizen are emphasized. The program uses literature, songs, and craft projects to explore citizenship—not only what it means to be a citizen, but also the rights and responsibilities that go along with citizenship.

Violence Prevention gives children an opportunity to discuss the growing problem of violence facing their schools and communities today. The program is designed to provide children with strategies to cope with problems they may encounter rather than resorting to violence. The lessons cover topics such as conflict management, mediation, decision making, and gun safety.

Mr. Fitness, the exercise specialist, spends an hour at each site a total of three times per week. His program focuses not only on getting the children to enjoy physical exercise, but also carries helpful, thought-provoking themes as well. Mr. Fitness emphasizes the impact drugs and alcohol have on the children's athletic abilities, and that to excel in sports it is important to say no to drugs and alcohol.

Tiny Tunes is a self-esteem program which uses music to encourage healthy self-concepts in preschool children. Tiny Tunes utilizes songs, music, dance, and verbal expressions to build confidence in children.

Why Be a Dragon Breath? is a smoking prevention program designed to teach children why they should not smoke or chew tobacco. The program explains the consequences of using tobacco and teaches children how to say no to the pressures of smoking.

Because Project Phoenix is communitywide, a growing network of community agencies (i.e., local, county, state, and federal) are being utilized to complement the programs offered by parks and recreation. The department provides facilities and participants; the complementing agencies provide expertise for programs. Examples of programs brought in by other agencies are:

Phonefriend (a presentation by Hopeline, Inc.) is a communication-based program which teaches children positive conflict management. The program shows children how to communicate their feelings effectively and how to resolve conflicts with friends, family, and teachers. Using interactive group games and role playing, Phone-friend also helps children to understand how to communicate effectively as part of a group.

Use It Again, Sam is an awareness program which teaches children the importance of recycling. Presented by the Wake

County Solid Waste Management Division, the program also teaches children about the three R's of waste disposal: reduce, reuse, and recycle. The program also offers children smart tips on how to select the products which are best for the environment.

Stop! Drop! Roll! is a fire education program designed to teach children what to do in the event of a fire. A puppet show format is used to present information on fire hazards, fire safety precautions, and personal safety.

DARE is a substance abuse prevention program which teaches children about the dangers of drug use. DARE officers from the Raleigh Police Department conduct the program, which extends the DARE programs that are presented in the Wake County Schools.

Southlight is a substance abuse prevention agency which offers programs that are designed to teach children about chemical substances abuse and prevention. In addition to providing children information about substance abuse, Southlight offers life-skills training which empowers children to say no to drugs and alcohol.

Motivational Reading, cosponsored with the Wake County Public Library, is designed to encourage children to read for pleasure. The program uses bookmarks, posters, library cards, and certificates as incentives to encourage children to read. These supplies are provided to participating playgrounds free of charge.

Staffing and Budget

Training and exposure to the program's purpose, goals, and opportunities are considered a "must." Two days of training for summer staff are given prior to the start-up date. Weekly staff meetings with specialists provide additional training. Staff can also check out videos, books, and syllabi. The curriculum is upgraded each summer. Approximately $1,000 is spent each year on curriculum development.

For summer 1994 the cost of the program was $34,020 for 14 leaders hired for nine weeks (eight-week program, plus one week of program preparation time) at $5.50 per hour. Mileage, supplies, and curriculum development expenses accounted for the remainder of the costs.

Program Outcomes

To complement the positive, favorable, yet subjective responses obtained from participants and citizens, the department sought a more objective evaluation to provide evidence to justify the program and insure its continuance and expansion. The Drug Education Center in Charlotte, North Carolina, provided a valuable resource for undertaking the evaluation. Dr. Sehwan Kim suggested the use of the Self-Concept Attitudinal (SCAT) Inventory to provide information about the program's impact in a practical and economical manner. The inventory is designed to measure attitudes of participants in seven areas: basic values, listening, MathMagic, reading, school, self-esteem, and substance abuse.

For 1991 and 1992 comparisons were made between "traditional" recreation sites not receiving the education program emphasis and those that did. At the beginning of the 1991 summer playground season, the SCAT Inventory was administered to two different recreational activity sites serving children ages 6–12. The test was administered a second time to the same groups at the end of each summer program. Group I participants received eight weeks of the structured educational component. Group II received less structured educational opportunities. The results of the posttest showed a significant improvement in every category for Group I, which consistently outscored those in Group II. The results were interpreted to mean that educational activities, when incorporated into summer programs, can make a positive difference in children's attitudes and better prepare them for school in the fall.

By 1993 and 1994 all summer programs were utilizing the educational component so no comparison sites were available. Only comparisons between educational component sites were possible. In general, children's scores improved over the summer.

Chapter 20
The Summer Search and
PRYDE Programs
in Oklahoma City, Oklahoma

Presenter:
Wendel Whisenhunt
    Assistant Director, Oklahoma City Parks and Recreation
    Department

Background

Since 1989 the Oklahoma City, Oklahoma, Parks and Recreation
Department has developed two summer programs in response to
critical youth issues. The first issue centered on the need to find
meaningful activities for children between the ages of 6 and 12 who
are too old to be in day care, but not old enough to be left at home as
latchkey children while parents and/or older siblings are at work.
This is a crucial age where choices and influences have lifelong
consequences. Some of these children are from homes which do not
provide a nurturing, positive environment.

    The second issue concerned at-risk youth between the ages of 8
and 13 who are particularly vulnerable and are most likely to engage
in illegal and destructive activities during the summer months. Allowing them to hang out at park and recreation facilities with no
planned or structured alternatives is not the answer. The majority of
these youth live in areas of the community where they are exposed to
daily influences of drugs, poverty, violence, and gangs. They face
strong peer pressure to join a gang where they are likely to become
increasingly resistant to authority and defy traditional rules and
values.

    In response to these two related youth issues, the Oklahoma City
Parks and Recreation Department developed the Summer Search,
and Parks and Recreation Youth Development and Enhancement
(PRYDE) programs. Oklahoma City has a population of 441,719 (in

1990), with 75% of the population Caucasian, 16% African American, 5% Hispanic, and 4.2% Native American. The median age is 32 years, with 18.2% of the population aged 5–17.

Summer Search Program

Objectives

The objectives of the program were:

(1) to provide supervised, structured, and meaningful interactive programs for youth during the summer months to avoid "leisure boredom" and produce long-term benefits;

(2) to foster, develop, and encourage the spirit of community involvement in a positive and constructive manner; and

(3) to promote self-development, self-esteem, and peer mediation as deterrents to delinquency and other social problems.

Program Planning

The Summer Search program was initiated in the summer of 1989 to serve children 6–12 years old by stimulating their interest in the fine arts and other activities, community involvement, and self-development. The challenge was to combine learning and fun in a package that this age group would find interesting and challenging. The proposed program syllabus included dance, music, art, and games.

The program had to provide an environment where parents felt their children were safe from the potential dangers of being left home alone, or from boredom and stagnation in a day care center which did not meet their interests or needs. Participants in the program may be signed in and out only by their parents or legal guardian.

Staffing

Twelve teens serve as instructors for dance, music, art, games, and other activities. The instructors serve as positive role models for the youth participants while learning how to promote peer mediation and community involvement. Recreation center staff and temporary summer staff provide direction, supervision, and guidance for the teen instructors, and have overall responsibility for the Summer Search program.

Marketing

Summer Search was promoted by posting information at the recreation center. The parks and recreation department's marketing coordinator highlights Summer Search in the spring *Activities Guide* which is published annually in December. The guide is distributed in all recreational facilities, schools, and city offices. Word-of-mouth success stories by the participants have also been effective in creating demand for the program. Summer Search is so popular that telephone calls for placements begin in January, and all openings are filled by mid-March.

Financing and Resource Acquisition

Participants are charged $15 per week to cover the expense of hiring additional staff and materials. Summer Search is self-supporting with 1994 expenditures of $7,020 and revenues of $9,600.

Measurement of Program Outcomes

Summer Search has been offered for six summers, and the level of interest increases every year. Initially 20 youth participated in the half-day sessions. In 1994 a full-day program for 65 youth was provided. The success of this program is not only verified by its growth, but also by the number of participants and teen instructors who return each year. Positive feedback from participants, parents, and the commitment of the teen staff validates the success of the program.

Program Description for PRYDE

The goal was to develop a program which would enable at-risk youth ages 8–13 to participate in organized training and educational activities at the recreation facility in their local neighborhood. The program needed to stimulate pride and interest in restoring and protecting their community, and to discourage youth from participating in activities that destroyed their neighborhood, and, often, themselves.

Objectives

Objectives of the program were:

(1) to provide a forum for promoting and developing positive
    leadership skills and a strong work ethic among at-risk youth
    during the summer through a structured volunteer program;
(2) to encourage youth to identify with and embrace a positive
    group as an alternative to joining a neighborhood gang to
    fulfill their need to belong; and
(3) to generate a sense of ownership and pride in their neighbor-
    hood and community center by the youth, and to encourage
    their parents and guardians to become partners in this feeling
    of community and volunteerism.

Key Players

Department personnel provided the impetus for developing and
implementing PRYDE at the community centers. The City-Wide
Neighborhood Initiative coordinated funding through a Federal
grant. An orientation and training session was conducted at the
beginning of the summer by park and recreation staff, the State Office of Volunteerism and other agencies who have strong youth and
adult volunteer programs. The Oklahoma City Parks Foundation
contributed to the program by purchasing 200 PRYDE logo T-shirts
for the participants.

Program Planning

Recreation administrative staff actively searched for a vehicle to
convey and develop a sense of community and volunteerism for
youth in the targeted age group. Many ideas and formats were generated, analyzed, explored, and discussed before a decision was
reached to proceed with the Parks and Recreation Youth Development and Enhancement program with the acronym PRYDE defining
the mission of the project.

   Program ideas were solicited from youth who attended activities
at the center to determine their interest in volunteering and participating in life-skills classes. The resulting strategy identified specific
job duties for the volunteers, guidelines for their behavior, goals of

the program, anticipated outcomes, ideas for training classes, evaluation processes, and recognition mechanisms for outstanding participants. In June 1992 one recreation center was selected as the trial site for PRYDE. Based on responses from participants and parents/ guardians, plans were made to expand PRYDE and offer it at 12 sites in the summer of 1993 and 14 locations in 1994.

Staffing

Staff at 14 different recreational facilities are responsible for supervising and directing the PRYDE program. Support is provided from administrative staff in the recreation division. A number of outside resources and agencies are utilized to provide some of the life skills and career opportunities training: Oklahoma City Metropolitan Library System, Eagle Ridge Mental Health, Oklahoma City-Oklahoma County Health Department, and Oklahoma City Police Department.

Marketing

Marketing for the PRYDE program is quite simple because of the program's success. The program is promoted through success stories on television, radio, and in the newspapers. Participants in the program wear T-shirts to identify them as members of the group which also generates interest from prospective participants. Field trips during the summer and other forms of recognition for the high-achieving participants serve as effective recruitment and marketing tools. A half-page promotional ad is included in the parks and recreation department's *Spring Activities Guide*.

Financing and Resource Acquisition

Participants in the program are not assessed a fee. The department uses $4,000 from a Federal grant that is coordinated through the City-Wide Neighborhood Initiative program. The funding covers the costs of incentives, T-shirts, pins, awards, supplies, and other items. Several individual facilities solicit donations to supplement grant funding. An end-of-summer celebration is funded by donations from outside businesses and agencies. In future years, plans are to expand this effort and solicit a community donor to sponsor the PRYDE program.

Measurement of Program Outcome

Center staff personnel believe PRYDE is one of the best programs offered to at-risk youth in the community, because they have witnessed how it builds life skills, teamwork, self-confidence, and increased involvement in the community and neighborhood. PRYDE youth display a keener sense of ownership and pride in their neighborhood and community centers than other young people at the recreational facilities who do not participate in the program. More parents and guardians have also begun to take pride in their neighborhood and to call in January to enroll their children for the summer program. In 1993 and 1994 more than 700 at-risk youth between the ages of 8 and 13 participated, and over 250 youth and adults attended the end-of-summer recognition event. Increasing numbers of parents and guardians and youth are requesting that the PRYDE program be continued throughout the school year.

Chapter 21
Summer Fun
in Wichita, Kansas

Presenter:
Bob Johnston
    Program Development Coordinator, Wichita, Department of
    Park and Recreation

Background

Wichita, Kansas, is a city of approximately 289,000 residents with a
median wage of $17,214 and a minority population of over 18%. In
1991, neighbors living in an area bordering McAdams Park Recreation Center (50% below the poverty level; 31% of residents below
age 17) began a campaign to reduce violence and crime committed
by gangs and young teens in areas surrounding the park. This campaign led to other surrounding neighborhoods becoming interested,
and it encouraged the formulation of the Northeast Task Force with
representatives from neighborhood associations, church groups,
nonprofit organizations, and interested community residents. Representatives approached the director of park and recreation for assistance and the department agreed to develop a plan of action to reduce
crime and violence using recreation staff, innovative programming,
collaborative efforts, and existing resources. The vision was to develop an expanded recreation program which would provide youth
ages 6–15 a positive recreation and educational experience, while at
the same time offering parents a safe and secure environment for
their children.

Program Description

Program objectives are to:

(1) provide Northeast area youth with positive alternatives to
    gangs, drugs, and violence;
(2) develop collaborative efforts between public and private agen-
    cies to facilitate financial support and volunteer staffing; and

(3) establish a program that is affordable and accessible to all who desire to participate.

Partners

Collaborative efforts were established with several organizations including Project Freedom, a coalition made up of over 700 public agencies, nonprofit organizations, and commercial businesses interested in finding solutions to drug and alcohol and violence problems in the community; Unified School District 259; Summer Youth Academy; McAdams Park and Recreation staff; McAdams Park Swimming Pool staff; Northeast Task Force; neighborhood volunteers; and the Wichita Department of Park and Recreation administrative staff.

Program Planning

A pilot program (Summer Fun) was developed and implemented in 1992. This program consisted of recreation opportunities that were not available at other recreation centers operated by the Department of Parks and Recreation. The Summer Fun program provided recreational and educational opportunities from 9 a.m. to 4 p.m. Monday through Friday with transportation provided to and from the recreation center from area school locations. Bus schedules were set up so participants had the option of either transportation to the center, breakfast, the morning program, and transportation back to its pickup site; or transportation to the center, lunch, afternoon program, and return to pickup site. The summer schedule is shown in Exhibit 21A. In addition to regular center programming, open swimming was provided at the neighborhood pool.

An annual Summer Youth Academy for 12- to 15-year-olds was housed in a school directly across from McAdams Park. This was a program for elite students because demand for the program exceeded the number of youth who could be served. The students engaged in academic work in the mornings; however, in the afternoon some were selected to assist as tutors, mentors and junior supervisors with the Summer Fun program.

The Summer Fun program was a success based on daily attendance totals. Satisfaction with the program was expressed at community and city council meetings. Perhaps the most outstanding

---

Exhibit 21A

Example of Summer Program Schedule

Aley/Stanley Summer Fun Program
June 13–August 5, 1994

Morning Schedule:

8:00 - 9:00 a.m.	Bus route to Aley/Stanley
8:00 - 9:00 a.m.	Breakfast Program
9:00 - 9:10 a.m.	General Assembly/divide into activity groups
9:10 - 10:00 a.m.	Swim Lessons
10:00 -11:00 a.m.	Swim Lessons
11:00 -12 noon	Swim Lessons
9:10 - 12 noon	Choose any scheduled activity (e.g., Ceramics, Archery, Craft-A-Week, Stained Glass)

Afternoon Schedule:

12 noon - 1:00 p.m.	Bus route to and from Aley/Stanley
12 noon - 1:00 p.m.	Lunch Program
1:00 - 1:10 p.m.	General Assembly/divide into activity groups
1:10 - 4:00 p.m.	Choose any scheduled activity (e.g., Video Movie; Archery; Nintendo; Basketball/ Soccer; Swimming)
4:00 - 5:00 p.m.	Bus route from Aley/Stanley to Franklin, Payne, McCormick, Harry Street and Woodman. Program Ends.

---

illustration of its success was the council's decision to provide an additional $100,000 to make this a totally free program.

The second year, 1993, the program was made available to other low-income areas where residents expressed concern that the same programming options were not available in their neighborhoods. In response, the department developed recreation and educational programming at three additional sites: Aley/Stanley Community Center (8% below poverty level), Colvin Community Center (43%), and Evergreen Recreation Center (16%). Program sites were selected because of the large Hispanic population in the Evergreen area and the large Asian population at Colvin. McAdams was targeted because of the African-American population, and Aley/Stanley was selected because of the number of low-income individuals in the immediate area of the community center. All program sites were in areas which had problems with neighborhood crime and gang violence and experienced the same problems that had led to the development of the original McAdams Park community program.

In 1994 the Council again allocated $100,000 for the program. The budget for the Colvin Community Center is shown in Exhibit 21B. This is typical of the budgets at the other three parks.

Exhibit 21B

Budget for Colvin Community Center

1994 Summer Fun Program Proposed Costs:
Part-Time Wages

12 Recreation Leaders	$17,400
3 Swim Leaders (Lessons)	1,800
1 Swim Leader (Open Swim)	200
Employee Benefits (.1175)	2,256
Bus Transportation	5,000
Video Rental	50
Commodities (Games and Equipment)	1,100
Assorted Craft Supplies	1,500
	$29,306

Daily attendance was monitored at each Summer Fun site. Aley/Stanley averaged 180; Colvin 300; Evergreen 175; and McAdams 375 per day throughout the eight-week program. Breakfasts and lunches, funded by the USDA summer lunch and breakfast program, were available to participants.

Program Outcomes

The Summer Fun program has been successful at each of the sites. The residents are pleased to have activities in the parks in their neighborhoods. Wichita Police Department reported that progress was made in providing positive alternatives to gangs, drugs, and violence. Their crime analysis summaries showed a reduction in arrests for youth ages 6–15 in three of the four areas where Summer Fun programming was provided. During the June 13 to August 15 time period, Aley/Stanley had 11 arrests in 1993 compared to 4 in 1994. Evergreen had 8 arrests in 1993 and 4 in 1994. McAdams, which has been influenced by this program since 1991, showed 3 arrests in 1993 and none in 1994. On the other hand, in Colvin, 7 arrests were made in 1993 and 12 in 1994. Thus, greater efforts need to be made in this area. Expansion of the program is planned in future years.

Many collaborative partnerships supporting the program have been established. Local churches have requested parks and recreation department assistance in providing activities for their youth groups. Several of these programs have been initiated as a direct result of the success of the Summer Fun program.

Chapter 22
Kids' Kamp
in Indianapolis, Indiana

Presenter:
Reginald Jones, Jr.
  Youth-At-Risk Supervisor, Indianapolis Parks and Recreation

Background

In 1993 Indy Parks and Recreation recognized a need to provide summer day camps for inner-city youth. The goal of the camps was to develop an affordable recreational opportunity for youth (ages 4–12), to provide structured programming, and services at a lower cost per day than was currently being charged. Four- to six-year-old youth and six- to 12-year-old youth were served separately to facilitate offering age appropriate activities.

Program Description

For summer 1994, Kids' Kamp was offered in 11 different communities, and efforts were made to improve the camp program through building partnerships and creating special events. The program's objectives were to:

(1) Provide quality programming to serve the specific needs of individual communities.

(2) Increase the number of volunteers who are more actively involved in camp programming.

(3) Improve the marketing strategy.

   This was accomplished through development of a brochure which was distributed at schools, neighborhood family centers, and door-to-door in selected areas. Door-to-door marketing was deemed essential to overcome people's tendency not to read mail-delivered brochures. After consulting with local neighborhood associations and area churches about which areas to target, staff went door-to-door, talked to people about the camp, informed people about the pricing structure and available scholarships, and solicited volunteers. The usual target areas were the six blocks in all directions from a local Kids' Kamp site. In addition, a special television spot was also developed along with a Kids' Kamp coupon for parents who could not afford the basic cost of the camp and needed to have their children attend at a discount.

(4) Keep the price of the camps affordable for inner city youth.

In 1993 the Kids' Kamp fee was $1 per day with a ratio of 1 staff member to 20 campers. In 1994, the fee was raised to $2 per day and the staff member-to-camper ratio was lowered to 1:12. Through the development of a work-relation program around the family centers, youth were able to earn money to pay for camp. Twenty-five percent of the campers were subsidized.

(5) Add additional structure and value to the camps.

Theme weeks, sporting tournaments, and arts and crafts were added. Sporting events included softball tournaments, flag football and track and field meets. Examples of theme weeks are:

- Week 1—Hip Hop Hooray
- Week 2—Let's Get Busy
- Week 3—Around the World in Five Days
- Week 4—Stars and Stripes
- Week 5—Express Yourself
- Week 6—Summer Olympic Fest
- Week 7—Love Our Earth
- Week 8—Championship Week

(6) Provide leadership training for staff.

Summer seasonal and full-time staff took part in a four-day camp training orientation. Training emphasized:

(a) recreational site rules and policies dealing with unsuper-
    vised sites, staff in uniform, and the need to walk the
    grounds daily for hazards;

(b) safety information, including how to handle injuries, ad-
    minister medication, file accident reports, and undertake
    maintenance of the facilities. All staff were certified in
    CPR, learned how to handle situations involving blood,
    and how to administer medications; and

(c) daily procedures including which sites were early drop-off
    points, opening and closing times for sites, weekly sched-
    ules for parents, and site staff meetings.

(7) Improve quality of management.

In order to hire better qualified staff and people who had an
interest in recreation and youth, pay rates were increased from
$5 to $6.50 per hour. Efforts also were made to recruit staff
from local colleges and public school systems and to include
individuals who had prior day camp experience.

(8) Build and expand collaborations with other youth-serving
providers such as churches, local businesses, and local professional athletic teams.

Examples of partnerships that were established included: Sun-
shine Promotions which donated 800 Janet Jackson concert
tickets in June 1994, Mayflower Bus Company which donated
free transportation to the concert for the 800 youth; Indianapolis Indians (minor league baseball team) which gave away
10,000 free tickets; and St. Rita's Catholic Church and St. John
the Baptist Church which together provided one meal for the
campers at one site every day for the eight weeks.

Areas of Concern

The 1994 program was successful. However, its success created new
challenges. More youth signed up for the camp than were originally
anticipated. This created unacceptable ratios of campers to counselors and raised concerns among the parents about camper safety.
These problems were addressed by hiring more staff. Due to the

number of campers, transportation also became a major problem. Because the fleet of vans provided by Indy Parks was not sufficient, school buses had to be rented, and since funds were not available in the original budget, funding was provided by the Parks Foundation and other providers.

Program Outcomes

In 1994 Kids' Kamp participation increased from 13,000 to 42,000 camper days (approximately 700 children per week). At the same time revenue increased from $14,000 to $48,000. The program was able to provide a well-rounded, positive recreational and educational experience to the youth of Indianapolis. End of year surveys showed that 98% of the parents and children rated Indy Parks Kids' Kamp as excellent, with affordability and quality of programming considered to be the best benefits.

Future Directions

Specific goals for the program in the future include:

- Better staff training.
- Stronger partnerships with the Police Athletic League, Indianapolis Public Schools, and neighborhood groups.
- A stronger marketing campaign. The Kids' Kamp marketing campaign began the first week in January with reminder cards mailed out by March 1, and a Kamp brochure mailed out by April 1. A collaborative partnership with two major radio stations was established to promote the Kamp.
- Additional training for full-time staff through off-season seminars and workshops.

Chapter 23
After-school and Summer Latchkey Programs
in Corpus Christi, Texas

Presenter:
Malcolm Matthews
  Director, City of Corpus Christi Park and Recreation Department

Background

Between 1980 and 1990 the sociodemographic profile of Corpus Christi residents underwent a major change. In 1980 over 50% of the population was Caucasian. By 1990 the ethnic composition of the 257,000 residents was 50% Hispanics, 44% Caucasians, and 5% African Americans. In 1980 the local economy was driven by the oil and gas industries and military bases. By the early 1990s both of these economic bases had substantially declined, reducing the number of high-paying jobs in the area. As the tax base dropped, school budgets were reduced, and extracurricular activities were terminated. At the same time, the lack of high-paying jobs required that there were more instances where both parents in two-parent families needed to be employed in order to make a livable income.

These conditions meant that a substantially increased number of employed parents faced the difficult decision of whether or not to let their children go home after school to an empty house. The Task Force for Latchkey Children was formed in 1985 as a result of a series of articles, "Who is Minding the Children," published in the *Corpus Christi Caller Times*. One local principal had estimated that as many as 65% of the children from her school were involved in self-care after school. "We have so many children in this situation that we require multiple telephone numbers, because we cannot reach parents at home."

> When at home, many latchkey children have admitted to being frightened, hiding in closets, and carrying baseball bats because they fear burglars, or watching hours of television because it provides a kind of companionship. (Quote from "Who is Minding the Children?")

Task Force members included representatives from the YWCA, YMCA, *Corpus Christi Caller Times*, Chamber of Commerce, United Way, Corpus Christi Independent School District, Area PTA Council, Memorial Hospital, Parkdale Bank, and the Corpus Christi Park and Recreation Department. The Corpus Christi Chamber of Commerce provided $5,000 for a contract with the Social Science Research Center at Corpus Christi State University to do a community needs assessment survey. Approximately 500 parents from across the community were surveyed. The study showed that a substantial number of Corpus Christi children went home to an unsupervised environment. Approximately 75% of the children were left alone for at least 15 minutes after school. The survey also showed that the problem cut across ethnic lines and was most prevalent in middle-income families, generally because of dual-income parents. The respondents indicated that the preferred solution was for supervised day care, not an extension of the school day, and that families would be willing to pay for the additional enrichment services.

Taking into consideration these findings, the Task Force concentrated its efforts on: (a) actual care of the child after school; and (b) education in self-reliance skills. The Park and Recreation Department joined forces with the Corpus Christi Independent School District (CCISD) to address the problem through the development of the Latchkey Program.

Program Descriptions

Pilot Program

The objective of the pilot program was to develop an organized, supervised after-school program for elementary-school-age children who would otherwise go home alone to wait for a parent to come home from work. That simple objective has not changed, but the means of meeting that objective have changed dramatically through offering expanded programs. CCISD gave complete support by making two elementary schools available for the pilot program. The pilot program was so successful, and demand for additional sites so high that the program was expanded into 12 schools during the next school year.

Current After-school Latchkey Program

The current program has expanded in the number of youth and families, school districts, and neighborhood elementary schools served. The after-school program currently is offered in CCISD and Flour Bluff Independent School District at more than 30 school sites, serving approximately 2,800 elementary-school-age children. The program has experienced a steady growth in enrollment. However, there have been occasional growth spurts. For example, during the 1994-95 school year, there was a 30% enrollment expansion which did not appear to result from any dramatic circumstance other than the growing needs of employed parents (see Exhibit 23A).

Development of the Summer Latchkey Program

For decades, the city park and recreation department offered a typical Summer Recreation Program at city recreation centers and school sites across the community. However, the traditional approach to

Exhibit 23A

Parents' Comments

When school started, my 78-year-old great-grandmother was taking care of my boys. She became ill and was hospitalized for three weeks. My children would walk home and wait, for 30 minutes to an hour, unsupervised outside my great-grandmother's home. The program was a real lifesaver for me. Knowing they don't have to walk home in the cold and rain . . . is such a relief to me. When I arrive at Latchkey, my boys are always doing educational things and they look forward to participating. Before this, they only watched TV and were not allowed to go outside until I got there. The program is providing quality after-school care which would otherwise not be affordable; and they would be unsupervised.

staffing, events, fees, and procedures associated with this program over the years resulted in declining participant and political support plus an overall lack of excitement about the program. This led the Recreation Division staff to ask themselves "What type of program would you send *your* child to?" The responses resulted in a new program which better meets the needs of today's youth.

In 1992 a Summer Latchkey Program was piloted at one elementary school. The commitment of the principal at the school to make the program work, made it a positive experience for all involved. The program is now in its fourth year and includes four schools. Elementary-school-age children are placed in groups of their own age and are offered the opportunity to participate in a variety of "classes" during the day. A "lesson plan" which utilizes a variety of activities, resources, and equipment at the particular school is developed prior to each Summer session. Resources and equipment include computers, cafetorium, classrooms, library, and playground. Lunch is provided daily and field trips are regularly scheduled. The park and recreation department hires and trains the staff (many of whom are teachers from the schools involved), develops and operates the program, and collects all fees which are designed to cover expenditures, similar to the after-school latchkey program. Further expansion to eight sites is anticipated.

Vacation Station

As another spin-off program, the Park and Recreation Department began offering a school holiday break program during the Christmas/ New Year's break. Due to the level of demand, the Vacation Station Program is offered only at two city recreation centers. Its mission is to continue childcare programming for those families who need it, with only a limited break in service.

The After-school Latchkey Program, Summer Latchkey Program, and Vacation Station have objectives which are directed at all their beneficiaries:

For the Participant:
  (1) Provide a safe, professionally supervised environment for children after school;
  (2) Provide quality recreational experiences and enhance the child's leisure skills;

(3) Develop basic survival skills necessary in today's society;

(4) Develop physical skills and coordination; and

(5) Develop the ability to express thoughts and feelings through activities such as art, computers, drama, and games.

For the Parent:

(1) Provide a safe haven for their children;

(2) Keep the monthly fee affordable;

(3) Provide a scholarship program for those unable to pay for the service; and

(4) Provide education in areas that concern the well-being of their children (e.g., drug education, child abuse).

For the School Districts:

(1) Reduce vandalism and loitering around the schools;

(2) Keep the cost of their cosponsorship to a minimum (only provide the facilities); and

(3) Involve programming for taxpayers' after-school hours (maximize capital investment).

For the Park and Recreation Department and City:

(1) Promote consolidation with other agencies to save tax dollars;

(2) Run the program on a self-supporting basis;

(3) Develop attitudes in future adults which support educational, quality of life and social issues;

(4) Provide recreational opportunities through city-sponsored programming; and

(5) Reduce crime.

Each of these programs has reduced registration fees for low-income families and for families with more than one child in the program, and offers snacks and lunches funded with grant assistance from the Texas Department of Human Services. Private grants and donations are also solicited. Each school site must be licensed with the Texas Department of Regulatory and Protective Services as a childcare facility. Licensing requires certain staff-to-participant ratios, adequate room space, and toileting facilities.

The needs of employed parents do not end after the school year. In fact, childcare is an even greater need during the summer and other holiday breaks from school. Offering these programs to the community year-round has resulted in strong support for the development of other youth and family-oriented city-sponsored programs.

Since their inception, these latchkey programs have received awards from the Texas Recreation and Parks Society, Public Technology Inc., the Texas Municipal League, the Corporate Fund for Children, as well as recognition from the Texas Attorney General's Office.

Chapter 24
KIDCO After-school and Summer Recreation Program
in Tucson, Arizona

Presenters:
Ronnie Lee Burton, Sr.
   Recreation Supervisor, *and*
J. M. Hayes
   Recreation Coordinator, Tucson Parks and Recreation

Background

> We know what causes gangs and juvenile crime and
> youth violence—poverty, broken families, poor or no
> role models, abuse, stress, hopelessness. We've pro-
> vided all the ingredients—our 'Field of Nightmares.'
> We built it. They came. We shouldn't be surprised.

The Presidio of *San Agustin del Tuquison* was founded as an outpost
of Spanish conquest in 1775. What is now Tucson, Arizona, recorded its first homicides less than seven years later. A citizen, a
soldier, and eight Apaches died as a result of what could be called
Tucson's first turf war.

Just over two centuries later the "Old Pueblo" was rocked by turf
wars between street tribes with a capacity for senseless violence that
would have confused both the Conquistadors and Apaches. And this
time, sadly, it was kids killing kids.

Only 4% of the population of Pima County, Arizona, lives outside the greater metropolitan Tucson area. Between 1991 and 1992,
Pima County Juvenile Court records indicated that murder or attempted murder by juveniles rose by 340%, aggravated assault was
up 94%, robbery climbed 42%, and rape increased 100%. A local
newspaper's youth survey showed 27% of teens feared being a vic-
tim of violence at school. Though Tucson's economy was improving, 22% of families and 32% of children in the city were living

under the poverty level. By January 1993 Tucson police had identified 72 distinct gangs operating in the city. They estimated that more than 100 gangs actually existed with 7,000 gang members and between 3,000 and 5,000 "wannabes." Approximately 10% of Pima County youth between the ages 5 and 17 were gang members or displaying gang leanings. As a result, Tucson Mayor George Miller declared his determination to make Tucson a "child friendly city."

In January 1993, NBC *Dateline* ran a segment about latchkey children that featured a Tucson single mother who was forced to leave her children home alone while she worked a minimum wage job. This unflattering national publicity, together with rising gang activity and youth violence, helped focus community interest on what city manager Michael F. Brown described as the generation of "least parented children in United States history."

KIDCO Program

KIDCO, an existing, free after-school and summer recreation program for elementary-school-age youth, was begun in 1989 and served fewer than 600 participants. By 1992 the summer program served almost 1,500 children at 12 sites, running for eight weeks, five days a week, three hours a day. The after-school program, also at 12 sites, ran 24 weeks, four days a week and two and a half hours a day, and served 1,800 children. When city council and the residents of Tucson chose to support the mayor and make Tucson a child friendly city, one of the programs they selected for additional funding ($500,000) was KIDCO. In summer 1993, KIDCO expanded to 29 sites for six hours a day, five days a week during its eight-week season, and served 2,300 children. Beginning that fall the program ran from school dismissal time until 6 p.m. at all locations on all school days.

The expansion continues. In 1994 KIDCO operated summer programs at 40 locations and the after-school program was organized at 27 sites during the fall semester. The summer program enrolled 4,000, the after-school program 2,500.

Objectives of the program are:

(1) to provide a free program for children who have completed kindergarten through sixth grade;
(2) to provide a safe, comfortable place for children, after school and in the summer;

(3) to provide an opportunity for kids to express themselves through various art forms, sports, and special events;

(4) to provide a place to practice physical fitness, experience healthy alternatives, and learn respect for the body;

(5) to provide an environment to promote self-esteem, encourage listening and caring, learn stress release, and reinforce positive values;

(6) to provide an opportunity to develop varied interests, to practice recreational skills, and to experience positive use of leisure time;

(7) to encourage time for friendships;

(8) to discourage drug and alcohol use and promote healthy life choices;

(9) to provide an opportunity for college students, and other citizens in the part-time work force, to develop and enhance important work skills, get job experience, and earn a salary as employees of the program;

(10) to provide an opportunity for teens to develop job skills and awareness of child development through a teen volunteer program;

(11) to provide an opportunity for other agencies to offer their programs in conjunction with KIDCO; and

(12) to expand days and hours of coverage, develop programming for kindergartners, and, where possible, provide an alternative to latchkey situations in the city of Tucson.

Key Players

Tucson Parks and Recreation Schools' Unit produces KIDCO in collaboration with the Arizona Commission on the Arts, Asarco, Children's Television Resource and Education Center, Girl Scouts of America, Heartsprings Inc., Metropolitan Tucson Family Resource and Wellness Centers, Our Town Family Center Inc., Pascua Yaqui Tribe, Pima County Interfaith Council, Primera Alta Consortium, Southern Arizona Ranchers, Tucson Cable TV Company, Tucson Fire Department, Tucson Police Department, Tucson Water Department, University of Arizona Department of Education, YMCA, and three of the city's school districts—Amphitheater, Sunnyside, and Tucson Unified.

Program Planning

In May 1992 Tucson's mayor and council held a joint study session with the Pima County Interfaith Council (PCIC) regarding PCIC's concerns about the city's services for children and youth. Areas of concern included children's needs for constructive recreational opportunities and skill building. It was recommended that free and low-cost after-school and summer recreation programs for youth be expanded.

KIDCO is usually located in neighborhood schools and is designed to offer varied recreational and leisure activities in a safe, comfortable environment. Children are offered a wide range of leisure time experiences—physical fitness; sports; arts; crafts; values, self-esteem building; self-respect, listening and caring skills; acceptable stress release; social skills; friendship; cooperation; and creative expression. Perhaps most important is that participants have fun.

No two KIDCO sites are identical. A typical school-year program begins at dismissal time with children checking in at the cafeteria or multipurpose room where the KIDCO program is located. Children are supervised by staff at all times. Children are normally gathered for a brief meeting for announcements, attendance, and a rules review. Groups are formed by age, ability, and shared interests for participation in preplanned activities which occur both indoors and outdoors. Groups are rotated every 30 to 45 minutes. The same activity may be offered to all groups but revised so that it is age or ability appropriate. The last half-hour of the day is normally a supervised, indoor clean-up and free-play time to facilitate parents coming to pick up the children.

Summer programming typically operates for six hours a day and may begin as early as 6 a.m. or as late as noon. Starting times reflect an effort to best serve neighborhood and parent needs. The summer format is similar to the school-year program, employing age-appropriate rotations. Tucson's summer climate requires adjustments. Most outdoor activities occur early in the morning or late in the afternoon depending on weather conditions. Many schools offer additional space which allows for an increased range of indoor activities. Breakfast and lunch are provided free to needy children at qualified summer sites. The range of activities is at least as varied as during the school year.

KIDCO strives to adapt to community needs. In one instance, efforts to implement the program at a Native-American village failed until consultations with the village council resulted in tailoring the program to the site's unique cultural situation. Staff from the village were hired, trained, and encouraged to adapt the program to the location.

Another adaptation was "KIDCO in the Mall" which operated from 9 a.m. to 1 p.m. at the El Con indoor shopping mall during the summer of 1994. An area once housing a decorative fountain was converted into a day camp for up to 60 children per day. Activities had to be modified and scaled to available facilities, but the program was both successful and popular.

Community interest and support has resulted in many special enhancements to the programs. Numerous partnerships, grants, training, and subprograms have been developed. The Arizona Commission on the Arts awarded an artist's residency to three sites. A cable TV corporation awarded a grant for participants to write and produce a video. Three school districts and one mall provide facilities at no cost. The Children's Television Resource and Education Center selected KIDCO to pilot their "Getting Along After School" program. Working with the YMCA, staff were trained to deliver the "On the Right Track" drug prevention program. An intramural sports program was implemented in conjunction with the school districts at two elementary schools. In cooperation with police and fire departments, many sites hold bike rodeos or participate in a citywide Safe Kid Bicycle event. Several behavioral health organizations provide training and staff counseling in behavioral modification techniques. When a $1.6 million Department of Education grant was received by the school districts, $135,000 was designated to enhance KIDCO at two sites.

Library-trained staff are provided with materials (including 150 books per site) so all children can participate in a summer reading program. School districts provide participants in low-income schools with free breakfast and/or lunch (Summer 1994—72,420 breakfasts and 132,840 lunches). Many agencies visit sites as guest speakers or presenters. The Girl Scouts provide materials for their "T. J. the D. J." programs. The city water department trained staff and printed material for an environmental education program. At one site near campus, the University of Arizona offered a bilingual lab, taught by university graduate students. All these partnerships have enhanced KIDCO programming at no additional cost to the city of Tucson or to the families who participate.

Recreation versus Day Care

The program is planned to be recreation, not childcare. In reality, however, the type of programming offered probably is not very different, but the intention in emphasizing recreation is to establish a different philosophical approach. According to program organizers:

> When you tell someone you provide childcare they usually think you're giving them the politically correct term for babysitting. Recreation, on the other hand, indicates you're doing more than just watching kids. We try to convey the idea that we're involving them in important and enriching character building activities that also happen to be fun.

> Our staff know we're hiring them as something more than babysitters. The kids come expecting to do and learn things, not just hang out. Parents are shown they're not just leaving their children with babysitters, but in the hands of recreation personnel. When we have to discuss significant behavioral problems, the distinction between childcare and recreation occasionally buys us a parent's cooperation instead of blame.

Staffing

Each KIDCO site is staffed with a recreation assistant (site leader) and recreation workers at the ratio of one staff person to not more than 20 participants. A typical school-year site has one recreation assistant and two recreation workers serving 60 participants. An additional worker is added to handle a typical summer program site with 80 participants. These staff are noncivil service, part-time, seasonal workers. They are expected to be certified in CPR and first-aid. Paid staff are supplemented with teen volunteers provided through Tucson Parks and Recreation's Teen program where they are screened and monitored. Occasionally, other volunteers are provided through the city's Civics program.

Paid staff are selected for their experience and aptitude and are trained by civil service administrators. Two expanded-program, year-round school sites are currently staffed with part-time civil service recreation assistants. The school's unit consists of a supervisor, six to eight coordinators who administer up to eight sites each, and the site staffs mentioned above.

Turnover at the site staff level is higher than desired because of the limited hours and wages available. KIDCO takes advantage of the young, but highly skilled work force available through students at the University of Arizona and Pima Community College, as well as parents reentering the work force and individuals recommended by schools and neighborhoods.

Site leaders are paid $5.94 an hour and staff $5.37. The wages are comparable with other local school-age care providers, but are below the level necessary to attract and retain committed professionals, so staff turnover is a significant problem. With staff costs the largest expense of the program, the current pay rates allow service to be extended to a larger segment of the community; however, the low salaries may adversely impact program quality. Tucson is firmly committed to the goals of the Wellesley College and the Dewitt Wallace Reader's Digest's *Making the Most of Out-of-School-Time (M.O.S.T.) Initiative* aimed at professionalizing school-age children's services. For example, site leader salaries have been raised at two of the year-round schools to civil service status at $7.64 an hour with benefits.

Marketing

KIDCO, a free program, is understandably popular and receives much word-of-mouth advertising. Tucson Parks and Recreation produces a quarterly class and program guide which provides information on sites, registration procedures, activities, and numbers to call for further details. The guide is delivered via the Sunday *Arizona Daily Star* newspaper (circulation over 175,000) and is made available at all recreation sites, libraries, and other city offices. Fliers are distributed at each site in advance of registration. Site newsletters regularly advise parents of program information. Tucson newspapers provide reports on the availability of children's programs to their reading public. Local TV and radio stations occasionally feature KIDCO in their news coverage.

Cost to Participants

Fees are not charged to participants because program personnel believe that the absence of this revenue stream enables more resources to be leveraged from other partners, thus permitting the program to do more for less. By not charging, a number of significant costs are curbed or eliminated. For example, since the city does not charge for KIDCO, the school districts are willing to contribute their facilities. Being free also leads to other contributed program enhancements, e.g., local behavioral health organizations help train staff and work to mediate health problems. Girl Scouts of America and 4-H, among others, offer no-cost programming at KIDCO sites. Private industries invite groups and conduct educational tours for no charge. Staff believe that many of these services would not be free if the program was not free to the community.

By not charging fees, the program is also able to eliminate the infrastructure necessary to collect fees. No personnel are needed to determine who pays what, calculate partial costs, or give refunds. Cash does not need to be handled at sites and bad check problems do not arise. The program administrator noted: "In our circumstances, we've decided the hidden costs of charging for services are just too expensive."

In addition, by not charging a fee, the program is not subject to childcare licensing standards—things like space requirements (so many square feet per child), and restroom locations. As a free program, KIDCO is able to use school facilities that are already deemed adequate for children's use.

Finally, KIDCO employees are not subjected to expensive background checks, health testing, or registering with an oversight agency. However, all staff who work with children are fingerprinted. While these savings may appear to avoid safeguards that protect the children, the interviewing and hiring process is designed to carefully screen applicants and the program is designed to prevent opportunities for staff to be alone with children. Additionally, workers are carefully monitored by site leaders and program coordinators.

Financing and Resource Acquisition

KIDCO is funded from city of Tucson revenues and is supplemented with grants from several agencies. The direct service cost of KIDCO sites has been calculated at $25,000 for a school-year site and

$10,000 for a summer site. In 1995 Tucson plans to staff 28 school-year sites and 41 summer sites at a total program cost of $1.1 million. KIDCO's summer cost per child per day is under $4, while the after-school cost per child per day is less than $3. The following is a partial breakdown of these costs:

Salaries:

Program Administration	$181,000
Office/Warehouse Staff	25,000
Summer Site Staff	221,000
School-Year Site Staff	335,000
Additional Coverage for Year-round Schools	15,000
Staff Orientations (minimum)	19,000
Drivers	17,000
Specialists	8,000
Special Events	11,000
	$832,000

Site Equipment and Supplies:

School Year	$70,000
Summer	72,000
	$142,000

Administrative Costs and Supplies	$126,000
Total	$1,100,000

Measurement of Program Outcome

Impact on Crime

Early indications were positive. Youth crime declined 52% in the summer of 1993 compared to the summer of 1992. Unfortunately, that trend did not hold for the whole year. Overall, youth arrests rose 17% between 1992 and 1993. In 1994 youth arrests were up 14% from 1993, which is higher than the 11% increase which the city was averaging at the start of the decade.

Pima County's youth crime statistics are complied for those ages 8–17. Most crimes are committed by youths at the higher end of this age group. For instance, in 1994 only 5% of arrests in Pima County were of children ages 8–11. While 77% were 14 or over. Thus, most juvenile crime is committed by youth who are older than the KIDCO target groups, which is first through sixth grade (ages 6–12).

Tucson Police Department records indicate arrests of children ages 5–13 rose from 1989 through 1993, but at a decreasing rate— 8%, 6%, 4%, and 1%, then fell 2% in 1994. Five- through 13-year-old victims of crime increased dramatically, 30% between 1989 and 1990, but they have fallen every year since by 0.3%, 5%, 4%, and 0.5%. These trends do not neatly correspond to KIDCO's expansion, but they do relate to the period when the city was exhibiting growing awareness of this problem and beginning efforts, like KIDCO, to address it.

Survey Data

More than 400 survey forms were returned from parents and guardians of summer 1994 participants. When asked to rate the program's quality, 61% called it excellent, 32% said good, while 8% indicated it was average. When parents were asked what changes they would like to see in the program, the most common answer was more hours every day, more sites, more weeks, more field trips, and more meals at more sites.

Some questions were raised about inexperienced, intolerant or inattentive staff. On the other hand, staff also received unsolicited praise: "Staff did a super job" and "staff exceptional" were typical of these comments. Parents were almost universally supportive of the program as a whole.

> "This program is the best a child could have...it keeps them active and away from trouble," one said. "A wonderful program," was repeated over and over again, and, we "hope it continues."

Access to Additional Funding

Another measure of the program's success is the amount of additional money and interest which it has generated. The Mayor and Council increased the cost of each round of golf by $1 to benefit youth programs, adding another $400,000 to Tucson Parks and Recreation's budget. The 1994-95 budget was increased an additional $1,600,000 for youth programs. The city manager appointed a task force to consider solutions to youth problems. The Pima County

Board of Supervisors approved $1,900,000 for youth programs. The City of Tucson held a successful $265 million bond election in May 1994 part of which was designated for recreation facilities.

The program has received national recognition. The National Recreation and Park Association (NRPA) selected Tucson's KIDCO program as one of 20 for a comprehensive study that highlighted successful agencies and facilities addressing community social issues. Of KIDCO and Orange County Florida's "Rec and Roll," Tice and Tindall (1994) said: "These programs epitomize the innovative spirit of recreation and park services and their essential niche within the community." The National Park Service has awarded Tucson Parks and Recreation an Urban Parks and Recreation Renewal Grant to produce manuals which will allow other locations to reproduce KIDCO.

What are some of the things that KIDCO is doing differently from other agencies which offer summer and after-school programming? First, there is a strong partnership with Tucson's schools. In nearly every instance, KIDCO operates in school facilities. Without them KIDCO either would not exist or would be very different in size and scope. Being in neighborhood schools means serving children in convenient and familiar locations. While programs are not offered in all of Tucson's schools, KIDCO has targeted the neighborhoods where poverty, crime, and other negative factors combine to put kids who live there most at-risk. Staff feel that if they were limited to city neighborhood and recreation centers, nothing approaching the same level of service and impact could be achieved. Initially, some principals were not thrilled at an outside agency using their schools, but the enthusiastic response of children, parents, and the community has converted nearly all into ardent supporters.

At a time when tax dollars are hard to come by and support for further government spending is down, Tucson has bucked the national trend for the good of its children and supported a program that works.

References

Tice, R. D. & Tindall, B. (1994). *Beyond fun and games: Emerging roles of public recreation.* Arlington, VA: National Recreation and Park Association.

Chapter 25
Approach to Gang Prevention and Intervention
in Fort Worth, Texas

Presenter:
Richard Zavala
   Director, Parks and Community Services, Fort Worth, Texas

Background

In 1991 a task force of city officials and community leaders undertook a study of ways to reduce juvenile crime in Fort Worth. The report concluded that a holistic effort was required involving law enforcement agencies, the business community, religious institutions, educational institutions, government, the media, and nonprofit organizations. In order to be successful, prevention, intervention, and enforcement efforts were needed (see Exhibit 25A).

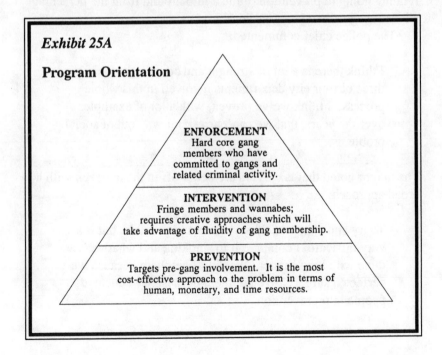

Exhibit 25A

Program Orientation

ENFORCEMENT
Hard core gang members who have committed to gangs and related criminal activity.

INTERVENTION
Fringe members and wannabes; requires creative approaches which will take advantage of fluidity of gang membership.

PREVENTION
Targets pre-gang involvement. It is the most cost-effective approach to the problem in terms of human, monetary, and time resources.

In fiscal year 1992 Fort Worth implemented a crime initiative called *Code Blue* based on recommendations from the task force report. To attack crime, $3.2 million was provided, 82% of which went to law enforcement initiatives. Of the total, $101,000 was allocated for late-night basketball on Saturday nights during the summer only. During the summer of 1992, over 8,000 young people participated in that program, with 7,200 and 8,200 participating in 1993 and 1994 respectively.

The results of the midnight basketball initiative were impressive. Based on crime statistics provided by the police department, in those areas where the midnight basketball program was provided, crime dropped 28% within a one-mile radius of community center program sites. As a comparison, at five other community centers where these programs did not exist, crime rose an average of 39%.

In the summer of 1993, the police, human services, and recreation departments put together a crime package that totalled $4 million, of which $2.7 million was requested for late-night programs year-round in the community. As testimony to the results that had been achieved through programs to date, the council approved a total of $1.5 million for all the programs in the package, with 87% of that funding going to prevention (quite a turn around from the percentage allocations just two years earlier).

The police chief commented:

> I think there is a lot of strength and advantage to having three or four city departments involved in this whole process. I think we've proven, with a lot of examples over the years, that we can't arrest our way out of social problems.

The mayor noted that taxpayers are better off in the long run with a broad approach:

> To try and change a lifestyle is not impossible, but it's very difficult. I compare it to smoking and what we've done with lung cancer. We didn't get there because we perfected surgery. We got there because we educated people into prevention.

In 1994 the Parks and Community Services Department received $702,000 for the remaining nine months of the budget year: $70,000 for youth sports programs, and $632,000 for late-night programming in five community centers, five nights a week, year-round, until 11 p.m. or midnight, depending on the night. For the next budget year, due to the success of the program, the total was annualized to $739,000.

After one year of operation the program yielded 75,000 units of service which works out to just under $10 a participant per year, 83¢ a month, or less than a nickel a night. This is considerably better than the $40,000 plus it costs to incarcerate a juvenile in Texas for a year.

The at-risk effort is centered around the two programs which are described in the following sections.

Year-Round After-school, Evening and Late Night Programs

This initiative is offered at five community Centers: Sycamore, Martin Luther King, Como, Northside and Worth Heights. The hours of operation are on Wednesday and Thursday, 3 p.m. to 11 p.m.; Friday and Saturday, 4 p.m. to 12 midnight; and Sunday, 2 p.m. to 10 p.m. Programs operate year-round.

Goals of the programs are:

(1) to provide social, educational, and recreational growth oppor-
    tunities for youth;
(2) to focus all efforts toward building and enhancing positive
    self-fulfillment, self-esteem, and well-being for youth;
(3) to provide structured, constructive, and innovative activities in
    a safe and secure environment during traditional and nontradi-
    tional times; and
(4) to maximize collaborations with other public, private and
    nonprofit agencies, and community groups.

Three leader positions are funded at each site with one program coordinator position funded to oversee the entire project. Security is provided at each center. Police officers involve themselves in the programs, many of them volunteering their time. Activities include: sports and athletics; educational programs such as tutoring, homework assistance, and GED training; recreational programs, such as photography, drama, art and music; programs on social issues such as drug and alcohol awareness, and AIDS education; parenting and job skills training, such as resume writing, employment interviewing, and career planning.

Comin' Up: A Youth Gang Intervention Program

Between 1987 and 1992 the number of gangs in Fort Worth increased from 77 to 211, while gang membership rose from 1,316 to 3,448. The goal of the Youth Gang Intervention Program is to impact positively the lives of youths involved in gangs by providing services and activities to reduce the level of gang violence. In August 1994 the city entered into a contract with the Boys Club of Fort Worth to manage and operate the Comin' Up program. The Parks and Community Services Department serves as the contract monitor and works closely with the Boys Club in the management of the programs. Initially seven sites were funded by a U.S. Department of Justice grant enabling the addition of two more sites. Of the nine sites, six are operated at Parks and Community Services' community centers.

With the assistance of the police department and other organizations and agencies, the program seeks to strategically identify specific gangs that are the greatest source of violence, and to target services for individual gang members that can have the greatest impact on reducing violence by their particular gang. Services are provided directly through the program as well as by a clearly defined network of service providers. A set of principles for dealing with the gang's problem is shown in Exhibit 25B.

Program Objectives

(1) To identify gang members in need of services by seeking referrals from the police, schools, juvenile probation, and other relevant agencies and organizations, (e.g., Parks and Community Services, churches).

Action Steps: The project will take referrals directly from agencies or organizations who can identify youth who need the

---

Exhibit 25B

Strategies that Must be Implemented by All Groups and Institutions that Deal with the Gang Problem

- Sensitivity training for all professional staff and constituents to respect cultural differences and ethnic diversity.
- Development of community-based partnerships to cut bureaucratic red tape and territorial barriers.
- Innovative and nontraditional methods of service and program delivery.
- Education of professional staff and constituents about gangs, their activities, and the related issues of violence, drugs, and weapon possession.
- Long-term commitment to solving the problem.
- Recognizing the value of *prevention,* and making it a high priority in programming and budgeting.
- Creation of more opportunities for building self-esteem and civic pride in youth.
- Creating and expanding mentoring programs for at-risk youth.
- Facilitating accessibility of services to youth and families who need them.
- Removing graffiti as soon as it appears to tell gangs they are not welcome.
- Commitment of resources (e.g., human, monetary, time) to provide long-term evaluation of prevention and intervention programs.

---

program, as well as receive feedback and information about program participants.

(2) To provide extended services in seven initial targeted areas that will attract 100 gang-involved youth at each site.

Action Steps: Seven area working groups will be developed to identify and target specific gangs and gang members for program participation. Gang affiliation will be verified by the police gang unit. Specific outreach strategies and time frames will be detailed in the action plan to reach targeted youth. Services will be provided late at night and will be interest-based.

(3) To identify and target 25 gang members at each site for more intense case management and service provision.

Action Steps: Twenty-five youth at each program site will be identified and targeted for more intense, expanded services. A needs assessment will be completed for each youth, and additional needs-based services will be provided directly by the program, as well as through referral services.

(4) To assess the needs and interests of each targeted youth, and develop specific plans of action to meet the needs of these youth.

Action Steps: A team including project staff, school officials, parent(s), police and/or probation officials, and any other relevant agency personnel will focus on the youth's needs, and on identifying services to meet those needs. The needs assessment will result in a service plan which can be tracked and routinely updated.

(5) To provide needs-focused services and activities (e.g., academic programming, employability and job development) directly through the project, as well as through a clearly defined network of collaborating organizations and agencies.

Action Steps: Sequential services will be provided so that mastered skills are built-on in a way that enable youth to succeed in school, in the workplace, and in the community at large. Services will begin with life-skills related services (e.g., communication and conflict resolution skills, academics) and progress to job skills and peer mediation skills. Interest-based activities will also be provided to support the needs-based services, including field trips, music, drama, and sports.

(6) To refer family members to appropriate services.

Action Steps: As needs assessments are completed and action plans are drawn up, program staff will identify any special

family issues, and identify referral resources to address these
family needs. This may range from drug and alcohol counseling to arranging for the academic needs of another family
member.

(7) To establish relationships and respect between youth from
different areas and neighborhoods in the city who would otherwise interact negatively or even violently.

Action Steps: As the program progresses and youth from the
different gangs are able to interact positively at each program
site, intersite activities will be planned. These activities can
range from social activities like dances and performances to
sports activities and community service activities where youth
work together on communitywide projects. The purpose of
these activities would be to develop an understanding between
youth from different parts of the city about common interests
and needs.

(8) To employ 14 program participants (two from each site) to
serve as part-time community outreach workers to enhance
access to and dialogue with gang-involved youth.

Action Steps: Two youth from each site will be hired part time
(25 hours per week) to serve as community outreach workers.
These youth will serve as liaisons and promote the program to
other youth in their community, and assist in mediating gang-
related issues that may arise.

(9) To support the development of truces among rival gangs as
issues arise and reduce random gang violence through peer
mediation and project staff involvement.

Action Steps: Program staff and community outreach workers,
through their established relationships with gangs, will promote truces between gangs, and mediate disputes when feasible and appropriate. Any mediation work would be done
with the knowledge and support of the police department's
Gang Unit in order to ensure that city efforts are coordinated.

Chapter 26
Mayor's Night Hoops
in Kansas City, Missouri

Presenter:
Nathaniel O. Wilkins
   Superintendent of Recreation, Parks and Recreation, Kansas
   City, Missouri

   With all of the problems and all of the challenges our
   children are facing today, if you were in their shoes,
   could you weave your way through, and become successful like you are today?

Background

In 1991 Kansas City, Missouri (population 434,829) Mayor Emmanuel
Cleaver called a summit of city leaders to develop a plan to combat
the challenges of limited recreation and employment opportunities
for youth ages 14–25. The Mayor had attended the 1991 Mayor's
Urban Summit where discussions were held about midnight basketball programs that had been instituted around the country. Mayor
Clever felt that midnight basketball could be as successful in Kansas
City as in Baltimore, Chicago, Detroit, and Atlanta. Instead, the
Recreation Division of the Kansas City Parks and Recreation Department took the lead in developing Kansas City Business Hoops, the
name emphasizing the collaborative funding relationship with busi-
nesses which was necessary to initiate the program. Eventually the
name was changed to the Mayor's Night Hoops Program.
   Ollie Gates, President of the Board of Parks and Recreation
Commissioners; Terry Dopson, Director of the Department; and
Nathaniel Wilkins, the Superintendent of Recreation, and his staff, all
helped to develop the program concept. Together they solicited
support from the Kansas City School District, Kansas City Police
Department, the Greater Kansas City Community Foundation and
Affiliated Trusts, Amateur Athletic Union (AAU), Dubuque Foods,
Price Chopper, KPRS Radio Station, Wilson Chapman Advertising,
Wings and Things, and others.

Program

During summer 1992, the Mayor suggested that the program operate Thursdays through Saturdays, 10 p.m. until 1 a.m. The program used Central High School, a newly constructed school district facility which was leased to the parks and recreation department to inaugurate the program.

The program operated from June through mid-August. The foundation of the program was deeply rooted in the old African proverb, "It takes a whole village to raise a child." Individuals and teams were recruited from area facilities, shopping malls and local basketball courts. Teams were registered through the AAU to ensure participant insurance coverage. Arrangements were made with the police department to use off-duty officers to patrol the parking lot and facilities to ward off any signs of trouble. Coaches were recruited from area parents and school organizations.

The season began and ended in a festive manner with contests such as three-point shootouts, slam dunk, and beat-the-clock contests. Area drill teams were asked to provide entertainment. At the closing banquet, participants were recognized with trophies and certificates of accomplishment.

The program recruited close to 200 participants and consisted of 16 teams (all male). By the summer of 1993 the Mayor's Night Hoops program grew to 480 participants playing on 48 teams including 6 female teams. The program provided learning opportunities, career exposure, and skill development. During 1993 volleyball was added, and the program was offered at three additional sites around the city: Don Bosco Youth Center, Central High School and Penn Valley Community College. Approximately 880 players were involved, with spectators numbering approximately 3,000. Spectators sometimes had to be turned away. Initially, spectators were charged $1 to participate in the program, but soon the leaders realized that the spectators were looking for some place to go, too! The building can provide a safe haven for parents, friends, and neighbors as well as for the players.

In 1994 the program expanded to include youth ages 10–14, Wednesdays through Fridays from 7 p.m. to 9 p.m. and on Saturday mornings. This was done since many older youth who participate in negative activities learned these behavior patterns when they were younger.

More than Just Basketball

An educational component was included in the development of the midnight basketball program. Participants learn about jobs, interviewing, interpersonal communication skills, HIV/AIDS, and drugs. While youth initially come to Night Hoops to play basketball, the education component gives them a chance to develop other skills. The classes expose participants to opportunities for personal development, motivational training, and entrepreneurial skills which can assist in developing self-worth and inner-strength (see Exhibit 26A). Educational sessions are kept to a maximum of one-half hour, since it is hard to motivate interest beyond that period of time.

According to Nathaniel Wilkins, Superintendent of Recreation:

> The program shows that recreation is a productive way of using city dollars and corporate support to benefit, involve, and create opportunities for our citizens. It is important to bring our youth together with strong adult

---

Exhibit 26A

Food for Thought

When you get what you want in your struggles for self, and
    the world makes you king or queen for a day,
Just go to the mirror and look at yourself, and see what the
    mirror has to say.
Whether it is your father, mother, sister, brother in life
    whose judgment upon you is passed.
The person whose verdict counts most in your life is the one
    staring back in the glass.
You may fool the world down through the pathways of life,
    and get pats on the back as you pass.
But your only rewards will be heartaches and tears if you
    cheat the person in the glass.
...Don't cheat yourself.

Comments by Nathaniel Wilkins

---

support to create a 'rite of passage' opportunity and to help them to understand and share adult responsibilities. We must take the time to instill values into young people, such as learning proper health and drug and alcohol-free lifestyles, and provide safe environments that are a positive alternative to gangs, drugs and violence. Night Hoops redirects frustrated energies in a positive manner. We are not just sitting back and hoping for a good summer. We are making it happen.

The goals of the program are:

(1) to develop a recreation program that utilizes basketball as a centerpiece or attractive incentive to achieve broader educational and entrepreneurial goals for youth;
(2) to raise the social consciousness of private businesses and the public sector concerning their need to be involved with a neglected segment of the population;
(3) to develop collaborative relationships;
(4) to develop a network of support services which would enhance and positively impact on participants' quality of life; and
(5) to develop opportunities for participants to train and develop skills in timekeeping, scorekeeping, and officiating.

Following the Rules

If a participant gets in trouble during a game, he or she is not necessarily kicked out of the facility. Participants are asked to leave only if they refuse to follow the rules and regulations. According to Wilkins:

It is easy to kick someone out. It takes some work to sit down with somebody and say, 'What's going on, why did you do that?' During the championship game, this kid gets angry; one point separates his team from the championship, and this guy gets fouled, but the referee misses the call. The player takes the ball and kicks it up in the air. We stopped the game and said, 'Hey, look, that's not necessary.' The player got angry, said a lot of choice words and left. Do you think he's going to be back in our program? Probably. But the next time what we will do is try to coach him to handle the situation better.

Wilkins also recounts a particular incident that illustrates the program's stance about teaching personal responsibility:

> One time we had a fight in the stands between some young people. And one of our people, who is on a police cooperative went up into the stands and said to all the group who were involved, 'All rise.' They all got up and were escorted outside, where he began to counsel them. The ones that didn't want to listen were asked to leave. People want to know what the rules are and what is expected; if you allow them to do the wrong thing, don't blame them. It is up to the program to provide guidance and set limits.

The program allows any person to enroll. When individuals become part of the program, they must attend and take part in the educational sessions; roll is called, but allowances are made for participants who have work obligations.

Police currently monitor the parking lot and enforce a security check to insure that people are not bringing weapons into the building. To help with security in the future, the program is considering creating an ID-card system although cost may be an inhibiting factor. This system would make it possible to monitor attendance and control who enters the building.

Staffing

The program is staffed by independent contractors who act as the program manager, commissioner, facility manager, chief of security, trainer, and assigner of officials. These contractors report to the recreation superintendent or his designee. In addition, volunteers are recruited as coaches. An advisory board is being formed to assist with fundraising and long-range planning.

Marketing

The mayor's office has helped promote the program with press conferences and news releases. Flyers are distributed throughout the community as well as in all community centers. The *Kansas City Star* has written about the program and profiled several participants. The local media have carried the opening gala as a lead story.

The program promotion effort was enhanced in 1993 by a promotion offered by Dubuque Foods and Price Chopper which provided a pair of quality tennis shoes to the program for every 50 pounds of hot dogs purchased at Price Chopper Stores during the months of February through May. Marketing of the program was also done through the use of a promotional video developed in-house by department staff. The video won an award for the best short story on a recreation program from National Recreation and Parks Association. Local radio station KPRS supports the program with a DJ as well as public service announcements. Word-of-mouth and personal contacts are also important for attracting participants.

Financing and Resource Acquisition

Presently, youth pay no fees for participating in the program. Major costs are covered by the parks and recreation operating budget; a donation from the Community Foundation and Affiliated Trust ($10,000); a grant from the State Department of Public Safety ($10,000); and a contribution from Don Bosco Youth Center ($5,000). The current program budget is $100,000; the allocation of that budget is shown in Exhibit 26B.

Exhibit 26B

Mayor's Night Hoops Budget Allocation for 1994

Security	$ 29,151
Site Staff	31,672
Management Staff	17,955
Uniforms	8,241
Equipment Rental	2,480
AAU Fees	4,975
Trophies/Awards	2,041
Banquet Costs	2,200
Miscellaneous Expenses	1,285
Total	$100,000

Measurement of Program Outcomes

The following factors are monitored throughout the program:

(a) the number of program participants;
(b) level of criminal activity in the areas surrounding program sites;
(c) the impact of the educational component;
(d) the number of businesses expressing interest in the program;
(e) the success ratio of job placements and referrals; and
(f) the number of young men and women in attendance at workshop sessions.

A review of juvenile apprehensions in the Central and East Patrol Divisions indicated a 25% decline during July 1993 compared to July 1992. The biggest declines were in violent crimes and property-related offenses. These divisions are the major areas in which the Night Hoops program operates.

One spin-off of the program has been the opportunity for some of the players to be trained as referees. Not only are they able to officiate during the times they are working Night Hoops, but they also have opportunities to officiate in other leagues as well.

In 1995 the Mayor's Urban Symposium and Tournament (MUST) was held in Kansas City. It provided an opportunity for community and political leaders to interact and exchange ideas on urban issues and concerns. MUST is the first national program to combine urban concerns and a national hoops tournament, with entrepreneurial training.

Chapter 27
A Collaborative Public/Private Street Outreach Partnership
in Olympia, Washington

Presenter:
Steven Zoet
 Recreation Services Manager, Olympia Parks, Recreation, and
 Cultural Services Department

Background

Olympia, Washington (population 36,740; 90% Caucasian) lies about
midway between Portland and Seattle on the I-5 corridor which
connects these two larger urban cities. Organized gangs within the
Tacoma/Seattle region recognize Olympia as a fertile area for the
recruitment of high-risk youth into gangs.

"Edge kids" are those in need of public or private assistance but
who are not likely to access public services until they have encoun-
tered the juvenile court system. Many are homeless, coming from a
dysfunctional or nonsupportive home environment. Most have little
or no connection to the education system, their families, or society at
large. Therefore, these youth are susceptible to the appeal of finding
a sense of acceptance and a fulfillment of basic needs through the
gang culture.

The city council, merchants, and residents watched as the number of edge kids rose with a resulting adverse impact on the urban
core. The kids hung out in large numbers at The Olympia Center,
which is the city's downtown community center, and while the center
has a youth lobby that houses some traditional recreation equipment,
serving this population was not the purpose for which it was originally designed. These youth became the source of numerous complaints from facility patrons and merchants in the downtown area.

The staff of the Department of Parks, Recreation and Cultural
Services recognized the severity of the problem. In 1991 Olympia
contracted with Thurston County Community Youth Services to
provide two social workers who possessed the skills and experience

necessary to identify and reach out to troubled youth. Their challenge was to meet youth where many of them live—on the street.

Rather than expecting those engaged in an unhealthy or alternative lifestyle to participate in traditional recreation programs and services, the outreach counselors met with youth one-on-one in the downtown area. Their charge was to identify and develop relationships with these youth and ultimately to connect them with appropriate public healthcare, job opportunities, education, recreation, and other social services. The objective was to break the pattern of homeless youth and then to help them avoid difficult circumstances and reversion to a recurring, unhealthy lifestyle. Fundamental underlying assumptions for the street outreach program included:

(1) providing proactive programs for troubled youth is more cost-effective than incarcerating them;

(2) given the high rate of recidivism, youth who avoid the juvenile justice system have a better chance of living a more rewarding and productive life than youth who do not; and

(3) street counseling is the most effective way to reach this high-risk population.

Program

Goals and Objectives

Two primary goals, each with underlying objectives, provide the framework for this successful program.

Goal 1: To promote greater integration of training, communication and information regarding downtown youth between Community Youth Services; Olympia Parks, Recreation, and Cultural Services; and Olympia Police Departments.

Objectives

(1) Implement a quarterly training program on how to deal effectively with downtown youth and their families, and how to provide referrals to needed services.

(2) Develop biweekly meetings with the parks, recreation and cultural services and police department supervising personnel to communicate emerging issues and concerns of the downtown youth population.

Goal 2: Expand and enhance case management, outreach, and advocacy for youth in the downtown area.

Objectives

(1) Expand hours and days of street intervention devoted to downtown youth.

(2) Develop and run special services and programs for street youth at The Olympia Center or another appropriate location. Community Youth Services staff will recruit and train street youth in a peer-helper model. The model is intended to encourage teens to assist one another.

(3) Recruit and train six volunteers to assist with street outreach.

Key Players

Community Youth Services, the police, and parks, recreation, and cultural services departments have a vested interest in the success of area youth. As a result, these agencies have developed a symbiotic relationship through which each relies on the assistance, cooperation, and support of the other. The collaborative effort has resulted in unifying the agencies in achieving a common goal of improved investment in area youth as an alternative to their entering the criminal justice system. Approximately $37,500 from the city's general fund is invested annually in this program.

Staffing

The street outreach program is sustained primarily through the efforts of two outreach workers employed and supervised by Community Youth Services with their salaries funded mostly by the city. They are an integral link with parks and police department staff. The outreach workers have established an informal, drop-in presence at The Olympia Center and have developed a sense of trust with the high-risk youth and center staff.

An additional objective of the outreach counselors is to develop programs and training for park and police department staff which address the changing issues and needs of troubled youth. By drawing on community resources, programs were instituted to help youth gain job skills, properly apply for and find employment, develop interviewing skills, learn skills needed for independent living, address safe sex, substance abuse, personal health, teen parenting, and other issues.

The outreach workers developed and facilitated special self-help groups at The Olympia Center and recruited and trained other youth to become volunteer peer helpers. Participating youth responded to the positive support by actively seeking counseling, medical assistance, and other services.

In addition to working the streets, the outreach workers frequent a teen center that operates Monday through Friday from 2:30 p.m. to 7 p.m. at The Olympia Center, as well as a Friday late-night program operating from 9 p.m. to midnight. Site capacity of approximately 150 is often met and staff hope to accommodate additional youth as more facilities become available to expand services.

Marketing

Informing youth of available services is not often done through any organized or traditional marketing effort. Street youth typically do not have access to the traditional forms of program or service information such as print, television, or radio. Postings in public places usually go unnoticed. Yet, many displaced youth have a highly developed network of communicating with each other on the street. As a result, most of those needing to connect with an outreach worker know how, when, and where to do so. Also, the outreach workers actively seek out youth on the streets, their environment, rather than expecting youth to come to them in an office environment or other more traditional areas of accessing social services.

Measurement of Program Outcome

According to tracking completed by Community Youth Services and the parks, recreation, and cultural services department, each month approximately 90 youth and young adults (1,080 annually) are directed into a social service program or to an agency that can begin to meet their needs. Approximately 15 homeless youth return home each month with the support of an outreach worker. Each month 8 to 10 youths are positively diverted from the juvenile justice system, i.e., a crime is prevented and the city saves the escalating costs of police and judicial actions including expensive incarceration.

Based on the annual operating costs of $37,500 and the assumption of 1,080 clients served, the city is spending approximately $34.72 per individual annually for diversion and services provided through Community Youth Services. With tight fiscal constraints and ever-escalating criminal justice costs, the city officials feel this is a good investment of public funds.

Section V
Targeted Settings

Chapter 28
Youth Recreation Program Housing Sites
in Boulder, Colorado

Presenter:
Patti Cummings
    Coordinator, Youth Recreation Programs, Boulder Parks and
    Recreation Department

Background

City of Boulder, Colorado, Public Housing has 485 units, with 67%
of the households headed by a single female and 258 children between the ages of 5 and 18. Seventy-two percent of the residents are
Caucasian, and 21% Hispanic. Boulder County has an additional 53
units—85% headed by a single female, 55% of the residents Caucasian, 40% Hispanic. These families have 91 children between the
ages of 5 and 18.

In the fall of 1991 the Resident Representative Council of the
Housing Authority of the city of Boulder conducted a resident needs
assessment. The results identified youth issues as the area of greatest
concern among residents. Of those who responded, 55% considered
unsupervised children a major problem, while 30% cited drug use
among teens as an additional problem needing to be addressed. Subsequent interviews with residents indicated a perception among the
youth that they had nowhere to go and nothing to do. As a result,
petty theft, vandalism, physical conflicts, smoking, and substance
abuse were becoming increasingly prevalent.

These results prompted a collaborative effort between residents
and staff of the city housing authority, Boulder County housing authority, and Boulder parks and recreation to develop a program that
would provide positive recreation alternatives for youth. In 1992 a
Youth Sports grant was received through the U.S. Department of
Housing and Urban Development to create the Youth Recreation
Program (YRP); a second grant was received in 1994.

Since an abundance of recreation resources are in the Boulder
area, program designers decided to avoid "reinventing the wheel" by
creating unnecessary and unproductive competition with existing

programs. Thus, programming efforts focused on establishing partnerships between the two housing authorities and three different youth-serving organizations: Boulder Parks and Recreation, Boulder YMCA, and the Boulder Chapter of the Sierra Club/Inner City Outings program. Other partnerships and collaborations have subsequently been formed, providing public housing youth the opportunity to participate in a wide range of recreation pursuits.

Program

Goal

The overall goal of the Youth Recreation Program is to increase resistance to substance abuse and other negative behaviors among public housing authority youth living in the city and county. Program objectives are:

(1) to develop a youth recreation program based on partnership and collaboration with existing recreation resources throughout the community, thus maximizing the beneficial impact on the youth while minimizing duplication of effort;

(2) to offer programs that will address the various needs of the youth, including their physical, emotional, and interpersonal needs; and

(3) to expand the horizons and knowledge of the youth participants and their families.

Program Management and Supervision

The management and supervision roles of each of the major sponsoring agencies are as follows:

City of Boulder Housing Authority

(a) To receive grant funds and serve as grant administrator.

(b) To monitor program for adherence to funding conditions and restrictions. Liaison to grantor (HUD Regional Office, Rocky Mountain West).

(c) To provide outreach assistance to city public housing sites.

(d) To serve in an advisory capacity to YRP coordinator.

Boulder County Housing Authority
(a) To provide outreach assistance to county public housing sites.
(b) To serve in an advisory capacity to YRP coordinator.

Boulder Parks and Recreation
(a) To oversee program planning and implementation process.
(b) To house and supervise YRP coordinator position.
(c) To coordinate billing procedures for program expenses.

Program Delivery

Delivery of recreation programs and services is accomplished through collaborative efforts between the Youth Recreation Program and many other agencies throughout the county. Currently the YRP has eight program areas that involve partnerships and collaborations with various individuals and community agencies:

(a) *Park and Recreation Districts*—Three park and recreation districts are actively involved in offering youth programs: Boulder, Lafayette, and Louisville. Boulder and Louisville both give 50% discounts to YRP participants.
(b) *Boulder YMCA*—The YMCA also offers a 50% discount for youth sports leagues and aquatics programs.
(c) *Other Programs*—Many providers work with the YRP to offer more specialized programs, such as dance, theater, music instruction, and martial arts.
(d) *Summer Camps*—Scholarships to summer camp programs are offered through the YRP, and are often supplemented by the providers. Camp providers include park and recreation districts, YMCA camps, church camps, Salvation Army, Boy Scouts/Girl Scouts, and private camps.
(e) *Sierra Club/Inner City Outings*—Sierra Club volunteers plan and lead wilderness outings. Activities include cross-country skiing, camping, hiking, whitewater rafting, and canoeing. Outing equipment was purchased with YRP grant funds and is owned and maintained by the Sierra Club.
(f) *Mentor Program*—Partners in Prevention (PIP) is a program that was developed in collaboration with Boulder County Partners in order to provide adult mentors to the youth, most of

whom live with single-parent mothers. The goal of PIP is the formation of 20 long-term adult/youth partnerships. Boulder County Partners matches YRP-referred youth with adult volunteers, and provides on-going counseling, training, recreation, and follow-up services in support of the participants.

(g) *Transportation Program*—One of the drawbacks of utilizing existing programs is the need for transportation to and from activities. One approach utilized to address this issue is the provision of bus tokens to participants. Tokens are purchased from the Rural Transportation District which subsidizes 75% of the cost.

In addition, more than 30 youth have received bicycles donated by GO Boulder, the city's alternative transportation program. These bicycles were given away by random drawing, along with new helmets donated by LT Helmets. More recently, funds were received from the Boulder Police Department to purchase 20 brand-new mountain bikes from Morgul Bismark Bicycles which provided the bicycles at cost. Youth earned the bicycles by performing 20 hours of community service.

(h) *On-Site Activities Program*—This is a volunteer-led program at the housing sites. Volunteer teams of two per site, work with youth to plan, develop and implement on-site activities at regularly scheduled times. Examples include games, team sports, arts and crafts projects, and field trips.

Program Planning

Final program decisions are made during quarterly meetings of the Youth Recreation Program Advisory Council whose membership includes representatives from both city and county housing sites; staff representatives of both housing authorities and Boulder Parks and Recreation; the YRP coordinator and her supervisor. The Council meets to review progress of the grant program, consider programming options, resolve issues related to program delivery and implementation, and set future program direction.

Karate is a good example of a program that YRP offers. Youth who want to get into martial arts have several options. The YRP coordinator explained:

They can take karate through the YMCA, or they can
take it through parks and recreation. The kids that are
very serious about it can go to a private martial arts
studio. The studios have been very good about enrolling
the kids and actually giving them free clothing. The kids
move through the various levels of the program if they
pass the requisite tests. And each time they have to go
through the testing process, they come back to me, and I
arrange to cover the costs. The program is really good
for the kids who stick with it; they're really into it; and
it's really turned their lives around.

One issue that has arisen when planning programs is whether to
mainstream the housing authority youth when they participate in
community programs, or to encourage the residents to take pride in
who they are by having housing authority teams enter community
leagues. At present this is a moot issue since the housing authority
program does not have funding to staff the formation of its own
team. The YRP coordinator stated:

There are advantages to mainstreaming in having residents get to know other kids and other types of people,
and not feel like they're a special population. I had a
mom call me in tears and say she could not tell the coach
of a community team that her daughter was in public
housing. So I had to find a way to pay for that without
the coach knowing.

Liability

Another issue that arises is liability. Again, the program has formed
collaborative arrangements to obtain the necessary coverage. In
general, all of the activity providers must have their own insurance.
For programs like outdoor adventure activities, the trip leaders are
covered by the Sierra Club's insurance policies and the youth are
covered by a supplemental policy. While rock climbing is not included, for other activities, the youth are covered from the time that
they depart until the time they come back. The trip leaders are covered even if they transport the youth in their own vehicles.

Staffing

Currently only the recreation program coordinator is paid directly from the grant. The coordinator acts as a liaison between program providers, the two housing authorities, and public housing residents. The coordinator also monitors safety procedures, tracks program expenditures and participation numbers, performs process evaluations, recruits and trains volunteers, researches future funding sources, and documents the program's progress.

Although there is only one official staff person, there are several other key players within the program. The supervisor (a staff member of Boulder Parks and Recreation) of the coordinator provides general program oversight, as well as program support. The program administrator (a staff member of the Boulder Housing Authority) is responsible for fiscal management of the grant. Other support is received from secretarial, reception, and financial staff members. With the exception of the grant administrator, all staff support time is donated.

At present, training for volunteers is not organized; however, it needs to be. At present one of the volunteers has over 20 years experience and has been helping orient volunteers by providing information on how to deal with youth, and the types of activities and games they prefer. In the future the program staff hope to offer more comprehensive training on how to identify signs of abuse and neglect.

Outreach

Program outreach is accomplished in several ways. A YRP brochure, printed in both English and Spanish is distributed to all resident families and provides a general overview of program offerings. In addition, newsletters are mailed each quarter that describe upcoming events and activities. Meetings are held at least twice a year at each housing site to encourage youth to register for available programs and to distribute 20-punch passes to their local recreation centers. Individual flyers are developed for all special events and new programs.

Media coverage of the program has been fairly substantial. The program has been highlighted by a local radio station and was the subject of several articles in the local newspaper. In addition, a taped interview describing the program was frequently aired on the city's cable channel.

Financing and Resource Acquisition

The HUD grant requires that approximately 50% matching funds be
provided from other sources. The matching amounts listed in the
YRP budget represent in-kind contributions such as staff and volunteer time, subsidies for registration fees and transportation, workshop
facilities, and office space and supplies.
    The budget breakout is:

Grant Funds	$124,748.00
Matching Contributions	$109,641.50
Total Program Size	$234,389.50

Measurement of Program Outcomes

The YRP has been able to reach over 60% of public housing youth at
some level over its first two years. This includes participation in
regular recreational programs, as well as wilderness outings, and use
of the recreation centers. Participation numbers are tracked throughout the year and included in quarterly reports to HUD.
    Anecdotal evidence of program success is gathered from inter-
views and written surveys of program participants and their families.
Housing authority staff are also consulted to see if there are changes
in the number of reports of vandalism and other on-site behavioral
problems. Unsolicited comments from parents regarding the impact
of the program on their children have also been received. Examples
of such letters are shown in Exhibit 28A (page 260).
    Evidence gathered so far indicates that incidents of problem
behaviors on the sites are generally down. Parents comment that the
opportunity for their children to participate in recreational activities
provides a diversion from boredom, increases their self-esteem, and
makes it easier for them to reject negative peer pressure. Residents
are also more familiar with the recreation resources that are available
to them and how to access those resources. Finally, participation in
Sierra Club sponsored wilderness outings is helping youth and parents alike to develop an increasing appreciation for the outstanding
natural resources of the Boulder area.

Exhibit 28A

Parent Letters

I just want to let you know how much I appreciate your program that is helping my kids get into sports and activities that I could not have been able to afford on my own. I see a *big* difference in my younger son—he is being consistent in going to his practices and games and his self-esteem has been boosted 100%! He has stayed out of trouble for the whole time he was in basketball!! It is very encouraging, and now he wants to join baseball, football, and so on. It is great. It is so good for him, he will probably keep the experience with him all his life! Please don't stop helping kids like mine because it does do a world of good.

I would like to thank you for helping my kids get into sports when I would never have been able to afford it myself. I am a single mom and the cost for sports is way more than what I could afford. But I want to tell you how it has helped my son James so much! I would have felt so bad if he had wanted to join all these sports and I couldn't get him in. It has improved his attitude 100%. He makes friends easier, does better in school, and all around feels better about himself. I can tell!! It's wonderful—first you helped us with basketball (I think) then with baseball and weight lifting. Now he's into football and wants to continue year round with all the sports. I am so proud of him and he has gained respect from other boys his age. Your program is invaluable (at least for us), and I hope you continue because for at least one child you helped, it is worth it. Thank you so much!

Chapter 29
Public Housing Drug Elimination Program
in Columbus, Mississippi

Presenter:
Evelyn M. Morris
Human Resources Director, Columbus Housing Authority

Background

The city of Columbus (population over 91,000) is located in
Lowndes County, Mississippi. Two state universities and two community colleges are located within a 25-mile radius. Columbus is
located in what is known as the Golden Triangle Area which includes
West Point, Starkville, and Macon, Mississippi.

The Columbus Housing Authority administers four public housing complexes consisting of 480 units. As of April 1, 1994, the complexes had a 98% occupancy rate, housing 1,289 residents, of which
615 were adults and 674 were children under the age of 18. The
average family size is three; 69% of the families are headed by a
single parent; and the average family yearly income is $4,800.
Ninety-five percent of the residents are African American.

Because there was a critical drug problem in the area, the Columbus Housing Authority implemented a drug prevention program.
A summer program was also developed to deal with the large number
of children who were left unsupervised during the day. In many
cases, children went all day without food. Thus, the program incorporated provisions to provide breakfast, lunch, and dinner if necessary.

Program Description

Program Objectives

(1) to decrease the amount of drug distribution, arrests, and use
among Columbus Housing Authority's residents;

(2) to reach and teach children at an early age through special activities about the dangers of drugs and drug use;

(3) to teach children and parents about the dangers of drugs and signs of drug abuse;

(4) to encourage parents to take an active role in the development of their children;

(5) to help children resist peer pressure to use drugs through the provision of group activities;

(6) to involve local law enforcement agencies in facilitating drug prevention and education programs;

(7) to recruit, train, and utilize community volunteers to assist with drug prevention, educational, and recreational activities;

(8) to secure additional funding from other agencies to combat drugs in public housing;

(9) to actively involve a variety of community entities in the implementation of the drug prevention program; and

(10) to institutionalize the drug prevention program.

Program Content

Specific program efforts consisted of making physical improvements to the housing units and grounds, implementing a security patrol, and implementing drug prevention, and recreation programs for youths and adults. Community agencies were actively involved in building a strong comprehensive program using a combination of both individual and group facilitators throughout the program. A drug coordinator was hired to provide drug education through counseling and group meetings with reinforcement through group activities. Residents received information through drug education and prevention workshops, seminars, and group sessions.

Programs for adults dealt with the dangers of drugs and provided them with the knowledge necessary to teach their children. This was done through the utilization of videos, literature, and speakers. Group meetings were held that involved community leaders and other program facilitators. Additionally, training workshops were conducted by experts in the field of drug education on-site and throughout the state. The elderly were educated by local health department personnel, doctors, and nurses on how and when to take their medication and to the dangers of becoming addicted to prescription drugs.

Children participated in cultural and recreational activities and received lessons on drug awareness, fire and bicycle safety, dealing with peer pressure, and increasing self-esteem. The program utilized special features such as puppet shows, sing-a-longs, and skits to provide drug education. These presentations were made in small groups to both children and their parents. Older children and teenagers participated in drug education lessons through one-on-one counseling sessions and group sessions. Field trips to "Youth to Youth" conferences, mental health community services, and public libraries provided preteens and teenagers with the knowledge and training to become peer counselors for younger children.

Summer day camps were established at the community buildings at Columbus Housing Authority sites. Children were registered in the program by their parents. Camps were held for eight weeks during the summer months. On-site food was provided for program participants by the State Department of Education's Bureau of Child Nutrition. Volunteers from the community and parents assisted with the educational and daily recreational activities. The day camps included lessons on safety, arts and crafts, exercising, self-esteem, decision-making and daily living skills, and drug education. Columbus/Lowndes Recreation Authority provided recreational activities which included soccer, summer baseball, T-ball, basketball, karate, and cultural activities. Some of these programs were subsequently extended throughout the year.

Neighborhood security was important to the program's success. Security was provided from 6 p.m. to midnight Monday through Friday and from 5 p.m. to 2 a.m. on Saturday and Sunday. In addition, improved lighting was installed throughout the housing project.

The overall project also provided employment opportunities for eight residents who were trained to provide leadership in various segments of the program. This group, along with other parents who received training as part of the program, are now available to provide long-term community support for the development and leadership of other programs.

Program Facilitators

Over 40 different agencies and organizations assisted in the development and support of the program. These included:

- Friendly City Resident Council of the Columbus Housing Authority;
- Columbus/Lowndes Recreation Authority;
- Columbus Police Department;
- Columbus Fire Department;
- Mississippi Assistance and Child Abuse Prevention Center;
- Lowndes County Health Department;
- Mississippi State Cooperative Extension Service;
- Golden Security Services, Inc.;
- Mississippi Department of Education, Bureau of Child Nutrition;
- Lowndes County Chancery Clerk;
- Lowndes County Department of Human Services;
- Lowndes County Board of Supervisors;
- City of Columbus Mayor and Council Members;
- National Bank of Commerce;
- Carter's Funeral Home;
- Columbus Art Council, Inc.;
- Oliver Miller and Associates;
- AME Church Volunteers;
- Mississippi University for Women; and
- Hardee's Restaurant.

Program Funding

In 1991 the Columbus Housing Authority received a Public Housing Drug Elimination Grant from the U.S. Department of Housing and Urban Development (HUD) for $233,464. Additionally, $27,000 was received from the Mississippi State Department of Education's Bureau of Child Nutrition. A variety of both public and private sector entities contributed funding of $2,000, as well as in-kind assistance. In 1994 an additional $144,000 was received from HUD.

Program Outcomes

The Columbus Housing Authority Drug Prevention Program was highly successful because of the abundance of support received from the community. The partnerships established in implementing the program were the most significant factor in its success. These partnerships helped sustain the program during the summer of 1994 when renewal of Federal funding from HUD was delayed. This support showed the willingness of other agencies and the community at-large to take responsibility for the program. Other specific outcomes were:

- The amount of drug distribution significantly decreased at public housing sites, and the number of arrests of residents and nonresidents for drug-related criminal activities was also reduced.
- Over 1,140 children living in public housing were educated about the dangers of drug and drug use. More specifically, children were educated on how to resist peer pressure to use drugs.
- Over 1,750 children and parents received special training about the dangers of drugs and drug use. Additionally, this involved educating them on the ability to identify drug types.
- A substantial number of parents were empowered to take an active role in the social and emotional development of their children. This was done through a series of lectures, field trips, summer camps, picnics, and group meetings.
- The program was institutionalized through the use of volunteers and other community resources.
- The Columbus Housing Authority actively recruited over 75 volunteers to assist with the implementation of the drug prevention, educational, and recreational activities.
- The Columbus Housing Authority successfully engaged the services of the Columbus Police Department, Lowndes County Sheriffs Department, and Columbus/Lowndes Metro-Narcotics Division.
- The Friendly City Resident Council actively participated in the development, formation, and implementation of the drug prevention program.

In recognition of its success, the program received the 1993 Distinguished Managers Award given annually by the United States Department of Housing and Urban Development at the Mississippi Association of Housing and Redevelopment Officials Annual Conference for outstanding implementation of a drug prevention program.

Chapter 30
Beyond School: A Pilot Project
in Calgary, Alberta, Canada

Presenter:
Dave Breckon
    Leisure Services Division Manager, Calgary Parks and
    Recreation

Background

Canada Employment and Immigration reports that 100,000 young
Canadians (30% of the total) leave school before they graduate.
Comparing lifetime incomes of dropouts who have less than nine
years of education with those of high school graduates reveals that
male dropouts receive 36% less and females 76% less income than
their high school graduate counterparts. Each student who drops out
costs society over $50,000 more for Social Assistance and Unem-
ployment Insurance Benefits over a 40-year period than students who
complete high school. Communities with high dropout ratios have
seen high numbers of daytime crimes and youth assaults.

Research in Calgary showed that programs targeting high-school
students (grades 10–12) to encourage them to continue in school
were in place. However, no programs existed which targeted junior
high-school students. In the high crime areas of the city the average
rate of absenteeism in the junior high school was 47%. Of those
students, 53% carried weapons on a daily basis. Youth gang research
indicated that students who could see no future in academics joined
gangs.

The Beyond School project was designed to be a proactive program directed at ninth grade students who had a high probability of
dropping out of school. This preventive program strategy was designed to help educate students and establish a commitment to school
before they reach the legal dropout age.

Key Players

The program was initiated and developed by Calgary Parks and Recreation and Canada Employment and Immigration. Ernest Morrow Junior High played a key role in obtaining additional grant dollars, incorporating the program into part of the school curriculum and promoting the program to the students. Community resource partners included the Calgary Immigrant Society, the Calgary Mennonite Centre for Newcomers, the Calgary Board of Education, the city of Calgary Probation and Social Services Department, the Alberta Teacher's Association, and the Boys and Girls Clubs of Calgary. Program participants included the Canadian Mental Health Association, Calgary Police, Outdoor Education Resource, Forest Lawn High School, the Career Clinic, and Alberta Fish and Wildlife. In addition, 17 community businesses were involved as project practicum agencies which provide work placements for the students.

Program Description

Students experiencing failing grades, poor attendance, and discipline problems were selected by administrators at the pilot school. Two groups of 15 students each participated in the program. Content of the 12-week program was designed to complement existing programs by developing awareness and relevancy between school subjects and career choices. Students participated in a series of 12 interactive two-hour life skills workshops and a subsequent one-day or eight-hour job shadowing practicum placement. In addition, students attended a 24-hour overnight campout.

Workshops were conducted during school hours for class credits in lieu of the students' regular curriculum. Program content focused on the life-skill areas of career and job explorations, personal development and self-esteem, as well as recreation and leisure education. A program called Explorations which focused on leisure education, social development, and job exploration had previously been developed by the department. Much of the content for the Beyond School program was developed from the Explorations material.

There were some critical components to the logistics of the program that encouraged students to participate in the class, continue with the program, and improve attendance in the rest of their courses. Students were made to feel privileged for being selected to join the program. After being sold on the advantages of being in the program, they were given the choice of whether or not they wanted to enroll. They received benefits such as soda and chips during class, free T-shirts, and an all-expenses-paid camping trip to the mountains if they finished the program. The program was fun, and it also provided a work experience of their choice which could help them in getting a job in the future. The students were required to sign a contract which they took seriously and perceived as official. The contract made them pledge that they would neither bring weapons to school nor come under the influence of drugs or alcohol. They also had to consent to being dismissed from the program if they attended the rest of their classes less than 90% of the time.

Staffing

Staffing was an integral component of the pilot program. The guidance counsellor from the selected school encouraged the school board to hire a contract project coordinator/instructor. In addition, the counsellor encouraged the school to allow another recreation department staff member to be involved in selection and training of the project coordinator. This allowed ownership of the program by the school, but simultaneously ensured that the leisure and lifestyle components were within the candidates' portfolio.

Financing

The financing of the program was a partnership effort. Canada Employment and Immigration had a one-time fund set aside to target at-risk youth. Additional funds were secured through a grant available from the Alberta Teachers' Association. Cosponsored dollars and services in-kind were provided through the Calgary Parks and Recreation Department. The total cost of the program was estimated to be $5,500. Future programs with 15 students in each class were projected to cost $2,000 per program.

Measurement of Program Outcome

The pilot project included a fairly detailed evaluation component. Based on the selection criteria for student participants, 60 students were identified as high risk for dropping out of school. Thirty were randomly placed into the program, as the test group, and, as the control group, 30 continued in their regular school activities. One semester later the control group recorded a dropout rate of 37% (higher than the national average of 30%). The test group, however, recorded a dropout rate of only 17%; thus showing a 20% reduction in the dropout rate.

Qualitative research was also conducted throughout and at the conclusion of the program. Students indicated they would recommend the program to their friends, and staff felt the program was worthwhile and should be continued. Staff noted improvements in students' attitudes, self-esteem, initiative, interpersonal skills, extroversion, confidence, pride in accomplishment, grades, and attendance. Subsequently, it was concluded that the Beyond School program does have the potential to increase substantially the percentage of students who continue from junior high school to senior high school, thereby increasing the probability of participants graduating from senior high school. The stories of Tom and Mary in Exhibit 30A offer testimony to the program's effectiveness.

Evaluation comments did indicate some areas that could be improved when the program is offered again. Participants felt that the program should have been 24 rather than 12 weeks long to allow more time to go into more depth on some subjects and to permit the utilization of more guest speakers. Teachers suggested that the program might run over at least two terms; possibly the entire year.

The Final Evaluation Report of the Beyond School program noted:

> If we reach only one student each time the Beyond
> School program is presented, we have the potential to
> realize savings of $54,500 nationally. This accounts for
> the dollars alone, not even taking into consideration the
> positive intellectual and emotional impact the Beyond
> School program has on the students, allowing them to
> maximize their potential as productive members of society. For each additional student we reach, the numbers
> just multiply.

Exhibit 30A

Tom's Story: A Participant's Reaction

Tom was a participant in the Beyond School program and was considered a high risk for dropping out of school. Tom's dream was to become a professional hockey player, but his parents were unable to pay for his participation in hockey. At the time this was an unrealistic goal. Tests indicated that Tom had an interest in becoming a sports announcer. As a result, the program facilitator used the Shadow Program to place him with the announcer of the Calgary Flames hockey team of the NHL for an internship.

Tom attended three NHL games in the media box and even got to announce part of a game on radio during one of his visits. The professional announcer gave him a tour through the TV station and introduced him to many aspects of broadcasting. The announcer also arranged for a tour of the dressing room for Tom to meet all the Flame players. Tom was overwhelmed.

Tom has become completely refocused. He is taking communications in school with the goal of becoming a sports announcer.

Mary's Story: A Parent's Perspective

Mary was a single parent living below the poverty line with a daughter who was having difficulty in school and had very little interest in continuing. Her daughter was asked to become a participant in the pilot program and, as a result, she has developed a much improved attitude towards school and her future.

Mary felt that the Beyond School program changed her daughter's life at a critical time. Her belief in the program and its importance in helping other kids was so strong, she started a fund which raised $5,000 for the program to help support its continuance in future years.

Section VI
Innovative Focused Programs

Chapter 31
The Oakland Summer Performing Arts Day Camp (OPAC)
in Oakland, California

Presenters:
Cleve Williams
    Director, *and*
Jennifer Koney-Li
    Visual Arts Coordinator, Oakland Office of Parks and Recreation

A recent publication by the Black Community Crusade
for Children looked at seven urban areas in the south,
east, and west. The report came to two conclusions
regarding actions that need to be taken: (1) youth need
more involvement with caring adults, adults who can
create a mentoring and positive relationship; and (2)
means need to be found to revitalize neighborhoods.
Both of these issues speak to the necessity of empower-
ing people to do things and take increased responsibility
for themselves. (Cleve Williams)

Many recreation departments have reorganized their administrative
structures in order to better serve the needs of at-risk youth. In Oakland, California, creative partnerships aimed at serving the needs of
at-risk children and youth have been forged between the Office of
Parks and Recreation, the Oakland Unified School District, nonprofit
organizations, churches, colleges, private industries, and the community at large. The overall goal is to establish the "building blocks"
necessary for human development from preschool through the teenage years. These building blocks consist of after-school programs;
education, health, recreation, social, cultural, and athletic programs;
employment and job preparation programs; and individual, family,
group, and peer advisory counseling.

To avoid fragmentation and to facilitate the coordination of efforts, an Interagency Youth Advisory Committee made up of non-profit, voluntary sector, law enforcement, and public education organizations is in the process of being established. In addition, the city has created an Interdepartmental At-Risk Youth Advisory Committee made up of representatives of the police department, health and human services, library, museum, and city manager's office. The Office of Parks and Recreation (OPR) is playing a lead role in the organization and leadership of these committees (see Exhibit 31A).

The OPR organizes its youth-oriented activities under three areas: extended school care; prevention and intervention services; and teen centers. *Extended School Care Services* are aimed at avoiding problems created by lack of parental supervision after school and during school holiday periods. Programs are offered for elementary- and middle-school children at a variety of sites including schools, the Oakland Public Library, several nonprofit agencies, and at Housing Authority sites. *Prevention and Intervention Services* consist of late-night recreation programs, the implementation of a teen curfew, youth outreach services, and programs that attract teens to constructive alternatives to gang and delinquent activities. Brief descriptions of these programs are given in Exhibit 31B, page 278. Seven *Teen Centers* offer places for teens to gather and interact in a safe, teen-centered environment.

One of the outstanding programs organized by the OPR is the Oakland Summer Performing Arts Day Camp (OPAC).

OPAC Program Summary

The Oakland Summer Performing Arts Day Camp provides a pivotal opportunity for Oakland-area 6- to 18-year-old youth to learn how to express themselves through dance, music, drama, and the visual arts. The program was established on the premise that cultures and societies have always created art as a vehicle for expression of their values, hopes, and beliefs. Every aspect of a person's life is touched by art in one way or another.

The curriculum encourages participation in the four artistic disciplines (i.e., dance, visual arts, music, and drama) and is taught by professional artists/instructors. Additionally, a Masters Camp component provides an opportunity for intensive training with artists-in-residence in the areas of dance, music, and drama, while exploring career possibilities in the arts through guest artist lectures,

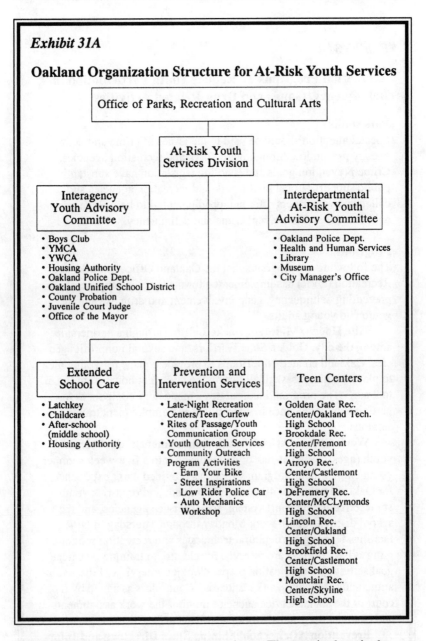

Exhibit 31A

Oakland Organization Structure for At-Risk Youth Services

Office of Parks, Recreation and Cultural Arts

At-Risk Youth Services Division

Interagency Youth Advisory Committee

• Boys Club
• YMCA
• YWCA
• Housing Authority
• Oakland Police Dept.
• Oakland Unified School District
• County Probation
• Juvenile Court Judge
• Office of the Mayor

Interdepartmental At-Risk Youth Advisory Committee

• Oakland Police Dept.
• Health and Human Services
• Library
• Museum
• City Manager's Office

Extended School Care

• Latchkey
• Childcare
• After-school (middle school)
• Housing Authority

Prevention and Intervention Services

• Late-Night Recreation Centers/Teen Curfew
• Rites of Passage/Youth Communication Group
• Youth Outreach Services
• Community Outreach Program Activities
  - Earn Your Bike
  - Street Inspirations
  - Low Rider Police Car
  - Auto Mechanics Workshop

Teen Centers

• Golden Gate Rec. Center/Oakland Tech. High School
• Brookdale Rec. Center/Fremont High School
• Arroyo Rec. Center/Castlemont High School
• DeFremery Rec. Center/McCLymonds High School
• Lincoln Rec. Center/Oakland High School
• Brookfield Rec. Center/Castlemont High School
• Montclair Rec. Center/Skyline High School

discussions, performances, and excursions. The curriculum is designed to expand appreciation of lesser known arts and cultures, thus fostering appreciation of differences between people and cultures. The program is conducted in a noncompetitive atmosphere without the judgment of "good, better, best." Schedules are coordinated with

Exhibit 31B

Recreation Programs To Reduce Youth Participation in Delinquency, Gangs and Drug-Related Activities

Philosophy

Special attention should be paid to the issues of crime and delinquency prevention through public park and recreation agencies. Crime prevention goals and enabling legislation have substantial public support. Local public park and recreation agencies and collaborative partners offer untapped potential to help abate criminal behavior and to prevent crime and delinquency.

Programs

The following are programs that the Oakland Office of Parks and Recreation (OPR) has implemented for the specific purpose of preventing delinquency, gang involvement and drug use among youth and young adults.

Nite Hoops (Midnight Basketball): Through a partnership among the city, Golden State Warriors, and several nonprofit agencies, Oakland created Nite Hoops to provide a place for young men to play organized basketball during the late night hours from 9 p.m. to 2 a.m. The program incorporates a mandatory component for participants' attendance in educational and employment training sessions.

Workreation (At-risk Youth Employment): OPR recruits youth (ages 14–18) at-risk of delinquency into a five-week summer youth employment program which has provided work experience for Oakland youth for 40 years. Delinquent and/or at-risk youth are referred by the court system, social service agencies, and the school district. Youth work Monday through Thursday in OPR facilities learning horticultural techniques and recreation programming skills. Fridays are reserved for classroom training on career goal setting, job application preparation, job interview skills, evaluation, and safety and work standards. Counselors assigned by the court or the social service agencies monitor the work assignments and evaluate the youths' work performance.

Prevention After-school/Shining Stars Directory and Information Referral: Oakland offers an after-school program including academic and arts-based programs at seven school sites for 600 middle-school and junior high-school youth; innovative youth

Exhibit 31B (Continued)

services are contracted through nonprofit agencies; the Shining Stars Directory of all local youth service agencies and programs is available for reference; and a computerized information retrieval system is operated by the Oakland Library.

Gang Prevention Outreach: Nontraditional outreach strategies are used by OPR to recruit youth who are at greatest risk of becoming involved in violence and crime to provide them with positive alternatives. The prevention and intervention services are aimed at attracting and recruiting youth (ages 13–21) who are "nonjoiners" of conventional recreation programs, but who exhibit behaviors that are early indicators of "dropping out," as positive, contributing members of society. Examples of the hard-to-reach youth are those engaged in delinquent activities, gangs, violent behaviors, drug use, alcohol use, truancy, vandalism, and dropping out of school.

Youth workers (intervention specialists) go to locations where these youth congregate, and talk with them on *their* terms and on *their* turf. They attempt to draw them into special nontraditional programs. Many of the programs are designed and developed by the youth themselves. The programs teach values and life skills including teamwork, individual responsibility, respect, leadership, conflict resolution, and self-esteem. The programs offer tutoring, remedial education, mentoring, counseling, cultural awareness, communication skills building, and recreation.

Youth Communications Group: This OPR program is specifically aimed at serving youth who are regarded as "troublemakers" and who congregate in groups in the community; get in trouble with police; and shun traditional recreation programs and facilities. Youth workers channel group activities toward increasing youth awareness of life options; motivating them to pursue positive alternatives in the community; getting them in activities where they see immediate and positive benefit to their own communities; and discussing the destructive outcomes of certain negative influences. The program also provides educational and tutorial assistance in reading, writing, math, and computer workshops in a nonthreatening environment; and provides weight-training and other recreational activities of interest to the youth.

Low Rider Car Club: The Low Rider Car Club program works with youth vulnerable to neighborhood gang involvement

Exhibit 31B (Continued)

and encourages them to participate in activities that "give something back to the community." The program educates and mobilizes at-risk youth to help eliminate neighborhood eyesores through graffiti removal and trash cleanup programs. The program's theme promotes safer neighborhoods and schools and increases the youths' connection with the community.

The Low Rider Car Club program builds bridges between troubled youth, police, and schools. Recently, the program symbolically adopted a neighborhood junior high school located in an area marred by heavy drug dealing, crime and gang activity. Members of the Low Rider Car Club, streetwise themselves, serve as mentors, teach troubled teens how to work on cars and find employment, and offer safe settings for recreational activities.

Earn Your Bike Program: The program offers unclaimed bicycles from the police department inventory and bicycles donated to needy youth (ages 9–18) who earn the bicycles by volunteering a minimum of 40 hours of community service (e.g., cleaning up city parks or erasing graffiti). Participating youth learn about the new Helmet Safety Law and how to repair bicycles and operate them safely. Youth also learn about self-esteem, discipline, taking pride in their community, and earning something valuable through hard work.

Broad Reach–Maritime Training: The training and job placement program gives Oakland at-risk urban youth/young adults (ages 18–25) a unique opportunity to experience the economic, entrepreneurial, and fun aspects of commercial fishing. Learning a trade, new skills (e.g., fishing, net hauling, boat handling, navigation, seamanship, boating safety, equipment nomenclature), discipline, and self-respect and being provided a new avenue for economic gain are the key prevention elements for these youth, many of whom deal drugs for a living.

Hard core, at-risk youth who are screened and referred by the Youth Communications Group program staff enter into the maritime training and on-the-job experience program in commercial fishing. Youth serve as crew members on a 26-foot Coast Guard–approved fishing boat guided by experienced fishermen. In the four-day training program, the youth crew members assist in operating the boat and participate in herring fishing in the San Francisco Bay area. The youth earn $10 per hour while in training and, after graduating, acquire the potential for earning $20 to $25 per hour.

Exhibit 31B (Continued)

This program offers assistance with job placement. The California Department of Fish and Game has agreed to help the Maritime Training Program in placing all graduates. OPR staff have conducted and videotaped job interviews with the youth, disseminated the interview tapes to potential employers, and secured job offers for some of the youth.

---

other community arts programs to avoid overlap and to encourage use of existing community art resources.

In 1991 initial funding and support for a pilot effort was provided by the mayor's office with some private monies used to supplement these city funds. After demonstrating success, the city council was approached for funding for future years. This pattern of action for initiating programs has been used widely in Oakland.

In 1992 the program operated at two sites and served 160 participants. By 1994 it had grown to include 700 participants ages 6–16 (320 for 2 sessions of 2 weeks each), together with 60 youth ages 12–18 in a Masters Camp.

The day camp operates from 9:30 a.m. to 3:30 p.m., with extended care available from 8 a.m. to 9:30 a.m. and after camp ends until 5:30 p.m. The day camp is held at a centrally located school site, accessible by public transportation. Fees are low to reflect the financial status of the participants: $20 per two-week session; $45 per one-week Masters Camp; $25 per week for extended care. In 1994 scholarships totaling $2,875 were awarded.

Objectives of the program are:

(1) to provide an affordable, accessible, high-quality creative arts experiences for Oakland-area children in a safe and nurturing environment in order to prevent crime and delinquency;

(2) to provide low-cost, safe, alternative childcare;

(3) to expose low-income inner city youth to the arts;

(4) to foster and nurture appreciation for all forms of creative expression, and, by doing so, to emphasize the importance of each child's vision and voice and improve his or her self-esteem;

(5) to teach and to practice good audience listening skills in order to develop an art audience;

(6) to introduce possible career paths in the arts; and

(7) to celebrate the diverse community that is Oakland through cultural arts expression.

Key Players

OPAC is planned in partnership with the Oakland Public School District, the mayor's office, prominent members of the local arts community (e.g. Michael Morgan, Director of the Oakland Symphony), Laney Community College, and the Cultural Arts Division of the OPR. Additional partners who help with implementation include the Federal Lunch Program, Summer Youth Employment Training Program (SYETP), Studio One Teen Club teaching assistants, community members, and parent volunteers.

Resource Assessment

Implementing OPAC required an assessment of currently existing programs, organizations, and material resources that could augment and benefit the program. To be successful it was necessary to be innovative and build on successes. Some of the resources used to foster development of the program have included:

- *Mayor's Office:* catalyst; spearheaded fundraising; increased visibility.
- *Parks and Recreation Department:* administrative coordination; determined structure; implemented program.
- *School District:* facilities; maintenance staff; loaned musical instruments.
- *Local Artists and Art Organizations:* curriculum recommendations; artist/teaching staff; guest artists; distributed brochures.
- *Local College:* curriculum recommendations; supported program.
- *Federal Government:* free lunch program.
- *SYETP:* provided recreation staff.
- *Teen Clubs:* provided teaching assistants; volunteers
- *Parent/Community Volunteers:* supervised lunch time and recreation program.

- *Local Businesses:* made in-kind donations; distributed programs.
- *Existing Art Education Programs:* used as augmentation, not competition. Program dates were planned with them in mind so as to build upon each other's efforts (i.e., Laney Orchestra Camp).

Collaborative Planning

Planning in partnership with the mayor's office, the city manager, council members, and other city departments proved to be fruitful, but required careful attention to communication channels and follow through. Being equally accountable for the outcome of the project, all players had to be equally invested and able to state their objectives and concerns from the start of the project. Some potential problems of collaboration have been: communication delays; lack of clear policy direction (mayor versus city council; council member turf issues); and coordination with the city manager's office (city manager versus mayor).

Additionally, it was important to get an early buy-in from the site organization (i.e., school district) where the program was held. Representatives needed to be involved in the planning process from the start. Facility-use decisions needed to be communicated to the site employees (e.g., principal, secretary, custodial staff) and agreements developed with the facility supervisor (i.e., custodian) stating when the site would be open and locked each day and the level of cleanliness required.

Staffing

The quality and reputation of a performing arts day camp is directly dependent upon employing an expert and experienced teaching staff who are not only well-established in their artistic discipline but who also have an interest and commitment to teaching their craft to children. Since the OPAC program is short and intense, experienced teachers are hired so that preparatory training is kept to a minimum. References are checked and interviews are carefully conducted. As part of this process, evaluation of the leaders' ability to work well with children, encourage creative growth, and patience and spirit required to pass on their craft is also necessary. Finally, instructors must be able to work well within a bureaucracy. Since much paper-work and structure is necessary to conduct such a complex program, cooperative and enthusiastic personalities are a necessity. Interviews also stress the need for staff to be dependable and fully responsible.

The program needs coordinators, besides a director, to take responsibility for such specific areas as: registration, lunch time, supplies and equipment, teaching assistants and volunteers, extended care, and final performances. The use of coordinators helps diminish the daunting magnitude of administering the project.

Staff Training and Orientation

Once instructors and staff have been hired and contracted, orientation meetings are held both to introduce the program organization to the staff, and for staff members to meet each other. Staff responsibilities are concisely laid out. A staff handbook has been developed. During training sessions plenty of time for questions is allowed. Agenda items include:

    I. Introductions of administration staff and the vision.
    II. Introductions of teaching staff.
    III. Site specifics and logistics.
    IV. Program description, daily schedule and staff responsibilities.
    V. Supply and equipment needs.
    VI. Final performance and art exhibit arrangements.
    VII. Getting paid/necessary paperwork.
    VIII. Questions.

Communication

With a large staff and a complex program involving many different key players, establishing effective communication channels is critical. Mechanisms used to facilitate good communication include:

- providing on-site staff folders for class registration lists and last-minute updates;
- placing a communication board near the staff folders for announcements;
- scheduling mid-program staff meetings and teacher appreciation gatherings;

- consulting expert teaching staff during the planning process; giving them evaluations to complete at the conclusion of the program; and recognizing their contributions; and
- sending meeting minutes and agendas to affected key players; keeping records.

Marketing

A descriptive, easy-to-comprehend program brochure is the primary promotion tool. The challenge with the program brochure is to describe an extensive program, while making the brochure visually appealing as well. Use of a logo and color printing helps. Review by potential recipients is also critical. Some additional considerations are:

- charging low or no registration fees;
- providing information on scholarships and application procedures;
- allowing students to select their classes with alternate choices;
- carefully tracking and honoring class limits; and
- inquiring about musical instrument needs on the registration form.

To date, marketing strategies have included mass mailings, distribution through the schools, classroom recruitment talks, fairs, recreation and art centers, local businesses, community cable channel, and radio community service spots. Efforts are made to reach those children who are hard to reach. A poster, designed by a camp class, is also used to promote the program.

Implementation

OPAC was implemented after careful research, planning, staffing, advertising, and registration. Organizing the students into age groups and classes was achieved through color-coded name tags imprinted with class numbers and names. A registration database was critical for tracking students and developing class rosters. Children were assigned to subgroups by age and artistic discipline. Having a large, wall-sized chart with class names, numbers, teachers, locations, and times provided a valuable central information source.

Ensuring the safety of every student is the primary responsibility of all staff at all times. Daily attendance, a simple check-in/check-out system for extended care, hall monitors, and plenty of lunchroom and recreation staff have combined to ensure that students are accompanied at all times.

Students and staff are reminded of the importance of daily clean-up. Nurturing a respect for the environment and site has helped to curb possible messes.

Methods currently used to measure program outcomes include: evaluation forms (parent/staff/class); the number of returning students; review of final performances and exhibitions (participation level); parent and student comments; and noting the level of excitement.

Budget and Financial Considerations

For 1994 the OPAC program budget was approximately $80,000. The following major expenses were incurred:

Instructor Salaries	$46,970
Administrative Support	6,350
Program Director	3,500
Security	1,875
Custodial	2,200
Extended Care and Lunch Time Recreation	11,550
Brochures and Printing	800
Supplies and Rentals	3,500
Scholarships	2,875

Chapter 32
Northern Fly-In Sports Camps
in Winnepeg, Manitoba, Canada

Presenter:
Neil Winther
  President, Northern Fly-In Sports Camps Inc., Winnipeg,
  Manitoba, Canada

Background

Approximately 80,000 of the one million people living in the central
Canadian Province of Manitoba are of Native ancestry. Thirty thousand of these Native people live in remote fly-in communities. Over
50% of these isolated Native people are under the age of 18 years.
Young Native men and women are highly overrepresented in the
criminal justice system. For example, while only 8% of Manitoba's
population is made up of native people, they account for 60% of the
total inmate population in Manitoba provincial jails. The physical
isolation and cultural differences have resulted in substantial differences between Native and non-Native people in Manitoba. The
problems were well-stated by Chief Dennis Shorting of the Little
Saskatchewan First Nation during his appearance before the
Manitoba Aboriginal Justice Inquiry:

> We find ourselves in the fertile breeding ground of
> crime: high unemployment, lack of educational opportu-
> nities, substandard housing, inadequate healthcare; tradi-
> tional, hunting, fishing and trapping rights being vio-
> lated; a shortage of recreation facilities; and being sub-
> ject to the law which many times we don't understand—
> laws which do not fit our culture, values and traditions.

Sports and Recreation Bridge the Gap Between Native and Non-Native Cultures

One organization which has bridged the gap between these two cultures and addressed the need for programs and training emphasizing

the value of physical activity is Northern Fly-In Sports Camps Inc. (NFISC). Beginning with a pilot project in 1986 involving two communities, NFISC has delivered 63 summer sports and recreation programs in 26 different remote communities in Manitoba, Ontario, and the Northwest Territories.

NFISC is a Canadian nonprofit corporation which strives to enhance the quality of life for Native children and youth living in remote communities through the implementation of summer sports and recreation programs and youth leadership training. The Sports Camps were founded in 1986 by a volunteer Board of Directors who represent the fields of physical education, recreation, law, crime prevention, education, Native studies, medicine, and business. Each member of the Board had either lived in a remote Native community, worked extensively with Native people, or is Native.

Program

After reviewing a number of program approaches, a sport model was developed based on the "humanistic physical education" approach first conceptualized by Hellison (1973), a physical education professor at the University of Chicago. Hellison's model capitalizes on the highly interactive and emotional character of "life in the gymnasium and on the playing field," using sport and physical activity as a medium to teach self-discipline and social responsibility. The program also addresses the six generally accepted theories of delinquency proposed by Cohen in 1959 (see Exhibit 32A).

Youth in remote settlements liked the idea of university students coming to their communities for the summer to teach them new skills, and parents liked the idea of youth being occupied with meaningful activities. The Royal Canadian Mounted Police (RCMP) saw the crime reduction benefits of the NFISC programs and began providing free air transportation for instructional staff. RCMP personnel joined the Board of Directors and became volunteer instructors. Soon other government agencies recognized that NFISC could offer a unique community-based training opportunity for Native youth and began supporting training initiatives.

The present summer programs include sports, aquatics, creative arts, and outdoor recreation. The *sports component* includes individual sports such as golf, bowling, badminton, and juggling; team competitive sports such as lacrosse, field hockey, and soccer; and

Exhibit 32A

Goals of NFISC Related to Theories of Delinquency

Reason for Delinquency	Goal of NFISC
Exposure to delinquent behavior models as social norms	Expose youth to positive role models (leaders) and positive peer pressure experiences.
Weak social controls	Provide programs and group determined standards for behavior. Individuals involved in a recreation program will have social controls placed on them by coaches and peers.
Rebellion against perceived unrealistic goals	Provide the opportunity for achievement of realistic objectives and increased activities which will reduce stress and frustration.
Boredom	Provide a variety of stimulating activities, thus offering something for everyone.
Need to assert masculinity	Provide opportunities for "power-brokers" and youth to work and play together on the same side. Provide opportunities for positive and constructive uses of power, strength, and aggression.
Labeling	Reinforce to youth that they are capable. Athletes enjoy status and with this staus comes the expectation to conform.

cooperative games such as tag, relays and obstacle courses. The *outdoor recreation program* teaches skills in the area of ecology, plant study, weather, orienteering, crafts, outdoor cooking, and astronomy. The *aquatics phase* focuses on boat safety, water safety, swimming, diving, water polo, synchronized swimming and aquatic fitness. The *creative arts section* emphasizes Native culture through local games, activities, crafts, art, beadwork, and moccasin making as well as singing, painting, and storytelling.

When possible, NFISC organizes a preplanning trip where meetings are held with the chief or mayor, school principal, RCMP members, and interested community members. The purpose of this meeting is to determine community needs and interests.

NFISC is available to First Nation and Metis communities who demonstrate community interest and support. In cooperation with NFISC, the host community advertises the program through various such as local television or word of mouth. The community also provides accommodation for the NFISC team, ensures equipment and facilities are available for the program's use and provides transportation where needed within the community.

Staffing and Funding

One full-time salaried employee, whose work is supplemented on occasion by outside expertise, is employed year round. During the summer months the staff expands to 14 to 20 people (depending on funding) who live in their assigned communities, coordinating and leading various activities. These instructors represent a wide cross-section of university faculties including physical education and recreation studies, native studies, fine arts, education, and music.

A variety of delivery models have been explored through the years. However, the most successful model has been a two-phase program involving instructor training and program delivery. The first component of this model is the instructor training session where ten to 12 local youth receive a one-week workshop outlining basic administrative and program planning considerations for the operation of children's recreation programs. This training session also offers instruction in specific sports and recreation skills and suitable instructional techniques for the presentation of these skills to children and youth.

The second phase of the program commences in week two when a team of NFISC instructors comes to the host community and joins forces with the ten to 12 youth who were trained in the first week. Working together with volunteer RCMP, nursing, and North West Company personnel, the multiactivity program is delivered to the children in the community. Although NFISC's on-site staff spend only four weeks in each community, the program continues under the leadership of the local youth, who are hired by the community for the summer.

NFISC staff usually live in homes that teachers within the local communities have vacated during their summer holidays. Food for the summer staff is donated by the North West Company, Inc. or purchased by NFISC. The instructional staff are given access to community facilities and equipment.

Over 50 program sponsors have donated $1 million in financial resources and $1.5 million in products and services over the last seven years. The largest financial contribution was made by the Manitoba Lotteries Foundation through the Manitoba Community Services Council, Inc. Host communities and the RCMP have made the most significant contributions in terms of products and services. Other support has come from the Government of Manitoba Departments of Culture, Heritage and Citizenship, Justice and Northern Affairs, Health and Welfare Canada, Employment and Immigration Canada, Manitoba Family Services, the Variety Club, Norman Regional Sport Association, Eastman Sports Development Council, and The North West Company Inc. The physical education and recreation studies program at the University of Manitoba has provided office space and administrative resources since the program was initiated in 1986.

Evidence of Program Outcomes

As a result of the NFISC programs, thousands of children and youth have benefitted from quality summer leisure-time programs. The activities provide a much needed break during the long days of summer and help to alleviate the boredom that is often associated with life in remote communities. An analysis of crime trends conducted in 1987 indicated that total crime for all remote communities north of the 53rd parallel showed an increase of 11%, while the four communities visited by NFISC enjoyed a dramatic 17% decrease. During the summer of 1989, the duration of the program was extended to two months. This program was delivered to eight communities and resulted in crime reductions of 20% to 78% during the period the program was in operation, when compared to years when the program was unavailable. The following table illustrates these dramatic crime reductions:

Crime Reduction Impact
of Northern Fly-In Sports Camps—1989

Community	Total Pop.	Pop. 0–19 Years	% Reduction in Crime
St. Theresa Point	1,724	1,005	- 20
Brochet	646	360	- 56
Oxford House	1,260	550	- 67
Pukatawagan	1,359	710	- 41
Gods River	314	154	- 78
Moose Lake	962	423	- 43
Gods Lake Narrows	112	52	- 41
Cross Lake	2,938	1,755	- 47
Average			- 49

A study conducted in 1993 assessed the effects of Northern Fly-In Sports Camps on the daily life experiences of young offenders and potential offenders who participated in the programs. Using beepers that enabled the sampling of mood states and activities at specific times of the day, the study compared the levels of satisfaction, challenge, and the youths' subjective states of mood in their daily life experiences during the camp and when the camp was not present in the community. The subjects were also asked about their feelings towards and contact with the Royal Canadian Mounted Police who participated as instructors in the program. Statistically significant results indicated that the program had a positive effect on participants' levels of happiness, enjoyment, interest, perceptions of leisure, and perceptions of the RCMP. Also, for some of the participants the camps relieved tension and anxiety regarding the well-being of friends. The RCMP were viewed both as more helpful, and more approachable when the camp was in operation.

There are also many benefits of the NFISC program both in terms of the community development, and the individual growth and development of participants. Some of these potential benefits include fun for the participants, the provision of new recreation programs, community development, youth training and employment, social development, skill acquisition, and reductions in crime rates in host communities.

Future Plans

The long-term goal of the NFISC Board of Directors was to transfer the Corporation's assets to an Aboriginal agency as soon as the program and training model were fully developed. NFISC is in the process of negotiating this transfer with the assistance of the Assembly of Manitoba Chiefs (see Exhibit 32B).

Exhibit 32B

The Assembly of Manitoba Chiefs fully supports the objectives and activities of the Northern Fly-In Sports Camps program. The obvious benefits of this program to First Nation communities and their youth are significant. More particularly, the crime-rate decrease in those participating communities justifies the program and the need for a more aggressive campaign to be undertaken is critical to ensure for its continued development. *Grand Chief Phil Fontaine, Assembly of Manitoba Chiefs, Winnipeg, November 1991.*

References

Cohen, A. K. (1959). The study of social disorganization and deviant behavior. In R. K. Merton, L. Brown, & L. S. Cottrell (Eds.), *Sociology today: Problems and prospects.* New York, NY: Basic Books.

Hellison, D. R. (1973). *Humanistic physical education.* Englewood Cliffs, N.J.: Prentice Hall.

Chapter 33
Outdoor Adventures: A Natural High
in Tacoma, Washington

Presenters:
Leanna Waite
    Program Coordinator, *and*
Michael Bradley
    Recreation Supervisor, Metropolitan Park District of Tacoma

Program Description

Youth Outdoor Adventures, an outdoor education and recreation
program targeted at inner-city, at-risk youth, was developed in 1992
with funding from the National Park Service (Urban Parks and Recreation Recovery Act). Other resources have been supplied by the
Metropolitan Park District of Tacoma and by a state of Washington
Criminal Justice grant.

Goal

The goal of the program is to supplement other park district and
youth service agency programs by:

(1) providing positive recreational activities for youth in the out-
    doors;
(2) providing quality and safe activities;
(3) providing outdoor education, safety, and environmental aware-
    ness; and
(4) introducing youth to recreation as a career.

Approximately 1,000 youth participate annually through various
avenues. Many enter through the park district's youth outreach
programs at several neighborhood community centers. Participants
also come from youth service agencies, including the Pierce County
Juvenile Court/Remann Hall, Eastside Boys and Girls Club, Faith
Group Homes, and Children's Industrial Home/Jessie Dyslin Boys

Ranch. Other youth participate through home school associations, after-school programs at Tacoma Public Schools, and other agencies.

Program Content

Youth Outdoor Adventures consists of outdoor educational skill workshops and outdoor adventure trips. *Skill workshops* occur weekly at five program sites. These 30-minute workshops introduce youth to outdoor environments, where they learn a wide range of basic outdoor skills, including such things as tent setup, hypothermia prevention, and water safety. Younger participants also learn camp songs and games while older youth focus on team-building.

Adventure trips, like the skill workshops, occur on a year-round basis. Following the public school calendar, activities range from a two-hour canoe outing at local Wapato Park after school to a full-day mountain bike ride on a nonschool day. Extended overnight trips lasting from two to six days are scheduled on weekends, nonschool days, winter and spring breaks, and during the summer vacation. All camping equipment, food, and transportation are provided, and trips are staffed by Youth Outdoor Adventures.

A unique component of this program is *Adventure Leadership Training*. This is an extension of the skill workshops and adventure trips and is targeted at youth 12–18 years old. Participants are selected based on their level of involvement in general workshops and adventure activities, interest in developing leadership skills, and a belief that they will benefit by participating in an outdoor leadership experience. Five-week classes offer participants the opportunity to become part of a team of six to ten youth. They participate in team-building games and activities, instruct and teach one another a variety of advanced outdoor skills, and help plan an adventure trip which they subsequently undertake. Following the conclusion of each session, participants instruct and lead (under staff supervision) an outing in which they teach a group of adults or other youth. For example, in a winter session, they may teach cross-country skiing skills to a group of adults and lead them on a day's outing. The program's specific objectives for 1995 were to offer 250 instructional trips and three Adventure Leadership Training Sessions. In total, the program sought to serve 3,000 participants and increase the number of Asian and female participants. Efforts were also made to develop an intergenerational program for seniors and youth.

Costs

Most programs cost $1 to participate for a single activity and $8 to $12 for a camping trip. If individuals do not have the funds, they can still participate. Those who cannot pay, however, are expected to do volunteer work to help meet some of the needs of the program. Volunteer work includes helping change bike tires, patching tents, cleaning coolers, or working around the community center.

Program Outcomes

The success of Youth Outdoor Adventures is reflected in the relationships which staff and participants share and its influence in the lives of participants. Although they come from diverse ethnic and economic backgrounds, a common thread ties participants together. Each faces challenges day after day. Poverty, drugs, alcohol, and gangs are a part of life for them. These youth survive on a daily basis. Their stories are told in Exhibits 33A, 33B (page 298), and 33C (page 299). For the youth described in the Exhibits and many others, Youth Outdoor Adventures is an experience that fosters pride, self-esteem, and success, and teaches hands-on skills. Participants develop respect for themselves, others, and the environment, often experiencing success for the first time.

Exhibit 33A

Sheilaigh is a 17-year-old single mother of two children. They live in a group home for unwed mothers. She has been in several foster homes, experienced physical and sexual abuse, and lived in poverty. But Sheilaigh and her small family enjoyed an overnight camping trip with Youth Outdoor Adventures. She swam in the calm Yakima River, went horseback riding on wooded trails, and canoed in a small lake. She is looking forward to participating in more outdoor activities with her children.

Exhibit 33B

Cory and his brothers and sisters had been in numerous foster homes, finally being reunited in one home two years ago. Their father had been killed years earlier in a drug-related incident and their mother is in a rehabilitation facility. Cory, 12, and his eldest sister, 17, walked from their new foster home to buy ice cream for his birthday. On the way, Cory's sister stopped to talk with some friends. Within that group were some known gang members. Before Cory and his sister left the group, a drive-by shooting took place. Cory's sister lay dying at his feet. That day, he lost the only mother he had ever known.

Cory showed up on a camping trip to Wenatchee State Park. He participated in river rafting, mountain biking, and camping—all new activities for him. He struggled with some of the expectations and the rules. But after a second trip, where Cory was given a chance to redeem his earlier behavior, he began to open up. He obviously had difficulty with male authority figures. He responded well, often going out of his way, to assist female staff. He was more comfortable in one-on-one activities with staff than in group activities with other youth. All of his actions pointed to a way of thinking that was not conducive to the group environment. Cory was uncomfortable—out of his element.

But that very discomfort allowed him to experience positive change in his life. He knew he was with people who cared about him. He was encouraged and recognized for the positive things he did. And he experienced thrills that will stay with him throughout his life. The smile on his face as he took a corner on a single-track bike trail was all it took to convince the staff that Cory had truly benefited from Youth Outdoor Adventures.

Exhibit 33C

Ming is a 16-year-old former gang member. He has been involved in drive-by shootings, has sold drugs to help put food on his family's table, and has seen his friends killed. He has stolen property, and he has run the streets.

River rafting, mountain biking, hiking, and lake swimming were "firsts" for Ming. Sleeping in a tent, cooking on a campstove, and sitting around a campfire roasting marshmallows were also "firsts" for Ming. His language was foul, and he wore his pants so that they sagged. He has been on numerous camping and day trips. He also has worked as an assistant on day trips with younger participants. Ming became a part of Adventure Leadership Training in the summer of 1994. Working with seven other teens, Ming became an important part of a team, showing his leadership potential when he discussed drug and gang issues with other participants. Ming was the most outstanding part of the team that session, not because of what he had done, but because of who he had become. He still struggles with the temptation, the urge, the draw to go back to the gangs. But he will not. And Ming's experience with Youth Outdoor Adventures allowed him to see something different in life. The outdoor bug has bitten Ming as well. What once was an unfamiliar environment is now comfortable for him. Ming is a likely candidate to advance through Youth Outdoor Adventures as a participant and to become a staff member.

Chapter 34
National Park Service Programs
in Washington, District of Columbia

Presenter:
Robert G. Stanton
  Regional Director, National Capital Region, National Park Service, U.S. Department of the Interior

Background

National Capital Region (NCR) parkland amounts to about 7,000 acres within the District of Columbia and almost 60,000 acres in Maryland, Virginia, and West Virginia. NCR has some 447 miles of parkways and primary roads, more than 150 statues, monuments and memorials, and serves more than 38 million visitors annually. Some 717 miles of trails and bike paths wind through NCR parks.

Park sites in Washington include the National Mall, the White House, Washington Monument, Lincoln Memorial, Thomas Jefferson Memorial, Vietnam Veterans Memorial, Mary McLeod Bethune Memorial, Frederick Douglass National Historic Site, Rock Creek Park (the country's largest and first urban park), Anacostia Park, George Washington Memorial Parkway, and the C&O Canal National Historical Park.

NCR sponsors and conducts numerous national celebrations—the Cherry Blossom Festival, Independence Day, and Presidential anniversary wreath-layings at the Thomas Jefferson and Lincoln Memorials and the Washington Monument. Birthday wreath-laying ceremonies are also held at the Mary McLeod Bethune Memorial, Frederick Douglass National Historic Site, and the Lincoln Memorial in honor of Dr. Martin Luther King, Jr. NCR also sponsors the National Christmas Pageant of Peace and other events of national and international importance.

NCR provides various visitor services through its concession operations. These include interpretive sightseeing, golf courses, transportation, tennis courts, several marinas, ice-skating rinks, horseback riding facilities, and food services. Fifteen concessions are operated at 40 separate locations.

Programs for At-risk Youth

The NCR also operates programs that serve the needs of at-risk youth. Program objectives include:

(1) developing and administering outdoor educational, recreational and cultural programs for Washington youth;

(2) forging partnerships with the District of Columbia Department of Recreation and Parks, school system, community organizations, private sector, youth organizations and others in order to achieve a sustained level of support and cooperation;

(3) offering expanded and, in some instances, new opportunities for youth to be gainfully employed in National Park Service areas and programs; and

(4) providing opportunities for participants to gain an increased awareness of the cultural diversity of outstanding citizens who contributed to the growth of the nation, and who are commemorated in units of the National Park system.

This final objective focuses on the benefits of parks to the participant's intergroup education. These benefits include:

(a) helping members of a group who are commemorated (e.g., Native American, Hispanic, Asian American, African American) gain a greater awareness and appreciation of their own heritage and take pride in knowing that others can share in their contributions or achievements;

(b) helping members of groups enhance their appreciation of each other's contributions;

(c) helping participants gain a sense of belonging, self-recognition and appreciation of the history and future of the United States; and

(d) using cultural and historic parks to serve as a bridge from personal lifeways to the group's cultural heritage.

Staff have been charged with the responsibility to develop exciting and innovative opportunities for youth to experience park resources and programs. Each manager within his or her authority and area of responsibility is required to develop programs with input from youth meetings, school teachers and administrators, and other community leaders. Managers are encouraged to use Congressionally approved appropriation authority to transport youth to nearby parks for educational and recreational programs.

In 1975 Congress authorized the use of funds to transport youth into the national parks as a part of their educational and recreational experience. NCR has been a leader in this effort with approximately 1,000 youngsters transported in 1994 from the city to parks.

Program Content

Parks as Classrooms: Activity-driven, curriculum-based education programs are offered to school groups in park settings. All parks take part in this program, but of particular note is the Model Elementary Science Outdoor Classroom Program at Fort Dupont, National Capital Parks—East. The program is part of a national effort to encourage active participation and utilization of national parks in furthering educational objectives.

Summer Camp: The Community Outreach and Special Park Initiatives (COSPI) Summer Camp program provides overnight camping experiences to six different community-based organizations located in Washington. Over 380 youths are served. Prince William Forest Park and Catoctin Mountain Parks were the two sites utilized for this program.

Sportsmobile: The COSPI Sportsmobile program provides activities for youth at National Park Service facilities. Concentrating on seven parks in the region, the Sportsmobile has provided additional resources to the parks while introducing urban youth to the enjoyment of open space. To date, the Sportsmobile has been utilized by 20 community-based organizations and served over 1,100 youth, ages 5–13. These organizations were able to enhance their summer day camp programs by utilizing the Sportsmobile.

Saturday Field Trips: The COSPI Field Trip program provides leisure activity to seven different community-based organizations located in the District of Columbia and one located in Montgomery County, Maryland. Over 250 youths are served. The C&O Canal and Great Falls Parks were the two sites utilized for this program. In addition to transportation, COSPI coordinates ranger-led programs at each park. Youth from Washington's Summer Youth Employment Program (SYEP) are used to maintain communications between the COSPI office and community-based organizations who participate in camping and Saturday field trip activities.

United States Park Police Explorer Post 1791: The Explorer Post, an affiliate of the Boy Scouts of America, has proven to be an asset to the police by providing assistance with crowd and traffic control at many special events, parades and other on-call assignments. Law enforcement explorers (young male and female adults between the age of 14 and 21) are provided with an opportunity to gain experience in the law enforcement profession. Ninety-seven percent are African-American students from the District of Columbia. Fifteen individuals participate in the year-round program.

Youth Conservation Corps (YCC): The Youth Conservation Corps is an eight-week summer park employment program for young participants (male and female) ages 15 through 18. In 1994 personnel from NCP—East, Central, Rock Creek, and Greenbelt Parks worked with individuals primarily from the District of Columbia metropolitan area. Ninety-eight percent were African American.

District of Columbia Summer Youth Employment Program (DCSYEP): The DCSYEP provides summer employment and training for youth within the District of Columbia between the ages of 14 and 21. For more than 15 years, NCR has worked with the District of Columbia in a partnership agreement that makes summer jobs available for District of Columbia youth. Funds for staff salaries are provided by NCR, along with training and orientation and day-to-day supervision. Other incidentals that are provided include transportation, safety work equipment, supplies and materials. In 1994 this program served 85 students for the six-week program.

District of Columbia Service Corps: NCR became a partner with the District of Columbia Service Corps in order to provide young people between the ages of 17 and 23 opportunities to work with the area's elementary and secondary schools and the campuses of the District's universities and colleges.

Consortium of Churches: NCR provides assistance to the Community Church Association (a consortium of churches in District of Columbia). The program consists of overnight camping, environmental awareness, and an overview of the National Park Service. The region provides transportation, lodging, and an interpretative program at Camp Round Meadow in Catoctin Mountain Park. A total of 250 African-American youth between the ages of 6 and 13 participate.

Chapter 35
Building "the Getaway"—Teen Playground
in Rockford, Illinois

Presenter:
Gayle Dixon
    Supervisor, Rockford Park District

Background

The Youth Recreation Council (YRC) was created by the Rockford,
Illinois, Park District to address the needs and desires of young
people in the Rockford Community and to provide youth with opportunities required for them to achieve productive and meaningful
futures. YRC held several sessions to identify teen needs and interests in the Rockford/Loves Park Communities. The Council was
also responsible for conducting two communitywide youth summits,
including one for at-risk students. At the summits, teens gave the
community an overall grade of D-minus in addressing the major
challenges facing youth. These challenges included illiteracy, crime,
dropouts, substance abuse, teenage pregnancy, employment, and
recreation. Results from middle-school and high-school surveys
found that 69% of middle-school youth agreed with the statement:
"Oftentimes I feel bored because there is nothing to do." Only a
slightly lower 61% of high-school youth reported they were bored.
Students complained that they felt isolated and disconnected from
the larger community. Teens throughout the community expressed a
desire for a safe, secure, place to go where they could enjoy themselves, hassle-free.

Program Description

Objectives

The primary objectives of YRC are to:

(1) serve in an advisory capacity on issues of concern and on activities related to use provided by the Rockford Park District;

(2) organize, provide, and conduct programs and projects of interest to high-school youth in the Rockford Park District planned and conducted by the YRC with advice and guidance from Rockford Park District staff;

(3) promote the development of leadership qualities in youth involved in the YRC organization and in participants in YRC programs;

(4) work with existing recreational agencies, youth groups, and recreational programs to improve overall youth programming and participation;

(5) develop new recreation programs for high-school age youth; and

(6) serve as a line of communication between youth and adults, and between youth themselves.

The YRC suggested a bold solution to teen needs in the Rockford community: teens would plan, design, build (including raising the needed funds and identifying donors of food, recruiting volunteers, tools, and materials) and program "the Getaway" teen playground, a first in the nation and modeled after the two successful Youth Playworks projects in town.

The YRC enlisted the services of a nationally recognized playground architect. Collaboration between the architect, the teens, and the community resulted in the Getaway being built entirely through volunteer effort. The Getaway is an economical, high-quality, custom-designed supervised play structure which offers a wholesome, unique community experience for teens.

Planning

The YRC, together with an adult community leader site committee, selected a wooded park picnic area in Blackhawk Park as the site for the innovative playground. Criteria used in the site selection process included: appropriate topography; visibility; compatibility with other park use; neighborhood support; safe accessibility; parking accessibility; mass transit availability; and easy accessibility for police, ranger, and emergency vehicles. The site is in the approximate geographic center of the community. The process of building a creative playground was divided into three segments. Each is described in the following paragraphs.

Design Day was the official kickoff of the community effort. On September 27, 1990, the architect evaluated the potential of the Blackhawk Park playground site and visited area high schools to solicit student input for the 64,000 square foot playground. Ideas included a large stage and dance floor, a changeable maze, a disorienting room with murals and mirrors, an obstacle course, teen-sized swings and slides, seating for hundreds of people, picnic areas, and a tree house. Ideas were collected and then transformed into a schematic plan drawing of the playground that depicts the dreams of the teens within the constraints of the site.

Organization Phase: A unique aspect of developing the playground was that it relied on the community to unite behind the project in support of the teens. Joint teen/adult committees were formed to secure all the tools, materials, volunteer workers, funds, food, and public relations needed to create the playground. A representative from each school served as committee coordinator for one of these core committees, and he or she was responsible for following through with the identified needs and requirements, and for obtaining additional student and adult volunteers to serve on the committee.

Construction Weekend: The construction phase was led by the architect. Due to the size and complexity of the project and the ages (13–19) of the majority of volunteer workers, a longer than average building schedule was planned:

Pre-Build	September 19–22	1991
Build I	October 2–6	1991
(Achieved 65% completion)		
Build II	April 23–26	1992
	April 29–May 3	1992

Fundraising

Two hundred thousand dollars were needed for construction costs. Fundraising was seen as an opportunity to generate support and enthusiasm among members of the community. Twenty-three grant/ foundation applications were submitted to local corporations and organizations. Individual donors, businesses, and service organizations also contributed. Coupon book sales and T-shirt sales also supported the fund drive. The Rockford Airport Authority aided the project by hosting the first major fundraiser at one of their airport hangars.

Volunteers

People of all ages worked each building day from 7 a.m. to 9 p.m. YRC members were trained in the necessary skills to be foremen on the site and to work with volunteer crews. Approximately 7,625 person days of volunteer assistance were contributed for sawing, hammering, drilling, and sanding, as well as food preparation, first-aid, and volunteer information. Typically, these playground projects utilize the skills of adults. However, the majority of these volunteers were teens (ages 13–19), some working with adults or parents, but many working in crews made up solely of teens. The volunteers included groups from all of the high schools, building classes, middle-school and elementary classes, clubs, sport teams, juveniles required to do community service, scouts, and youth church groups.

Food

Feeding workers was a major factor in convincing the three-hour shift volunteer to increase his or her commitment to three days. The total cost of food was zero. By showing commercial businesses that this was a widespread community endeavor, large donations of food were acquired from local restaurants, wholesalers, supermarkets, and fast-food franchises to provide on-site meals during the building phase.

Tools

The task of the tools committee was to assemble all the tools necessary for construction of the playground, to ensure that these tools were distributed efficiently and in a safe, serviceable condition throughout the building period, and to return tools to their owners after construction. Sources of donated tools included contractors, utility companies, public works departments, rental firms, parents, and tool companies.

Materials

The duties of the materials committee were to seek donations of specified supplies and materials to use during construction. A donation of supplies was considered to be more valuable than a cash donation because it helped foster greater community commitment to the project. Sources of donated materials included lumber yards, gravel and concrete suppliers, hardware and discount stores, steel companies, manufacturers, and paint, plumbing, auto parts, and garden supply stores.

Public Relations

Public relations efforts helped establish the validity and uniqueness of the project. These efforts helped arouse the enthusiasm of the community and elicit community pride (see Exhibit 35A). The sense of community was a key in securing donations of money, materials, tools, and volunteer help.

Exhibit 35A

The Getaway

What has	*Where can* teens go
142 doors	to hang out with friends
750 poles	to loiter without hassle
1,450 pounds of galvanized nails	to hide in a maze
3,040 gallons of sealer	to swing from monkey bars
3,700 feet of utility poles	to dance to live bands
and a sound system that	to sit under the stars
will knock your socks off?	to just be themselves?

Ongoing Guidance for the Program

The YRC remains the controlling force of what happens at the Get-away. It is responsible for soliciting input from respective schools, making the decisions, and formulating future direction as the project proceeds. It has selected peak teen use times, including supervised hours, times, and season length. It is directly involved in creating and selecting the activities that are programmed and help the Get-away staff implement their ideas.

Young adults (ages 13–19) have priority at the Getaway. The playground is open daily to the public, but special teen hours are reserved each evening. Supervised teen activities are programmed from Memorial Day to Labor Day.

With the expansion of teen programming within the Park Dis-trict, the operation of the Getaway teen playground has now become the responsibility of a full-time Pre-Teen/Teen Program Supervisor. The evening operation is run by two seasonal part-time facility man-agers and four teen technicians. The Rockford Park Rangers are responsible for security.

Youth must show a picture ID or purchase a Getaway ID to enter the facility. Promotion efforts center around flyers outlining the program. Individual event flyers publicizing specific events rely on teen distribution and word-of-mouth. Summer Hot Night Events are publicized through public service announcements and local newspa-pers and the Rockford Park District calendar of events and seasonal brochures.

Financing and Resource Acquisition

Revenues:

Rockford Park District 1991	$30,000
Capital Improvement Program 1992	58,000
Youth Recreation Council Fundraisers	8,298
Cash Donations from Local Individuals and Businesses	4,758
Trusts, Grants, Foundations	54,200
In-kind Value of Donations of Materials/ Equipment	35,613
Total:	$190,869

Expenses:

Architect Fees	$43,407
Material Costs	112,495
Equipment	7,819
Supplies	5,590
Promotion	2,676
Maintaining Facility	<u>4,425</u>
Total:	$176,412

1995 Operating Budget

Revenues:

Individual Recreation Fees	$1,000
Miscellaneous Recreation Fees	1,000
Concessions	3,000
Sponsorships, Donations	<u>2,000</u>
Total:	$7,000

Expenses:

Personnel:

Regular Salaries	$21,912
Seasonal Salaries	15,500
Employee Benefits	<u>8,931</u>
Subtotal	$46,343

Supplies:

Operating Supplies	$3,050
Food/Beverage (Resale)	2,875
Maintenance Supplies	3,600
Program Supplies	<u>3,700</u>
Subtotal:	$13,225

Contracted Services:

Entertainment	$10,900
Transportation	7,888
Advertising	3,000
Electricity	5,000
Other Professional Services	<u>7,350</u>
Subtotal:	$34,138

Total:	$93,706

Measurement of Program Outcome

Although it took a little longer than anticipated, the teens' dream of a place of their own became a reality with completion of the Getaway teen playground. The program effectively met the goals and objectives of the YRC. The group responded to needs expressed by high-school-age youth in the community when they selected building a teen playground as their number one priority. Leadership qualities were developed among YRC members through their work as chairpersons of their respective committees.

YRC members studied the community to identify existing recreation agencies and programs and youth groups to enlist their support and dedication to the project. Many of the groups which became involved in the overall building have remained involved with the Getaway's operation, and are helping to improve youth programming and participation. With the completion of the Getaway, the YRC now has a location for developing many new recreation opportunities for high-school-age youth.

Chapter 36
Youth-In-Action
in Lebanon, New Hampshire

Presenter:
Cindy Heath
   Recreation Director, Lebanon Recreation Department

Background

For several years, community groups, local businesses, parents,
social service agencies, and city officials had attempted, with little
success, to involve the high-school-aged population in Lebanon,
New Hampshire, in a series of safe, supervised recreational activities
during the evening and weekend hours. Teen dances and drop-in
hours at the community center were sparsely attended; nonalcoholic
nights at local restaurants were frequented by people who had purchased or consumed alcohol prior to attending; and athletic programs
reached only a small percentage of the student population.

A successful teen volunteer program, Youth-In-Action (YIA),
had been operating in nearby Hanover, New Hampshire, for ten years
under the leadership of a parent volunteer. This visionary parent saw
the need for high-school students to use free time in a constructive
and useful manner to benefit themselves and their community. The
vehicle for achieving this goal was the creation of volunteer opportunities. Students had a choice in how to spend their time which was a
critical element in the program's success. They were provided with
positive role models, opportunities to be responsible contributors to
their communities, and a useful entry on their job resumes. Almost
50% of the students in Hanover were participating in the program.

The Lebanon Recreation Department staff and a group of parent
volunteers decided to start a YIA program in Lebanon (based on the
Hanover model) with the additional goal of integrating students in
the two communities through volunteer service. One major difference between the approach taken by the two communities was that in
Hanover the program was basically run by a single person, whereas

in Lebanon an advisory committee was used together with the resources of the Lebanon Recreation Department. Lebanon is a community of 12,000 people. The Recreation Department has a staff of
3.5 FTEs and is supported by approximately 250 volunteers.

Program Content

Objectives

The mission of the program is to reach as many high school-aged
young people as possible with a diversity of opportunities to experience involvement in community service. Program objectives are:

(1) to create a spirit of cooperation and good feeling within school
     communities;
(2) to include adults in the Upper Valley community as coworkers
     and role models in community involvement;
(3) to develop service activities that meet real needs (i.e., make a
     difference) while providing opportunities for good social inter-
     action between peers and nonpeers;
(4) to plant the seeds of good habits and future involvement in
     community service;
(5) to work in partnership toward common goals with established
     community programs; and
(6) to give young people a way to stretch, grow, learn, and dis-
     cover their capacity to care about others.

Key Players

A committee of parent volunteers, school representatives, the recreation director, and two members from the Hanover YIA program
were involved in developing the Lebanon program. Parent volunteers were solicited by advertising a series of informational meetings
to describe the program, and an advisory committee was formed
from interested parents willing to commit to a year of service. This
advisory committee conferred with, and received total support from,
the high-school principal, staff, class advisors, and interested parents
prior to implementing the program.

Program Planning

Weekly meetings of the advisory committee were held in July and August of 1993. As the Hanover program had been coordinated exclusively by one person, and the Lebanon program was to be coordinated by a group, the first step was to identify the organizational structure of the committee and responsibilities of committee members. Job descriptions were developed as follows:

- *Program Coordinator*—maintain student data base, receive project requests, provide orientation for committee members, track project requests;
- *PR/Communications*—send press releases, appear on radio and television talk shows;
- *Record-Keeping*—take minutes at meetings, coordinate photography at YIA projects, clip media announcements about YIA;
- *Telephoning Students*—contact students by phone regarding project opportunities;
- *Meeting Facilitator*—keep meetings on track, provide refreshments;
- *Hanover Liaison*—attend monthly network meetings, report back to Advisory Committee on project collaborations and fundraising ideas; and
- *Project Coordinator*—oversee specific projects from start to finish.

In the two-year history of the program, the roles have evolved to include a volunteer program coordinator who manages the student data base, processes project requests, and sets meeting agendas. The recreation director facilitates meetings and handles program publicity, and the remaining committee members handle all student telephoning.

The next step was to identify projects on which Lebanon students and Hanover students could collaborate as a means of beginning interaction between students from the two towns. Collaborative events included a welcome BBQ at the start of the school year, leaf raking for senior citizens, Community Mixer Dance, Community Harvest Dinner, and hazardous waste recycling.

Finally, a series of meetings with school officials were held to outline the YIA concept, request bulletin board space in the school, set up meetings with students for the first of the year, and review student and parent survey forms (see Exhibit 36A, pages 317 and 318).

Service clubs, community foundations, and the city contribute to the program. The total budget for fiscal year 1993-94 was $2,000. Of this amount, the city portion was $500; sponsors contributed $1,500. Since the program is coordinated entirely by volunteers, the major expenses are office supplies, food for two BBQs (beginning and end of the school year), community dinner supplies, and T-shirts for participating students.

Agencies needing volunteers contact the program coordinator with a project request, detailing the time, date, number of students needed, and description of the service required. The program coordinator contacts advisory committee members on a rotating basis, each of whom has printouts of the student survey data base detailing students' interest areas. The committee member then arranges for the appropriate number of students to volunteer. Requesting agencies are required to provide training on-site or prior to the experience as necessary (see Exhibits 36B and 36C, pages 319 and 320, respectively). Projects in this realm include recreation department sports tournaments and special events, blood bank volunteers, childcare for social service agencies, and community fund-raisers.

In addition, students and advisory committee members select projects for the entire YIA membership to participate in, such as community dinners, park decorating, clean up days, leaf raking, bulb planting, and the make-a-difference day program.

One of the more exciting programs that Youth-In-Action sponsors is the Good Times program, in which high school students are matched with elementary school students who are at risk. Youth-In-Action students take the participants bowling, to movies, sledding and spend time mentoring them when possible. Youth-In-Action funds the activities, as well as a monthly gathering for all involved. The beauty of the program is that it doesn't cost very much money. It doesn't cost money to volunteer, and the students come away feeling that they've made a difference in their community, or in someone's life. [More details of the Good Times Program are given in Exhibit 36D, pages 321 and 322].

Exhibit 36A

Youth-In-Action Interest Survey

Name:_____ ☐ Fr ☐ Soph ☐ Jr ☐ Sr Locker #___
Street Address:_____
Town, State and Zip Code:_____
Mailing Address (if different):_____
Telephone Number:_____
Did you participate in YIA last year?
    ☐ Yes ☐ No

T-Shirt Size: ☐ Medium ☐ Large ☐ Ex-Large ☐ XX-Large

    Please give us some idea of what you might be interested in volunteering for this coming school year so we can develop our program.
    Indicating interest on this sheet does *not* obligate you. You may be called with more details and given a chance to make a commitment if you have the time and interest.

Community Events such as:
☐ Christmas in October   ☐ Halloween Haunted House
☐ Breakfast with Santa   ☐ Halloween Fantasy Castle
☐ Holiday Celebration at the Mall   ☐ Opera House activities
☐ 4th of July Celebration   ☐ Audrey Prouty Bike Ride (in July)
☐ Crop Walk

Youth-In-Action Fundraising Activities such as:
☐ Car washes
☐ Benefit dinners, bake sales, etc.
☐ Raking leaves, car work, etc.
☐ Rent-A-Kid (your name kept on
    file and matched with people
    calling in looking for reliable,
short-term help, such as babysitting, and odd jobs. The amount you would be paid would be negotiated between you and the employer)
☐ Sell popcorn at games, parades

If you think your parents/guardians may be interested in helping the Advisory Committee with any YIA projects, please let us know.

    ☐ Yes   ☐ No

Other Helpful Information:
Communication is a major problem! We will use locker notices, bulletin boards, the mail and phone calls. Unless indicated, we plan our calls between 7 a.m. and 10 p.m.

    ☐ OK   ☐ not OK (let us know when we can reach you!)

Exhibit 36A (Continued)

General Events and Activities such as:

☐ Alumni Day Celebration
☐ Art Activities
☐ Bicycle Rodeo with LPD
☐ Blood Bank (help with equipment)
☐ Blood Bank (provide childcare after school)
☐ Boxboard Recycling
☐ Build Low-Income Housing
☐ Bulletin Board-upkeep at High School
☐ Childcare
☐ Children's Library Help
☐ Children's Playgroups
☐ Chore Corps (chores for Senior Citizens)
☐ Community Dinners
☐ Community Mixer (for adults with mental retardation)
☐ Computer Skills
☐ Concession Stands
☐ David's House
☐ Drama
☐ Driving
☐ Earth Day Clean Up
☐ Food Drives (for local food shelves)
☐ Fundraising for community groups
☐ Gardening
☐ Good Times—Big Brother/Sister program (open to Sophs., Jrs., and Srs. only)
☐ Green-Up Days
☐ Heavy Work

☐ Helping out in a pinch
☐ Helping with children
☐ Hospital
☐ Kids 'n' Cops
☐ Make-A-Difference Day
☐ Montshire Museum (overnight chaperone)
☐ Music Activities
☐ Outdoor Work (e.g., lawns, raking, snow shoveling)
☐ Peer Support
☐ Photography
☐ Publicity (e.g., posters)
☐ Public Speaking about YIA
☐ Recycling (and other environmental concerns)
☐ Senior Citizens
☐ Senior Citizen Fundraiser Dinner
☐ Senior Citizen Partnerships
☐ SHARE (carry Senior Citizen bags)
☐ Ski Lessons at Storrs Hill
☐ Social Events (such as BBQ for high-school students)
☐ Special Olympics
☐ Sports
☐ Telephoning
☐ Tutoring children
☐ Videotaping
☐ Other:_____
_____

Please list your involvement in after-school and community activities:

Exhibit 36B

Good Times Program

Your First Meeting and Getting Started

Don't get discouraged if your companion or the parent(s) seem shy, hesitant, or unresponsive at first. They may have had many bad experiences in the past...it takes time to build trust!

Your first meeting with your companion will be on _____. We will all meet as a group that day, getting to know each other, playing a few games and sharing refreshments. If you don't meet the parents the same day as your companion, it is a good idea to speak to them on the phone in order to introduce yourself to them. You can then meet them in person at a later date. Let them know when you will pick up the child, what the two of you will be doing (ask permission when appropriate), where you can be reached, and when you will return. Your first meeting will be very important. It will set the tone for your relationship.

Here are some suggestions to help you get over that first hurdle:

(1) Think about the meeting before you go. What will you say and do when meeting your companion and his or her family?

(2) Introduce yourself to everybody. What do you enjoy doing? What is your family like? What activities are you involved in?

(3) Explain why you are excited about being involved in Good Times.

(4) Try to direct your conversation to your companion as much as possible right from the start. Let him or her know right away that you are a friend and that he or she is your primary interest in that home.

(5) Try to determine common interests.

(6) At the end of the visit, and on each following visit, set a specific time and place for your next visit. It is really important for you to know your schedule ahead of time so definite plans can be made at the end of each meeting. Call sometime during the week before your next visit to confirm the next meeting and just to chat.

Exhibit 36C

Good Times Program

Emergency Procedures
When you and your companion are together, safety is of prime importance! Here are some common sense reminders:

(1) *Always* wear safety belts in the car. Do not drive the car until both of you are buckled in. Make no exceptions to this rule!
(2) If the weather is bad or even questionable, make other plans and don't drive.
(3) If going skating, make sure the ice has been tested and is strong. Don't go skating on a pond alone...make sure there are others besides you and your companion. Don't skate on the river.

If an accident should occur while you and your companion are together, you will first need to assess any injury. If you question your ability to treat the injury, *don't take any chances!* Call 911 immediately, and then call the parents. Stay with the child until the parents arrive (this may mean riding in the ambulance). During this time (if you are not injured), try to remain calm. Your companion will need you to stay centered and in control. Reassure him or her that help is on the way and that you will stay with him or her until his or her parents are there. When the parents arrive, the responsibility will shift to them, but be willing to help out (e.g., perhaps by remaining with the child while they make phone calls).

When you get home, do something to help yourself...e.g., talk it over with your parents, take a walk, take a long, hot shower, listen to music. Take care of yourself...we need you as a part of this program! Once things are under control, please call us and report the accident. Youth-In-Action assumes responsibility for you and your companion, so we will need to know ASAP about incidents such as accidents, and injuries.

Exhibit 36D

Good Times!

Introduction

Commitment: If you're at this meeting, you've already made a commitment to this program. You are being asked to serve as a stable and mature role model for the child with whom you are matched. We know you understand the important role you will play in the life of another person.

Consistency: Contact your young companion weekly. We ask that you see him or her weekly, also. Understandably, conflicts may arise which may force you to cancel or reschedule. In such cases, be considerate of your companion and offer an explanation. If there are several weeks between meetings, you should keep in contact by phone or letter. *We stress consistency.* Promises not kept, disappointment over visits not made by a separated parent, hurt caused by casual commitments from adults—all these may be a regular part of your companion's life. Please, try not to make impossible promises. Be on time and plan activities together so they can anticipate future meetings and have a feeling of responsibility. This will encourage them to trust you, other people, and finally themselves.

One-on-one: You should spend time with your companion alone. Other sisters and brothers of your companion should only be included on special occasions, not on a regular basis. Another aspect of this to consider is involvement of your friends. Attending an occasional athletic event, concert, etc. is fine, but please remember to put your companion first. Consider your relationship with your companion an important event.

Set a good example: Remember that you are under the scrutiny of the child and the family. Everything that you do is noted, analyzed, and sometimes imitated.

Try to let your companion make his or her own decisions: Give advice sparingly. Share your growing experiences with her or him, but don't preach. Providing a good friendship is the best contribution you can make. Your relationship may produce a change in your companion, but don't become frustrated if the change isn't immediate, or if you don't even see the change. Your involvement may be planting the seeds for future growth in your companion—growth that you may not witness. And remember, change takes time.

Self-esteem: Try to accept your companion for who he or she is. When he or she begins to see that you do, he or she may open up and/or be influenced by your attitudes and behavior. A positive self-image and confidence may be lacking. Your good example and age will bring

Exhibit 36D (Continued)

respect from your companion. He or she may talk to you as he or she could to no other adult. Listening and being patient can build a very constructive relationship between you and the child who really needs you to be a part of his or her life.

Use money sparingly: You can't buy friendship or provide the material things that your companion may lack at home. Use money sparingly during activities and buy small gifts only on birthdays and very special occasions. Learning to have fun without spending a lot of money will help the child integrate the experiences with you with those at home.

Limits: Don't be afraid to set limits. Limits can and should be set on the amount of time you will spend together, the number of phone calls from the child that will be acceptable to you, and the behavior while he or she is with you.

Involvement of the family: Even though the parents of your companion have granted permission for you to be with their child, the arrangements may nevertheless be threatening to them. The parents' reactions will be as varied as the matches. Do try to remember, however, that your relationship with the child is the most important thing. Most parents are supportive. Be courteous and tactful when speaking with them. Inform the parents where you will be taking the child and when you expect to return. Always ask their permission. As a rule, do not run errands or do favors for them as you may find yourself with more responsibility than you care to handle. Also, do not take sides in family disputes. Call us if you encounter any problems or have any concerns.

Parents' responsibilities: Leave to the parents the disciplining of your companion, conferring with school personnel, arrangement of medical diagnosis or treatment (except in emergency situations when the child is with you). If you feel the parents are neglecting some area of need, please talk with us about the best way of handling the situation. We will encourage parents not to use the "treat" of a visit with you as a reward or take it away as punishment. However, they may still do this, especially as your relationship becomes important to the child. Let the coordinator know if this happens often. The parents will be responsible for having the child ready when you come to pick him or her up.

Stay in contact: It is very important that we stay in touch with each other while you are involved in this program. Please call me once a week to let me know how things are going, to discuss concerns and share successes. We'll also be meeting once a month as a group (at a time to be decided upon during this meeting) so all of us, old and young, can have some fun together. If something about the relationship should be of concern to you, let our coordinator know while there is still time to straighten things out. Don't feel as though you can only call me once a week. Especially contact me if you think the parent or child is trying to terminate. This can be traumatic for the child if it is not handled properly.

Youth-In-Action students also participated in planting over 3,000 daffodil and narcissus bulbs at the local hospital. The students got together with the members of Youth-In-Action from a nearby town on a Saturday morning and planted 3,000 daffodil bulbs under the direction of a volunteer landscaper from Holland. The students felt like they were contributing, and came away having been mentored by the adult leaders who worked with them.   —Recreation Director

Marketing

Getting the word out to students was accomplished by visiting directly with them in class meetings at the beginning of the school year to explain YIA and distribute a student and parent survey form and information sheet. These materials further described the goals of the program, gave students a list of youth volunteer opportunities, invited parents to become involved, and required parental permission (see Exhibit 36E, page 324) for their participation. A Welcome BBQ (with food and supplies donated by local merchants) was held for students from Lebanon and Hanover. Icebreaker games were played; small group discussions were held to outline program goals; and community service ideas were solicited from the students—all facilitated by one advisory committee member and a Hanover Youth In-Action student. (Important Note: advisory committee members spent the afternoon baking hundreds of brownies, which bonded the group very nicely, and gave the house an enticing aroma for the students' arrival!)

Following the Welcome BBQ, project requests were solicited from community agencies, and students were directly telephoned by advisory committee members to solicit their involvement in various projects. Students' interest areas were determined from the completed survey forms turned in at the high school. As the community became aware of the program, students were invited to speak at service club meetings, on the radio and television, and at neighboring communities interested in starting the program. Comments like, "Youth-In-Action is the best thing that ever happened to me in high school," verified the value of the program for students.

Exhibit 36E

Youth-In-Action Parental Permission Form

Youth-In-Action is a program in which high school student participants donate volunteer service to the community under the direction of volunteer adults.

Participant's Name: Parent/Guardian Name:

_____   _____
(please print)   (please print)

    I, the parent/guardian of the above named person, give my permission for his/her participation in any and all activities of the Youth-In-Action. I do further release, absolve, indemnify, and hold harmless the organizers, sponsors and supervisors, any and all of them. In case of injury to my son or daughter, I hereby waive all claims against the organizers, the sponsors, and any of the supervisors appointed by them.

    Please list any preexisting medical concerns:

    I give permission for any adult supervisor to seek emergency medical attention for my child.

    I give permission for my son/daughter to be photographed at YIA activities and to have these photos reproduced for public use in the promotion of YIA.

    All participation in the Youth-In-Action program, and all services and manner of rendering services under the program shall be subject to the complete discretion and judgment of the program's advisors and directors.

    If the participant operates a motor vehicle in the course of participation in Youth-In-Action activities, the undersigned participant and parent(s) certify that he or she is covered by a family insurance policy providing both collision and liability coverage when operating the motor vehicle. No auto insurance is provided by Youth-In-Action.

    Occasions may arise when students are transported to activities by other student volunteers. I take responsibility for my son or daughter's action regarding this issue. Often, transportation provided by an adult will also be available.

    While participating in YIA activities, students are prohibited from involvement with alcohol, tobacco or other controlled substances.

    Lebanon High School supports the involvement of the students in YIA, but is not a sponsor or organizer of this program.

    We may receive requests from other agencies for help with community projects separate from Youth-In-Action activities. Do you give permission for us to give them your student's name? ☐ Yes ☐ No

_____   _____
(signature of participant, date)   (signature of parent/guardian, date)

A newsletter was developed, highlighting service projects the students had completed or in which they had taken part. It was distributed to school board, city council, supporting businesses and service clubs, students, and the media.

Measurement of Program Outcomes

The outcome of the program is determined by:

(a) follow-up telephone calls to agencies requesting volunteers in order to verify student participation, and monitor the quality of student performance;

(b) feedback from students sought at the opening and closing BBQs to solicit volunteer program ideas;

(c) monthly meetings held among advisory committee members to manage communications with students, progress on projects, and concerns that may arise in the course of carrying out a project; and

(d) monthly network meetings held with the Hanover Youth-In-Action advisory committee to plan joint projects among students.

Chapter 37
Parks Department's Summer Jobs Programs
in Tampa, Florida

Presenter:
Diana Kyle
   Deputy Director, City of Tampa Parks Department

Background

In 1992 the Tampa Parks Department initiated what would become three summer employment programs designed to provide youth ages 14–18 with positive work experiences, marketable skills and supplemental learning opportunities. The program initially drew on the experience of the city's Private Industry Council which had been providing job opportunities for youth through the U.S. Department of Labor's Summer Youth Employment Program and Job Training and Partnership Act since the early 1980s. When federal guidelines changed to require remedial classes for participants in the Summer Youth Employment Program, the Council saw participation drop from 150 youth to five. Classroom instruction, unfortunately, conflicted with available work shifts for youth. To avoid this problem, the Parks Department developed construction crews. Because the targeted sites were in operation all day, youth could attend school for two hours each morning then invest several hours on site in the afternoon.

   In 1993 there was on construction crew of fifteen youth, ages 14–18. In 1994 a second crew was added for a total of 30 youth. Under the guidance of a professional carpenter, crews worked 20 hours per week, four hours each day, constructing boardwalks and fishing piers. Two hours each day were devoted to expanding computer sills at a local vocational school. Under the general heading of "STEPS Toward Environmental Partnerships" (STEPS), the Parks Department currently coordinates three separate job programs: Operation Brightside, Environmental Services Program, and Youth Construction Crew.

Operation Brightside

Program Description: Thirty-five hours per week on the job (seven hours a day) working with grounds maintenance crews raking, weeding, and picking up litter in parks, recreation centers, and the cemetery. One crew worked in a large cemetery taking pictures of headstones, drawing maps, and doing surveys. Information was entered by these young adults into a computerized data base inventory. In addition, the program includes three hours per week of evening training on ethics, heritage, pride, self-esteem, hygiene, good eating habits, pregnancy, and the importance of a good education.

Target Population: Minorities 14–18 years of age with a minimum 2.0 grade point average, good attendance at school, responsibility, good attitude, and a mixture of low-income and middle-income households.

Budget: funded by Anheuser-Busch ($50,000 for salaries); Tampa's Urban League ($6,600 administration); and the city of Tampa ($5,204 for supervision). Total cost was $61,804 for 25 participants, or $2,472 per person. (Three dropped out but three more were added.) Total cost does not include in-kind use of equipment (e.g., mowers, weedeaters). Participants paid for their own safety shoes.

Environmental Services Program

Program Description: Twenty hours per week on-the-job working with parks grounds crews in a mentorship capacity on Tuesdays, Wednesdays, and one-half day on Thursdays. Participants were also involved 12 hours per week (six hours every Monday and Friday) in a customized training program learning to read and do math, utilizing grounds maintenance type problems and activities. Participants learn how to open a bank account, how to use a computer, to design a landscape plan, and to identify plants. Participants were also exposed to professionals who gave them information about different careers, e.g., forestry, drafting.

One of the keys to the success of the program was meeting with crew supervisors ahead of time, outlining the program and getting their commitment to be involved. Participants also had to be committed to the program since many had to catch a bus at 5:30 a.m., five mornings a week, in order to report to work at 6:30 a.m. Bus passes were provided.

Target Population: Job Training Partnership Act (JTPA) standards—low income, at-risk, in trouble with the law, poor grades, ages 16–20.

Budget: funded by the city parks department ($1,000 for supervision), the Private Industry Council ($23,350 for salaries and administration) and a Teacher Quest Grant ($1,440 for salaries). Total cost of $25,790 for 11 participants, or $2,344 per person, includes bus passes and safety shoes ($55 per person). The above cost does not include in-kind equipment (e.g., trucks, mowers). Six participants dropped out, of whom two had to drop out to go to summer school in order to graduate, and one dropped out due to complications related to pregnancy.

Private Industry Council Construction Crews

Program Description: Twenty hours per week 10 a.m. to 2 p.m. constructing boardwalks and fishing piers in a park with a carpenter as foreman. Twelve hours per week, two hours per day, at the local vo-tech learning to read and write with a standard computer program working at their own pace.

Target Population: Students 14–18 years of age. JTPA criteria—low income, at-risk, in trouble with the law, low grades.

Budget: funded by the Private Industry Council ($27,900 for administration and supervision), the city of Tampa ($20,000), and the city of Tampa Parks Department ($3,444—supervision). Total cost was $51,344 for 15 participants, or $2,090 per person not including wood ($20,000 of this is the price of wood and other materials for constructing docks, boardwalks, and other projects) including safety shoes ($55 per person). Five participants dropped out.

Evidence of Program Effectiveness

Some of the comments from the kids afterwards were "I loved the program because it taught me that I could be treated like an adult." Some of the quotes in the newspaper were: "I loved the program because now I know I have a choice!" "I can either go to college, or I can work for the parks department!" All three programs have worked out well and have been expanded. The Parks Department has approval to hire 19 of the best participants to work on Saturdays and half days on Sundays throughout the school year. This will be offered as a reward to the most reliable and hard-working participants in the summer programs. Two participants have graduated and are now full-time park employees. Both are enrolled in a two-year horticulture program at the local community college.

Chapter 38
*Drug Free Youth In Touch (D*FY*IT)*
in Joliet, Illinois

Presenter:
Ronald Dodd
> Director, Joliet Park District

> This program has brought together youth, educators, law
> enforcement, the medical community and business
> people in a positive way, underlining the importance of
> remaining drug free. We recognize its success by nam-
> ing Joliet [D*FY*IT] as winner of the 1992 Governor's
> Cup signifying the effort most symbolic of the spirit of
> Illinois volunteerism. (The Honorable Jim Edgar, Gover-
> nor of Illinois)

Background

D*FY*IT is an approach to drug and alcohol prevention which rewards students who are staying clean and enjoying life drug free. It
makes it cool to be clean!

When a group of students from Whitehouse High School, Tyler,
Texas, appeared on ABC TV's popular *Good Morning, America* to
talk about D*FY*IT, phones started ringing and questions started
pouring in to D*FY*IT national leaders. The questioners ranged
from a school principal in California to President Bush's former drug
czar William Bennett. "What," they asked, "is D*FY*IT and how
can we get it into our schools?"

The Tyler, Texas, D*FY*IT (Drug Free Youth in Texas) Program
in its first year, through positive peer pressure influenced more than
3,000 Smith County, Texas, high school students to be voluntarily
tested by urinalysis for drugs.

Bringing the Program to Joliet

In the fall of 1991, a community activist brought the D*FY*IT idea
to the Joliet, Illinois, Chief of Police. With police leadership, an

implementation committee was formed that included parents, public and private school staff, chamber of commerce representatives, healthcare professionals, the media, and the police. Joliet's Drug Free Youth In Touch (D*FY*IT) program started in 1992 and is modeled after the successful Tyler program.

Program Description

Joliet area D*FY*IT is guided by a Board of Directors made up of community leaders, students, school officials, and parents. However, implementation is through individual school-based chapters that are run *by* students *for* students.

At the heart of the program is a simple urinalysis test for drugs and alcohol. When students pass the drug test, they receive membership in their local school chapter and are entitled to all its benefits and privileges, free of charge. Subsequent random testing is required to maintain membership. The membership card is recognized by area merchants for direct discounts on merchandise, or on services such as a round of golf, admission to the indoor ice skating arena, and general recreation programs. Other businesses that wish to participate can provide direct donations or sponsorships to the D*FY*IT program.

Testing kits are acquired from companies that have a national reputation for providing quality diagnostic drug abuse products to government, business, and industry. Testing of students is conducted by volunteers who have been trained by professional laboratory staff from St. Joseph's Medical Center and Silver Cross Hospital. These professional staff are also available to provide quality assurance in the testing process.

To date over 2,000 students at three high schools and one junior high have become members of D*FY*IT. Membership in D*FY*IT is free to all students, and none of the costs of the program come out of the school budget. Money is obtained through fund-raising events, the sale of banners and bumper stickers, and charitable contributions.

The urine testing is legal, because the program is voluntary. If students are under 18 years of age, written permission must be obtained from their parents or guardians. Confidentiality is assured by using social security numbers, not names, when urine samples are submitted. If a test result is positive, the designated student chapter representative and the counselor meet with the student. Students who fail the first test get a second chance. Counseling is generally mandatory if a student fails twice. Students suspended from D*FY*IT are encouraged to join again. Requirements for reentry are determined by each chapter. Test results are not available to the public or the police. The goal of D*FY*IT is to eliminate drug use, not to prosecute abusers. In most chapters, results are not communicated to parents, but each chapter determines its own policy.

Membership in D*FY*IT can be revoked if alcohol abuse occurs or if a student commits an alcohol-related crime such as driving under the influence of alcohol. Policies on alcohol are usually determined by members of the student leadership panel.

Getting Started

The D*FY*IT program should be announced at a special rally or school assembly. The media, including local newspapers, radio and TV stations, should be alerted well in advance and invited. D*FY*IT banners, posters, bumper stickers and T-shirts can be distributed to help publicize the program.

The Key Role of Merchant and Business Participation

In June 1992, Joliet area D*FY*IT received the prestigious Illinois Governor's Cup Award being cited as the state's best example of the spirit of community volunteerism. D*FY*IT is a community effort. The support of area merchants and businesses, through the offering of discounts to D*FY*IT members, direct donations to sustain the program, and the sponsoring of materials (e.g., shirts, posters, mailings) is critical. Over 100 area merchants and businesses presently participate in the program.

Examples of merchant participation in D*FY*IT range from 2-for-1 offers to direct discounts on merchandise. Student members of D*FY*IT can be helpful in making suggestions. By offering fun, unique discounts, or other incentives to D*FY*IT members, merchants know D*FY*IT kids will keep coming back.

D*FY*IT also pays businessmen additional dividends because the D*FY*IT card can serve as an additional "recommendation" to employers who are evaluating students who apply to work in their businesses.

Section VII
Europe and Africa

Chapter 39
At-Risk Youth Programs
in South Africa

Presenter:
Rita Horn
> Director-General, Department of Sport and Recreation, Republic
> of South Africa

> Successful sport and recreation programs for the youth
> of South Africa are a prerequisite for ensuring a safe
> environment and a prosperous future for all the people of
> South Africa. (Rita Horn)

Background

South Africa has a predominantly young population. Persons
younger than 30 years presently constitute approximately 66% of the
country's population. Taking into consideration the widespread
involvement of youth in political violence and crime, the threat to the
future posed by rampant youth became obvious and could not be
rationalized away. Add to this the cultural and ethnic diversity in the
country, and it becomes abundantly clear that it is a complex situation which requires delicate management. Therefore it is imperative
that youth, many of whom are marginalized, be reached and brought
back into the mainstream of society.

Within the South African context, those between the ages of 15
and 30 are loosely defined as youth, and they constitute 29% of the
total population. Various social and political factors have contributed
to the shaping of the future of South African youth. These factors
include inadequate education resulting in unemployment and poverty; the forced removal of people from traditional tribal territories;
the pass system (domestic identity document, also called passbook or
reference book, carried by black citizens in South Africa); and the
system of migrant labor that resulted in family and community insta-
bility, coupled with the diminishing role of the parent in the immediate family circle. Because most work opportunities are in the city,

parents have to leave home in the traditional Black townships located outside the cities very early in the morning, and return late at night. During the day they have no idea of the whereabouts of their children. Under these circumstances, violence and crime have flourished.

Unemployment

The number of people who are unemployed in South Africa is disturbing:

	Unemployed	Percent of Group
Whites	209,260	8.4
Blacks	2,968,539	37.1
Asians	66,091	16.3
Coloureds	341,847	23.4

(Official figures in October 1993: provided by National Statistical Services; former independent homelands not included)

Unemployment is high especially among Blacks. This figure is reflected in the overall violence and crime rate. The above figures could be a gross underestimation of the situation for two reasons: first, because the former independent homelands are not included, and unemployment is rife in these predominantly rural areas; and second, no comprehensive head count has as yet been undertaken to determine the exact population of South Africa. Previous census reports failed to accomplish this task. The Human Science Research Council (HSRC) estimated South Africa's population figures for 1995 as being:

Whites		5,168,700
Blacks		35,585,200
Asians		1,030,900
Coloureds		3,528,600
	Total	45,313,400

Considering the large percentage *registered* as unemployed in the Black community, the estimates of the HSRC give rise for concern. It *therefore* becomes obvious that strong emphasis should be placed on programs targeting especially the youth belonging to this group in order to present them with quality of life experiences as well as opportunities to improve their physical environment.

Recognition by Government

In 1987 the President's Council Committee for Social Affairs tabled a comprehensive report on the youth of South Africa. Unfortunately, in spite of all the hard work and submissions by all the persons and departments concerned, the report was basically shelved. Various attempts over the next few years by the Department of Sport and Recreation for example to obtain funding for youth programs were ignored.

Although the African National Congress (ANC) promised youth in the preelection period that they would receive preferential treatment, other seemingly more urgent matters of State had to be dealt with first. In December 1994, however, the ANC adopted a proposal which provides for the establishment of a portfolio for Youth Affairs. The 16th of June has also been declared Youth Day and a national public holiday by Parliament.

At present, the Government of South Africa lacks a formal policy geared specifically towards youth. Although this situation is not desirable, the implementation of national programs is subject to the availability of financial and human resources. These resources have been stretched to their limit even before the election of the present Government of National Unity. Basic needs, such as healthcare, housing, water, electricity, and also education, receive preferential treatment at this time.

The Reconstruction and Development Program (RDP), which has as its goal the uplifting of communities is the yardstick for all expenditures by the Government. This program envisages a national youth service program and the establishment of an autonomous National Youth Council in which youth would be represented.

Programs

State Departments

The Department of Sport and Recreation is engaged in development programs targeted specifically at youth. But due to a lack of funds these programs usually operate on an *ad hoc* basis with limited funding. A more holistic approach to the problem as well as sufficient

funding by the Government is essential to address the youth problem.
A recent meeting hosted by the Department of Education for the
government departments involved in youth affairs, was a positive
step towards creating an awareness among the various departments
for their programs aimed at addressing the youth situation. Departments already involved are sport and recreation, health, welfare,
labor, education, correctional services, police services, and environmental affairs.

Nongovernmental Organizations (NGOs)

The National Youth Development Forum (NYDF) and the National
Youth Service Initiative (NYSI) are strong NGOs that have focused
efforts on training youth in various areas of service. Simultaneously,
youth are provided with basic education on-site. These programs
include training in building skills, childcare, and catering. The youth
earn a stipend and also receive suitable clothing and meals. Trainees
receive formal accreditation from recognized institutions after
completion of the various programs which last between a minimum
of six months and a maximum of two years. Their intention is to
establish a closer relationship with the government. For instance, the
Department of Public Works should become involved in a building
program; the Department of Education in the provision of facilities
and training; and the Department of Health in offering training in the
administration of health programs, as well as the training of nutri-
tionists and healthcare workers. During their period of training,
youth stay in their own communities. They are, therefore, able to
contribute on a continuous basis towards the uplifting of their communities.

The former Gold Shield Award, now the President's Award Program, is another NGO which aims at encouraging responsible citizenship amongst youth by way of service, hiking expeditions, skills,
and fitness training. The Minister of Sport and Recreation has accepted the position of Chairman of the governing body of the
President's Award Program.

Other NGOs that utilize outdoor recreational pursuits to develop
leadership abilities with youth are the Wilderness Leadership School,
Lapalala Wilderness School, the Outdoor Adventure Association of
South Africa, the Rural Foundation, Voortrekkers, Land Service
Movement, Boy Scouts, and Girl Guides.

NGOs, parents, and churches need to form partnerships with the state and the private sector to address the needs and problems of youth. This can only be achieved if all the efforts employed complement one another and are coordinated and geared towards developing the youth of South Africa.

The Future

The Department of Sport and Recreation will focus on mass out-of-school youth involvement in sport and physical recreation, catering to marginalized youth. The Department recognizes that sport and recreation have a strong mass appeal and an inherent ability to override social and cultural differences. On the playing fields all people are equal, and this phenomenon may serve as the basis by which other social issues and ills can be addressed. Once attracted by sport and games, the young person can also be exposed to other areas such as health, education, and job training. These could be presented in collaboration with sport and recreation programs.

The Department of Sport and Recreation intends to employ a two-pronged approach. Programs need to be presented on a continuous basis by the existing provincial structures and personnel, in conjunction with sports and recreation governing bodies. These programs may serve to identify sport and leadership talent and also to "keep youngsters from falling into mischief."

Young people will also need to be taught the skills to effectively function as sport and play leaders and even be employed in this capacity by local authorities, sport governing bodies, and NGOs. To recruit volunteers to assist in this training is of primary importance. Since these qualifications need to be recognized on a national level, formal certification and accreditation of leaders is imperative.

Chapter 40
Rescuing Young Offenders with
Recreation Programs
in the United Kingdom

Presenter:
John L. Crompton
  Professor, Department of Recreation, Park and Tourism Sciences, Texas A&M University

Background

The Solent Sports Counseling Project is probably the best known sport and leisure program aimed at preventing criminal youth behavior in the United Kingdom. This project is focused on Portsmouth, Southampton, and Basingstoke (cities in the County of Hampshire) located on the south coast of England.

The project was initiated in 1985 with a grant of $150,000–$200,000 per year for a three-year period, primarily provided by the British Sports Council. This is an independent body which is funded annually by central government, similar in concept but not content to the National Endowment for the Arts in the United States. The Sports Council supports and provides development of sport and physical recreation for all levels of ability and at all levels of government. It has a wide range of responsibilities and programs; amongst them is a mandate to support research and demonstration projects. The Sports Council's Research Unit monitored and evaluated the project for its three-year duration. The material in this article is drawn from that evaluation, from a report undertaken by the Centre for Criminology Research at Oxford University, from subsequent material provided by the project's director, and from discussions with one of the project's managers.

The project had its genesis in a local court in Southampton which established a pilot program to provide "sports counseling" for first-time offenders and young people at risk. The intent was to offer them the opportunity to take part in sports and to introduce them to sports clubs and facilities. The initial success of this small-scale program encouraged the Sports Council to support it financially on a larger scale as a demonstration project.

The initial idea of working closely with the courts and for the courts to refer offenders proved difficult to implement, and it became obvious that links with the Probationary Service were a far more satisfactory means of recruiting participants. As the project proceeded, there was an increased belief among the staff that participation should be voluntary. They came to recognize the importance of participants being involved because they want to be, rather than because they have to be.

Program Description

Project Objectives and Staffing

The broad aims of the project when it was launched in 1985 were:

(a) to enable an experiment to be conducted whereby first offenders with a spark of interest in sports may be given a chance to develop that interest in a constructive fashion with a view to introducing new purpose to their lives; and

(b) to develop participation amongst an isolated element of the 15–24 target age group which includes many unemployed persons.

The emphasis in sports was subsequently broadened to embrace other types of leisure pursuits. Within these overall aims, the following operational objectives were defined:

(1) to provide a program of sport and leisure activities using resources in the local area;

(2) to develop the goodwill and cooperation of appropriate agencies within the local community, and whenever possible use resources on a shared basis;

(3) to reduce the rate of appearance and reappearance of clients in court;

(4) to enable participants to develop social skills through the medium of sport and leisure activities;

(5) to foster the self-confidence of clients through the medium of sport and leisure activities;

(6) to facilitate clients participation in sport and leisure activities
     at their own level in a friendly and supportive environment;
     and

(7) to introduce participants to various facilities within the local
     community so that the activities introduced through the project
     may be continued on completion of their program.

The annual budget for the project was approximately $200,000
of which approximately $140,000 went for staff salaries and other
support costs such as training and travel. The other main budget
items were rent for premises ($12,000), office support costs ($4,000),
equipment ($30,000) and travel and activity costs for the clients
themselves ($14,000).

The staff consists of three separate teams based in the cities of
Portsmouth, Southampton, and Basingstoke. Each team is comprised
of a senior leader with two assistant leaders, while a central project
office in Southampton houses the project director and an administrative assistant. The project director reports to senior probation officers in Portsmouth, Southampton, and Basingstoke. Local advisory
groups were also established in each area to advise the project director.

Staff, who brought a wide variety of background experiences to
the project, were recruited and trained. Their objective is to build
relationships with participants rather than to arrange activities for
them. A strength of all the staff is that they are good communicators
which is a vital asset for establishing the necessary rapport with
participants. Staff training courses addressed personal development,
management, sports specific qualifications, first aid, working with
voluntary groups, racial awareness, and drug and alcohol abuse. The
director insists on the primacy of a client centered approach. In an
interview, he was quoted as saying:

> Our project works very much at the client level.
> Recently...staff had laid on an expedition. They were
> just about to go away...and I asked them how many
> people they had. They replied, 'Two.' I told them that
> we usually took eight. They said the people didn't want
> to go. I asked why were we doing the expedition then?
> 'You work to the needs of the people,' they replied.

Efforts are made to supplement the professional staff with volunteers who can organize specific recreation sessions or work one-to-one with clients. The quality of service offered to clients is perceived to be very important, and volunteers of the necessary caliber are not easy to find. However, several individuals have been found who have volunteered assistance, including a 67-year-old man who taught lawn bowls once a week and a lady who was a tennis coach.

Working with the Clients

The client profile is distinctive: over 92% of the clients are male; 66% aged between 17 and 21, and 86% of them unemployed. The nature of the participants' offenses vary widely. Many have a record of several different kinds of offenses, but the leading categories of the convictions were burglary (19%), stealing from or taking automobiles (16%), stealing from retail stores (31%), and other miscellaneous stealing (28%).

Following an initial referral, each client is contacted by a member of the project staff and a program of activities is arranged. The initial contact is crucial:

> At Solent Sports Counseling Project (SSCP) a relaxed and informal 'softly, softly' manner is used as an initial befriending technique. The aim is to 'sell' the project counselor as someone the client can trust and who may be able to help them. Young offenders are therefore likely to be introduced to SSCP via a (not too early) morning telephone call asking them whether they would like to come out for a few hours and attend a session of their choice. If clients choose 'fishing,' they are likely to spend the morning out fishing with a SSCP staff member. Although some clients complain that 'it is all a bit vague, what they are trying to do,' many respond with initial enthusiasm, while yet others are at least curious. Client and counselor work out the content of the treatment program until mutual agreement is reached. To ensure commitment to the program, many assessments are based largely on the client's own appraisal of his or her abilities and inclinations.

The project staff place emphasis on establishing an individual relationship with each client, both in terms of counseling and the development of an activity program. Defining a clear "pathway" for each client is fundamental to success.

The client's work program includes three distinct stages. First, an *initial commitment* is vital. Both the staff and the probation officers are anxious not to push clients into an involvement; the clients have to possess a "spark of interest" and some sort of drive or ambition. In some cases, the staff realize that prospective clients are not suitable and that the project would do nothing for them.

The middle stage for each client is a process of *self-assessment*. Success at this stage for many clients is measured by the extent to which they have established appropriate links beyond the project (i.e., with sports facilities, sports clubs, informal groups).

The most difficult stage facing the project is *defining the limit of its involvement* with individual clients. To address this problem a definite program is developed for each client at the initial commitment stage which involves a half- or full-day session once a week for a period of eight weeks. Although it is not necessarily appropriate for clients to complete such a program, all are aware at the outset that, at the end of the eight weeks, the project has no further obligation to continue its involvement with them. In practice, many clients are sufficiently motivated to maintain their links with the project on an informal basis. In other instances, the staff have the option to offer a further eight-week option to clients when further involvement seems likely to pay dividends.

Several bases have been established around the three main centers, including satellite locations in the suburban areas. Participants construct their own program from a choice of more than 30 sports; indoor leisure activities such as music, computing and model building; and courses in health and first aid. Teams have been organized in local leagues for tenpin bowling, indoor cricket, and indoor soccer. The project has established links with existing community facilities to take advantage of the equipment and facilities available, and it places some participants in local sports clubs, assisting in most cases with their initial joining fees.

Clients are coached in individual sports and encouraged to work towards recognitions where they are appropriate (e.g., swimming, lifesaving awards). Each client is counseled to participate in a variety of activities, some new, with at least one activity taking place

each week. After the introductory weeks, most clients go on to specialize in two or three regular pursuits. In addition to the program of
activities, each client undertakes a basic health test (e.g., blood pressure, lung capacity, fitness questionnaire) and is given advice on
good hygiene, good eating habits, and basic information on drinking
alcohol, smoking, drugs, and sex education. Results from these tests
show that the majority of clients smoke heavily, drink alcohol
heavily if money is available, and take little care of their bodies.

Some clients participate in team games against inmates in a local
prison, which are played at the prison's facilities. The clients selected are those who are in the most danger of receiving prison sen-
tences should they reoffend or breach the terms of their probation.
The staff believe the experience "inside" is an eye-opener for some
of them.

Benefits Received by Clients

The probation officers have identified a number of major benefits
that clients receive from the project. One noted, "We are dealing all
the time with damaged people." The project's approach allows clients to build self-esteem, substantially in many cases. Particularly
for drug abusers and socially inept clients, this aspect of the project
is considered to outweigh all the other benefits that might occur.
Partly linked to self-esteem, the development of self-awareness is
considered important for certain clients. Many develop a more disci-
plined attitude as a result of the project; others have broader horizons; some develop greater awareness of health and hygiene factors.
Gains in confidence emerge from their having done something on
their own for themselves. Many clients live in unstable environments, endure hardships in their upbringing, are often involved in
broken homes, and feel society has somehow let them down. This
gain in confidence helps to break this attitude.

The provision of an adult role model who cares about them is a
vital beneficial outcome of the project. Many clients are "adrift from
adults" and some have consciously rejected the adult world. The
leaders often bridge this gap by being positive role models. Similarly peer group socialization introduces clients to new social networks and the "camaraderie" associated with the project's activities
often leads to the development of new friendships. For certain clients, the project provides the chance to achieve, in some cases for the
first time. Most of the probation officers contend that gaining a

sporting award, certificate, or trophy is a major factor in encouraging clients to achieve in other areas of their life. Two presentation evenings a year are held to recognize individuals who have completed the program by awarding certificates for a variety of achievements. Family, friends, and probation officers attend, adding to the sense of achievement for those receiving the awards.

Evidence of the Project's Success

The Sports Council's independent monitoring report concluded that the project worked well and effectively met its objectives. The authors stated:

> The degree of support from within the probation service is immense; the reaction of outside agencies is both complimentary and enthusiastic; the clients themselves view the sports leaders as valued friends and confidants and in many cases have continued their sporting interests; sporting organizations, both public and private, have generally responded well to the project's ideals; and finally, the re-offending rates show some conclusive successes.

The report includes a number of individual case studies which effectively highlight the profound effect of the project on some of the clients' lives. The cases also illustrate that the project has an impact on a wide range of client types. However, it emphasizes that many of the positive results require time and patience to achieve maximum benefits, both of which have implications for the number of clients with whom the leaders can realistically work at any one time.

Constructing recidivism rates is difficult because British confidentiality laws constrain the police on the type of data they can reveal. Nevertheless, on the basis of a sample of clients' records, the Sports Council report was able to conclude that:

> Almost half the clients have maintained a trouble-free record since being involved with the project....In some cases the project has had significant successes in helping to halt long-time criminals with histories of serious crime.

The success of the project in the eyes of those engaged in probation work can be gauged by the spread of similar type programs into other jurisdictions in England including Somerset, Leicester, Dorset, Greater Manchester, West Yorkshire, Coventry, Northumbria, and North Kent. Probation officers feel that clients are not capable of getting into the social structure of sport on their own and that leaders are the key to integrating them. This type of project was one of the few tangible things they have to offer people, and the leaders have the time to do the job properly. As one officer noted, "It's starting where people are at, particularly the young clients."

A final convincing piece of evidence regarding its value came at the end of the three years for which the project was funded by outside grants. At that time, Hampshire County Council agreed to provide full funding for the project as a regular budgeted item and fully integrated it into the Hampshire Probation Service.

Although close relationships with probation officers are a key to the project's success, there is a firmly held belief by all parties involved that the project should remain separate from mainstream probation work. If it was seen as part of the probation service, there would be an image problem. This is not as likely to occur if those ties remain flexible and loose.

One of the major problems faced by the project's staff is getting the general public to appreciate the value of the project. The Director commented:

> Whenever I go to speak at these meetings, people say
> things like 'it's not fair that young offenders should have
> all these facilities—my son never gets a chance to do
> any of these activities.' I tell them that there is a differ-
> ence—'you care about your son, he's got love.'

The project director, Keith Waldman, would be interested in sharing more detailed information on the project and in interacting with individuals in North America who are involved in at-risk youth programs. His address is listed in the presenters section at the end of this book.

Appendix

Appendix

List of Colloquium Presenters

Dr. Delores M. Andy
Associate Professor
Temple University
Seltzer Hall- 062-62
Philadelphia, PA 19122
(215) 204-1941

Mr. Reco Bembry
Teen Programs Coordinator
City of Seattle Department of
    Parks and Recreation
100 Dexter Avenue North
Seattle, WA 98109
(206) 684-7186

Mr. Michael Bradley
Supervisor
Metropolitan Park District of
    Tacoma
4702 S. 19th Street
Tacoma, WA 98405-1175
(206) 305-1025

Mr. Dave Breckon
Manager, Leisure Services
Calgary Parks and Recreation
P.O. Box 2100, Stn. M
Calgary, Alberta T2P 2M5
Canada
(403) 268-4743

Mr. Ronnie Lee Burton, Sr.
Recreation Supervisor
Tucson Parks and Recreation
900 S. Randolph Way
Tucson, AZ 85716
(602) 791-4845

Mr. Ronald W. Chase
Director, Cincinnati Recreation
    Commission
805 Central Avenue
Cincinnati, OH 45202
(513) 352-4004

Mr. Robert Chavez
Social Services Division
    Manager
City of Commerce Youth
    Diversion Program
Commerce City Hall N. Annex
5550 Harbor Street
Commerce, CA 90040
(213) 887-4460

Mr. John Christian
Director
City of Sunnyvale Parks and
    Recreation
P.O. Box 3707
Sunnyvale, CA 94088-3707
(408) 730-7516

Dr. John L. Crompton
Professor, Department of
    Recreation, Park and
    Tourism Sciences
Texas A&M University
College Station, TX 77843-2261
(409) 845-5320

Ms. Patti Cummings
Coordinator, Youth Recreation
    Programs
Boulder Parks and Recreation
P.O. Box 791
Boulder, CO 80301
(303) 441-3400

Mr. Mark Deven
Superintendent, Anaheim Parks,
    Recreation and Community
    Services
200 S. Anaheim Blvd.
Anaheim, CA 92805
(714) 254-5243

Ms. Gayle Dixon
Supervisor, Rockford Park
    District
1401 N. 2nd Street
Rockford, IL 61107
(815) 987-8845

Mr. Ronald Dodd
Director
Joliet Park District
3000 W. Jefferson St.
Joliet, IL 60435
(815) 741-7275

Mr. David L. Fisher
Superintendent, Minneapolis
    Park and Recreation Board
400 South 4th Street, Suite 200
Minneapolis, MN 55414-1400
(612) 661-4888

Ms. Jean H. Fountain
Director, Parks and Recreation
North Miami Parks and
    Recreation
776 NE 125th Street
North Miami, FL 33161
(305) 893-6511

Mr. Kelvin Fountano
Recreation Program Coordinator
City of Sunnyvale Parks and
    Recreation
P.O. Box 3707
Sunnyvale, CA 94088-3707
(408) 730-7514

Mr. J. M. Hayes
Recreation Coordinator
Tucson Parks and Recreation
900 S. Randolph Way
Tucson, AZ 85716
(602) 791-4845

Ms. Cindy Heath
Recreation Director
Lebanon Recreation Department
P.O. Box 1207
Lebanon, NH 03766-4207
(603) 448-5121

Ms. Rita Horn
Director-General, Department of
    Sport and Recreation
Private Bag X896
Pretoria 0001
Republic of South Africa
(012) 314-6345

Mr. Robert P. Humke
Director, Madison School-
  Community Recreation
  Department
1045 E. Dayton Street
Madison, WI 53703
(608) 266-6073

Mr. Petty Hunter
Assistant Director
City of Houston Parks and
  Recreation
2999 S. Wayside Drive
Houston, TX 77023
(713) 845-1232

Mr. Bob Johnston
Program Development
  Coordinator
Department of Park and
  Recreation
455 N. Main
Wichita, KS 67202
(316) 268-4361

Mr. Reginald Jones, Jr.
Youth At-Risk Supervisor
Indianapolis Parks
1426 W. 29th Street
Indianapolis, IN 46208
(317) 327-7218

Mr. David A. Jordan
Youth At-Risk Coordinator
Portland Parks and Recreation
1120 SW 5th Avenue,
  Room 1302
Portland, OR 97204
(503) 823-6973

Mr. Jack Kardys
Executive Assistant to the
  Director
Metropolitan Dade Park and
  Recreation
50 SW 32nd Rd., Bldg. 1
Miami, FL 33129
(305) 857-3350

Ms. Jennifer Koney-Li
Visual Arts Coordinator
Oakland Office of Parks and
  Recreation
1520 Lakeside Drive
Oakland, CA 94612-4598
(512) 238-3092

Ms. Diana Kyle
Deputy Director
City of Tampa Parks
7525 North Blvd.
Tampa, FL 33604-1231
(813) 931-2117

Ms. Carol P. Langley
Program Supervisor
Education Development
City of Raleigh Parks and
  Recreation Department
P.O. Box 590
Raleigh, NC 27602
(919) 831-6640

Mr. John Lawrence
Recreation Supervisor
City of Sunnyvale Parks and
  Recreation
P.O. Box 3707
Sunnyvale, CA 94088-3707
(408) 730-7340

Mr. Malcolm Matthews
Director, City of Corpus Christi
  Parks and Recreation
  Department
Box 9277
Corpus Christi, TX 78469
(512) 880-3464

Ms. Gloria Morehouse
Director of Membership
Pacific Peaks Girl Scout Council
5326 Littlerock Road SW
Tumwater, WA 98512-7394
(206) 475-0307

Mr. Pierre Morin
Superintendent
Montreal Sports and Recreation
7400 St.-Michael, #202
Montreal, Quebec J4K 3C1
CANADA
(514) 872-2459

Ms. Eveyln M. Morris
Human Resources Director, The
  Housing Authority of the
  City of Columbus
1515 4th Street South
Columbus, MS 39701
(601) 328-4236

Ms. Cynthia D. Peters
Recreation Supervisor, City of
  Phoenix
Parks, Recreation and Library
  Department
2705 N. 15th Avenue
Phoenix, AZ 85007
(602) 262-7383

Ms. Kristin Renzema
Teen Coordinator
Longview Parks and Recreation
2920 Douglas Street
Longview, WA 98632
(206) 577-3345

Mr. Jim Stamborski
Superintendent
City of North Miami Parks and
  Recreation
776 NE 125th Street
North Miami, FL 33161
(305) 893-6511

Mr. Robert G. Stanton
Regional Director, National Park
  Service
U.S. Department of the Interior
1100 Ohio Drive, S.W.
Washington, DC 20242
(202) 619-7000

Mr. Al Tufono
Sr. Recreation Specialist
City of Seattle Department of
  Parks and Recreation
100 Dexter Avenue North
Seattle, WA 98109
(206) 684-7097

Ms. Daul Valenzuela
Recreation Manager
City of Scottsdale Human
  Services Division
P.O. Box 1000
Scottsdale, AZ 85252
(602) 994-2457

Ms. Leanna Waite
Program Coordinator
Metropolitan Park District of
    Tacoma
4702 S. 19th Street
Tacoma, WA 98407
(206) 305-1025

Mr. Keith Waldman
Project Director
Sports Counselling Project
27A Hanover Buildings
Southampton SO1 1JU
England

Mr. Wendel Whisenhunt
Assistant Director, Oklahoma
    City Parks and Recreation
    Department
301 W. Renn Avenue
Oklahoma City, OK 73102
(405) 297-3995

Mr. Nathaniel O. Wilkins
Superintendent of Recreation
Kansas City Parks and
    Recreation
5605 E. 63rd Street
Kansas City, MO 64130
(816) 871-5600

Mr. Cleve Williams
Director
Oakland Office of Parks and
    Recreation
1529 Lakeside Drive
Oakland, CA 94612-3092
(510) 268-3092

Mr. Neil Winther
Acting Associate Dean, Faculty
    of Physical Education and
    Recreation Studies
University of Manitoba
Winnipeg, Manitoba R3T 2N2
Canada
(204) 474-9255

Dr. Peter A. Witt
Department Head
Department of Recreation, Park
    and Tourism Sciences
Texas A&M University
College Station, TX 77843-2261
(409) 845-7324

Mr. Richard Zavala
Director, Fort Worth Parks
    and Community Services
    Department
4200 S. Freeway, Suite 2200
Fort Worth, TX 76115
(817) 871-5711

Mr. Steven Zoet
Recreation Services Manager
Olympia Parks, Recreation
    and Cultural Services
    Department
222 N. Columbia
Olympia, WA 98501
(360) 753-8380

Other Books
from Venture Publishing

Evaluation of Therapeutic Recreation Through Quality Assurance
edited by Bob Riley

The Evolution of Leisure: Historical and Philosophical Perspectives—Second Printing
by Thomas Goodale and Geoffrey Godbey

The Game Finder—A Leader's Guide to Great Activities
by Annette C. Moore

Getting People Involved in Life and Activities: Effective Motivating Techniques
by Jeanne Adams

Great Special Events and Activities
by Annie Morton, Angie Prosser and Sue Spangler

Inclusive Leisure Services: Responding to the Rights of People with Disabilities
by John Dattilo

Internships in Recreation and Leisure Services: A Practical Guide for Students
by Edward E. Seagle, Jr., Ralph W. Smith and Lola M. Dalton

Interpretation of Cultural and Natural Resources
by Douglas M. Knudson, Ted T. Cable and Larry Beck

Introduction to Leisure Services—7th Edition
by H. Douglas Sessoms and Karla A. Henderson

Leadership and Administration of Outdoor Pursuits, Second Edition
by Phyllis Ford and James Blanchard

Leisure And Family Fun (LAFF)
by Mary Atteberry-Rogers

The Leisure Diagnostic Battery: Users Manual and Sample Forms
by Peter A. Witt and Gary Ellis

Leisure Diagnostic Battery Computer Software
by Gary Ellis and Peter A. Witt

Leisure Education: A Manual of Activities and Resources
by Norma J. Stumbo and Steven R. Thompson

Leisure Education II: More Activities and Resources
by Norma J. Stumbo

Leisure Education Program Planning: A Systematic Approach
by John Dattilo and William D. Murphy

Leisure in Your Life: An Exploration, Fourth Edition
by Geoffrey Godbey

A Leisure of One's Own: A Feminist Perspective on Women's Leisure
by Karla Henderson, M. Deborah Bialeschki, Susan M.
Shaw and Valeria J. Freysinger
Leisure Services in Canada: An Introduction
by Mark S. Searle and Russell E. Brayley
Marketing for Parks, Recreation, and Leisure
by Ellen L. O'Sullivan
Models of Change in Municipal Parks and Recreation: A Book of Innovative Case Studies
edited by Mark E. Havitz
Outdoor Recreation Management: Theory and Application, Third Edition
by Alan Jubenville and Ben Twight
Planning Parks for People
by John Hultsman, Richard L. Cottrell and Wendy Zales Hultsman
Private and Commercial Recreation
edited by Arlin Epperson
The Process of Recreation Programming Theory and Technique, Third Edition
by Patricia Farrell and Herberta M. Lundegren
Protocols for Recreation Therapy Programs
edited by Jill Kelland, along with the Recreation Therapy Staff at Alberta Hospital Edmonton
Quality Management: Applications for Therapeutic Recreation
edited by Bob Riley
Recreation and Leisure: Issues in an Era of Change, Third Edition
edited by Thomas Goodale and Peter A. Witt
Recreation Programming and Activities for Older Adults
by Jerold E. Elliott and Judith A. Sorg-Elliott
Reference Manual for Writing Rehabilitation Therapy Treatment Plans
by Penny Hogberg and Mary Johnson
Research in Therapeutic Recreation: Concepts and Methods
edited by Marjorie J. Malkin and Christine Z. Howe
Risk Management in Therapeutic Recreation: A Component of Quality Assurance
by Judith Voelkl

A Social History of Leisure Since 1600
    by Gary Cross
The Sociology of Leisure
    by John R. Kelly and Geoffrey Godbey
A Study Guide for National Certification in Therapeutic Recreation
    by Gerald O'Morrow and Ron Reynolds
Therapeutic Recreation: Cases and Exercises
    by Barbara C. Wilhite and M. Jean Keller
Therapeutic Recreation in the Nursing Home
    by Linda Buettner and Shelley L. Martin
*Therapeutic Recreation Protocol for Treatment of Substance
    Addictions*
    by Rozanne W. Faulkner
*A Training Manual for Americans With Disabilities Act Compliance
    in Parks and Recreation Settings*
    by Carol Stensrud
*Understanding Leisure and Recreation: Mapping the Past, Charting
    the Future*
    edited by Edgar L. Jackson and Thomas L. Burton

 Venture Publishing, Inc.
1999 Cato Avenue
State College, PA 16801

Phone: (814) 234-4561; FAX: (814) 234-1651